GMO FOOD POISON HANDBOOK

'Genetically-Modified' Agriculture and Animals

Charles W Sutherland

Library of Congress Cataloging-in-Publication Data (forthcoming):

Sutherland, Charles

ISBN – 10   1494975327
ISBN – 13   978-1494975326

Printed in the United States of America

First Edition

Cover design and creation by Daniel Sutherland

To Daniel and Nathaniel,
and their generation

Per aspera ad astra

"Cultivators of the land are the most valuable citizens."

– Thomas Jefferson

"Men become accustomed to poison by degrees."

– Victor Hugo

"The American chemical industry, which now dominates agriculture, has achieved something never before accomplished in history: humans who are simultaneously overfed and undernourished – and slowly poisoned – on a global scale."

– Author

TABLE OF CONTENTS

PART 2 – 181
ANECDOTAL EVIDENCE
of
GMO HEALTH DANGERS
REVEALED in SCIENTIFIC ARTICLES and INDIVIDUAL STUDIES

9

FOREWORD

Bon appétite!

GMO crops are *scientifically created to <u>be</u> poisonous and to <u>absorb</u> poison*!

This book is about *chemically-created* GMO 'food products' which many chemical companies and food distributors would like you to believe are 'real food.' However, by the time you finish reading about any of them, you will probably lose your appetite.

'Genetically-modified organisms', GMOs, are chemically-created seeds into which poisons have been forcibly inserted in order to *kill* crop-eating insects, and, GMOs are chemically-created seeds into which chemicals have been forcibly inserted in order to *absorb* and resist the poisonous herbicides that are sprayed on them to kill weeds and other pests. These genetically-modified, chemically-created, poison-filled seeds have been spread into the global food supply by massive corporate marketing, government corruption, academic connivance, professional intimidation, and deceit.

The resultant GMO crops and 'food products' are unhealthy – for the environment, for insects, for animals, and for people, especially the unborn. This should not be any surprise, because it is not a secret:

The chemical companies openly boast about their laboratory successes in *creating* food seeds which *are* poisonous and which can *absorb* poison.

How poisonous?

"GM foods pose a serious health risk in the areas of toxicology, allergy and immune function, reproductive health, and metabolic, physiologic and genetic health."

That was the official announcement in a May 2009 press release by the American Academy of Environmental Medicine (AAEM), an international association of physicians and other professionals in the

11

United States dedicated to addressing the clinical aspects of environmental health. It was the formal conclusion of AAEM's research which resulted in a final position paper entitled,

'The American Academy of Environmental Medicine Calls for Immediate Moratorium on Genetically Modified Foods.'

Dr. Amy Dean, Member of the AAEM Board and Public Relations Chair, stated,

"Multiple animal studies have shown that GM foods cause damage to various organ systems in the body."

"With this mounting evidence, it is imperative to have a moratorium on GM foods for the safety of our patients' and the public's health."

The president of AAEM, Dr. Jennifer Armstrong, added that,

"Physicians are probably seeing the effects in their patients, but need to know how to ask the right questions. The most common foods in North America which are consumed that are GMO are corn, soy, canola, and cottonseed oil." [1]

The AAEM further stated: **"Therefore, because GM foods pose a serious health risk in the areas of toxicology, allergy and immune function, reproductive health, and metabolic, physiologic, and genetic health, and are without benefit, the AAEM believes that it is imperative to adopt the precautionary principle..."** And added,

"When an activity raises threats to the environment or human health, precautionary measures should be taken, even if some cause and effect relationships are not fully established scientifically. In this context, the proponent of an activity, rather than the public, should bear the burden of the proof (of the safety of the activity)." [1] [2]

[1]   http://www.aaemonline.org/gmopost.html
[2]   http://www.aaemonline.org/gmopressrelease.html

INTRODUCTION

Natural cross-breeding vs. 'foreign' genes

All genetic engineering requires the manipulation of DNA. When a gene is transferred between organisms that could be conventionally bred, like different kinds of plants, animals or fish, the process is known as *cisgenesis*. When a 'foreign gene' is taken from one species of a plant, animal, or bacteria and implanted or inserted into another species, it is called *transgenesis;* the gene involved is called a *transgene*.

In 1994 the *chemical* industry began transferring 'foreign genes,' including insect-killing bacteria, into food seeds in order to create a new kind of hybrid 'food product.' Because these *chemical* companies created 'genetically modify organisms,' the result is called 'GMO's.

Renowned scientists from around the globe now say the chemical companies are poisoning the food supply of the US and the world. Because the chemical companies are altering nature itself, critics say GMO stands for "God Move Over."

Led by Monsanto, the creator of such toxic chemicals as sulfuric acid, Agent Orange, and PCBs, other chemical companies have also created 'genetically modified organisms' (GMOs). These crops are now spreading around the world at an accelerating rate.

The various monitoring organizations, including the Center for Food Safety *(USA)*, currently estimate that 85% of corn produced in the United States is genetically modified, as are 95% of sugar beets, 91% of soybeans, and 88% of cotton (which many food products use as cottonseed oil, and which some animals eat). Other GMO 'food products' include alfalfa, canola oil, fish, milk, papaya, peas, potatoes, tomatoes, and zucchini. Over 70% of processed foods on grocery store shelves are estimated to contain some form of GMO ingredients!

These GMOs and the resultant GMO 'food products' are now spreading around the world. According to research scientists around the globe, these crops are poisoning the people who consume them, poisoning the animals that eat them, contaminating the soil in which they are planted, poisoning the water into which the rain washes the toxin residue of these plants, and poisoning the air with the toxic herbicides sprayed on these plants.

Variations and derivatives of these products are incorporated into thousands of 'food products' of every kind: packaged foods, breads, pastries, cereals, soups, cooking oils, condiments, milk, milk products, ice cream, yogurts, meats, pasta, snacks, soft drinks, beers, wines, and other liquids – all created with ingredients from the basic GMO crops.

The average consumer has no idea what chemicals are contained inside of any of these 'food products.' And, Monsanto and the other chemical companies spend millions of dollars each year on political campaigns and legal fees to **prevent** any government agency from requiring labels put on the chemical contents of these 'food products'!

One of the most common GMO ingredients is high fructose corn syrup which is used in virtually hundreds of 'food products' including cereals, liquids, soft drinks, crackers, snacks – and baby foods.

Another GMO crop which is found in various 'food products' is GMO soy. It is in virtually all soy products, including soy milk – and baby foods.

The GMO industry has also 'injected' their chemical ingredients into cows, through the bovine growth hormone (rBGH), which directly affects milk and various milk products, such as cheese. And, GMO ingredients are now even found in certain major brands of yogurt.

Although Monsanto is the principal producer of GMO seeds, other major companies which produce GMO products are Dow, DuPont, Bayer, and Syngenta. There are also many smaller companies as well.

The eight largest food companies which use or distribute GMO products are Mars, General Mills, Kraft, Nestle, Pepsico, Kellogg's, Coca Cola, and Unilever. [1] These companies make up over 90% of the food sold at your grocery retailers. [2]

The number of all of the 'food products' containing GMOs, and the percentage of GMO ingredients in these various products, is impossible to know. Part of the reason for not knowing is that the chemical companies which produce GMO seeds, and their distributors, refuse to label GMO products.

As of this writing, there are 64 countries around the world which ban GMO crops or require that the contents of the resultant 'food products' be labeled. The US and Canada are not among them. [3]

[1] http://www.undergroundhealth.com/the-8-biggest-food-companies-in-the-world-who-use-gmo/
[2] http://www.whydontyoutrythis.com/2013/06/comprehensive-list-of-gmo-products-and-companies.html
[3] http://www.labelgmos.org/the_science_genetically_modified_foods_gmo

Research Studies on GMO Toxins and GMO 'Food Products'

There are hundreds of studies conducted by research scientists around the world regarding the toxicity of GMO 'food products' and their affect on human health. So far, none of them has been a study of longer than three years. However, the results reveal short-term damage to health and suggest significant long-term toxicity.

The on-going studies referenced in this *GMO Food Poison Handbook* have been conducted, at different times over the past two decades, by medical doctors, academicians, and research scientists from various government agencies, universities, laboratories, and research institutes in **30** countries, including **Argentina, Australia, Austria, Belgium, Brazil, Canada, China, Egypt, England, France, Germany, Ghana, Greece, Hungary, India, Ireland, Italy, New Zealand, Northern Ireland, Norway, Paraguay, Poland, Russia, Scotland, South Africa, Spain, Thailand, Turkey, United Kingdom, and the United States.**

There are other studies, done by Monsanto, Syngenta, Dow, DuPont, Bayer, and other chemical companies. However, the results of many (or most?) of these studies have been concealed from the public. Outsiders don't know how many internal studies have been done by the chemical companies. Furthermore, the results of other studies by the GMO companies and their paid academic 'consultants' have often been falsely reported by the companies, in order to conceal negative facts. [1][2]

To distract from their own false reporting, the GMO companies and their highly-paid public relations firms and 'academic consultants' attempt to systematically discredit research scientists who reveal the harmful consequences of eating GMO 'food products.'

Among the many attacks to discredit those who criticize Monsanto was the public relations offensive against the renowned scientist Dr. Arpad Pusztai of the famed Rowett Institute in *Scotland* who was the first to challenge the health effects of Monsanto's GMO potatoes. A similar public assault was directed against Dr. Ignacio Chapela of the

University of California in the **United States** who challenged the health effects of Monsanto's GMO corn in Mexico (his family was also threatened in this matter).

Even the most basic facts are misrepresented by the chemical companies. The oft-repeated claims by Monsanto that there is no difference between their GMO corn and regular corn has been demonstrated to be false for many years, including in a recent study entitled, '*2012 Nutritional Analysis Comparison of GMO corn versus Non-GMO corn.*' [3]

This misleading claim that GMO food is 'equivalent' to real food is largely because of a man named Michael Taylor, who sometimes (officially) works for Monsanto and sometimes (officially) works for the US government. In the 1990s, when he was Deputy Commissioner for Policy at the Food and Drug Administration (FDA), he saw to it that GMO 'foods' were declared to be "substantially equivalent" to real food. Therefore, no testing was required!

Mr. Taylor is the personification of a personal 'revolving door' between government and big business – in this case the big agricultural companies (called 'Big Ag') that determine most US agricultural policies. With the support of Monsanto and the chemical companies, and 'Big Ag,' in 2010, the US president 'officially' put Mr. Taylor in charge of "protecting" our foods…!

A comprehensive report on various GMO studies is provided by Earth Open Source in an article entitled *GMO Myths and Truths.* This report summarizes the claims of the chemical companies that produce the GMO crops and the various studies which reveal their toxicities. [4]

N.B. As a matter of interest it is useful for you to know that Mr. Taylor began his incestuous career as an attorney for the Department of Agriculture (USDA) in the late 1970s; then in the 1980s he was a private lawyer – representing Monsanto; then from 1991- 1994 he was 'officially' a US government official as Deputy Commissioner for Policy of the Food and Drug Administration (FDA) – when the FDA officially declared that Monsanto's GMO 'foods' are "substantially equivalent" to real food and the FDA approved the bovine growth hormone (rBGH) for cows; then from 1994 to 1996 he 'officially' moved back to the USDA again; then from 1998 – 2001 he was 'officially' made Vice President for Public Policy at Monsanto Corp.; then, he became a private attorney and consultant, promoting "food safety" among other things; then, in 2009 the president, Barack Obama, 'officially' appointed him as Senior Advisor to the FDA Commissioner; finally, in 2010 Barack Obama 'officially' created a new US government position just for him at the FDA called Deputy Commissioner for Foods.

[1] http://www.salon.com/2013/06/27/study_monsanto_gmo_food_claims_probably_false_partner/
[2] http://www.blindbatnews.com/2013/05/false-flag-bio-war-gmo-creates-superbugs-destroying-our-food-sources-india-says-gmo-research-fradulent/21093
[3] http://www.momsacrossamerica.com/stunning_corn_comparison_gmo_versus_non_gmo
[4] http://earthopensource.org/index.php/reports/58

Anecdotal Evidence of GMO Dangers Revealed in Scientific Articles and Individual Studies

In addition to the multitude of research studies, there is a plethora of anecdotal information around the world which connects the GMO industry to various biological and medical maladies – but data which lacks a specific, scientifically-demonstrated link.

Many new biological and environmental problems are directly associated with GMO crops, even though they cannot yet be scientifically connected. Some of these reports are included herein. However, since the results were not the conclusions of specific scientific research studies, they are listed separately.

This information is analyzed in publications by leading medical doctors, academicians and journalists, many of whom have spent years studying this field. This will provide the reader with further information, and sources for further investigation.

What are GMOs ('genetically modified organisms') and why were they created?

GMOs are called 'genetically modified organisms' because they come from food seeds which are 'genetically modified' (altered) by chemical companies through a chemical-laboratory process.

Monsanto genetically modifies (altered) crops by forcibly **inserting into** seeds a poison from soil bacteria called *Bacillus thuringiensis* (*Bt* toxin), which kills insects by causing their stomachs to explode. The resulting 'food products' are called GMOs.

Secondly, Monsanto genetically modifies crops by **inserting into** 'food seeds' chemicals to **absorb** the poisons in Roundup that farmers spray on their crops. These chemically-modified crops had to be able to *absorb* the poisons of the pesticides and herbicides sprayed on them and not die. Thus, the crops become 'Roundup Ready' crops. The resulting 'food products' are also called GMO crops.

How many of these are the *same* crops, and/or how many different chemicals and poisons are in various crops... only Monsanto knows. And Monsanto refuses to allow any 'labeling' as to the contents of the 'food products' which are produced from these GMO crops. (There are now several other chemical companies which also produce GMO crops: they also opposed 'labeling.') What we know for sure is that these crops have been injected with toxins and chemicals to kill plant-eating pests and to resist herbicides, and – **these crops have the ability to continually generate their own poisons.** Thus, when eat GMO 'food products' we are ingesting poison.

In a paper entitled *Health and Environmental Consequences of Genetically-Modified Foods, Biopharming, and rBGH,* Dr. Martin Donohoe of Portland State University in Oregon *(USA)* summarized the general nature of these crops:

"Genetically-Modified Foods:
* 68% herbicide resistant
* 19% produce their own pesticide
* 13% produce their own pesticide and are herbicide-resistant" [1]

Another main GMO chemical is 'bovine growth hormone' (rBGH) which is injected into cows in order for them to produce more milk. Although this chemical stimulates milk production, it creates numerous biological-medical issues for the cows. AND, it creates serious medical issues regarding the milk which those cows produce.

Apart from natural breeding, historically there were some attempts to 'chemically alter' genes. However, modern GMO 'food products' were originally created in the 1990s to increase the sales of Monsanto's best-selling herbicide, Roundup. The various chemicals in Roundup, particularly *glyphosate*, were killing the food crops as well as the weeds on which they were sprayed. So to prevent the collapse of Roundup sales, Monsanto needed to create a plant which could *absorb* these poisons and not die. This began the modern 'genetically engineering process' of altering food seeds.

The important aspect to GMOs is that they are "patentable." In 1980 the U.S. Supreme Court, in a case called Diamond v. Chakrabarty, upheld the first patent to be filed on a newly created living organism. This organism, created by General Electric, was a newly-created bacterium for digesting crude oil spills which were affecting coastal waters. The Court ruled that if the 'organism' is truly "man-made" (even through genetic engineering), then it can be patented. This "opened the flood gates" to 'genetically-engineer' (and patent!) all types of bacteria, cells, seeds, plants, and even animals.

With this open road, Monsanto and other chemical companies developed a whole variety of chemically-altered 'food products' which are on most grocery shelves today.

It would be useful to observe how these scientific developments specifically affected the food industry. Since food health is monitored, and partially controlled, by the Food and Drug Administration (FDA), their approval is required to sell food.

The process of inserting chemicals into food seeds to alter them was approved by the FDA during the period 1991-1994. At that time, with only minor evaluations, the FDA officially declared these chemical 'food products' to be "substantially equivalent" to real food. (This is when Michael Taylor, an occasional officer of Monsanto, was Deputy Commissioner for Policy of the FDA).

In 1993 the FDA also approved the use of a genetically engineered hormone created by Monsanto, a recombinant Bovine Growth Hormone called rBGH (or sometimes called rBST) to be injected into cows in order to increase milk production. (This was also approved in 1993, when Michael Taylor was Deputy Commissioner for Policy at the FDA.)

Monsanto, and the other chemical companies, have tried to morally justify creating chemical crops by saying it is for the benefit of mankind, namely to produce higher crop yields. Monsanto and its shareholders make a similar claim for 'bovine growth hormones,' rBGH, in cows, namely to increase the milk supply.

Although the GMO crops are chemically-created to resist the toxins in herbicides and pesticides, Monsanto and the other chemical companies make the illogical claim that chemically-created GMO crops therefore *reduce* the need for herbicides and pesticides, rather than allow the use of stronger toxins to be sprayed. Logically, the opposite has proven to be true, and Monsanto's claims have been shown to be false:

- As the soil and crops develop a resistance to Roundup and the other toxins, more and more toxic pesticides and herbicides are required, and in greater strength.

- Even more troubling and dangerous, research studies now reveal that the insects themselves are developing a resistance to Monsanto's poisons, and are evolving into stronger species.

In 1970, Monsanto combined *glyphosate* with other chemicals and brought it to market under the trade name 'Roundup' and sold it to farmers. Roundup is a broad spectrum systemic herbicide used to kill weeds. *Glyphosate* is absorbed into plants through their foliage and translated to growing points in the plants. There it inhibits an enzyme

21

involved in the synthesis of internal chemicals in the plant, thereby preventing the weed's growth and causing its death.

But … Monsanto apparently overlooked the fact that Roundup would not just kill weeds, but also kills other plants too, namely crops. So, sales to the farmers were negatively impacted.

To increase the sales of Roundup without killing crops, Monsanto developed a method to insert chemicals *inside* of the food seeds – chemicals which would allow the plants to absorb *glyphosate* without killing the plants. Those seeds, under the trade name 'Roundup-Ready seeds,' became the first 'genetically modified organisms', GMOs.

What is *glyphosate*?

Glyphosate (a combination and contraction of the natural amino acid gly[cine] and phos[phon]ate) is a broad-spectrum systemic herbicide to kill weeds.

Its mode of action is to impair the cytochrome P450 (CYP) gene pathway which creates enzymes that help to form and break down molecules in cells. *Glyphosate* also inhibits some of these enzymes involved in the synthesis of certain aromatic amino acids, including aromatase, an enzyme involved in the biosynthesis of estrogens by the aromatization (altering) of androgens into estrogens *(androgens control male characteristics, and are the precursor of estrogens, the primary female sex organs, essential in both the menstrual and estrous reproductive cycles).*

Another function of these enzymes is to detoxify xenobiotics, in order to prevent infections and diseases. *('xeno' is the Greek word for 'foreign' and 'bio' for 'living'; hence, xenobiotics are 'foreign' intruders such as diseases, carcinogens, and chemicals).*

Thus, these are essential and significant components of human chemistry. Obviously, any alteration of the P450 (CYP) gene pathway, and the genes involved, interferes with the normal growth, development and functioning of our body. The implications are enormous.

Studies reveal that human exposure to *glyphosate* decreased levels of the amino acid tryptophan. *(Amino acids … hundreds of them… are biological compounds involved in neurotransmitter transport and biosynthesis, and, as proteins, are involved in cellular development, and the development of muscles and other tissues.)* Trytophan itself is involved in the signaling of the neurotransmitter serotonin… associated with a number of cerebral and mental issues, including depression and Alzheimer's, and obesity.

Because *glyphosate's* mode of action is to inhibit enzyme development and growth, it is believed to only be effective on *growing* plants; it interferes with the growth process of *growing* plants, causing them to die. *Glyphosate* (Roundup) is sprayed on crops to kill the weeds around them. The GMO crops themselves are protected by chemicals inserted into them by Monsanto: hence, "Roundup Ready" crops.

However, besides inhibiting *growing* plants and causing their deaths, no one knows for sure if the accumulation of *glyphosate* has an effect which prevents growth in the first place. So far, studies suggest that it *does* have such an effect, particularly if it accumulates in body organs.

This raises another fundamental question: if Monsanto developed GMO crops (Roundup Ready plants) to resist *glyphosate*, what protects those plants and animals which are *not* treated to resist this poison: the natural bacteria in the soil and water, nature's animals (insects, bees, birds, etc.), and human bodies? After all, *glyphosate* **is** poison! The answer: they have no protection from this poison!

Glyphosate is absorbed by the GMO crops which eventually result in 'food products.' It is also absorbed in the soil, with the accumulated amounts increasing every year. Two fundamental questions, then, seem to be:

'What amount' of *glyphosate* is toxic to soil bacteria which are essential for the growth of flowers and crops?'

'What amounts of *glyphosate* are toxic to bees, birds, animals…and to humans, particularly embryos and fetuses, when we eat them?'

Among the other questions are:

(1) What various chemicals did Monsanto insert into those seeds?

(2) What internal, natural chemicals and bacteria inside of the food seeds were removed, displaced, or killed when Monsanto's genes and chemicals were inserted into those seeds?

(3) When these plants are sprayed with Roundup, how much *glyphosate* is absorbed into those *glyphosate*-resistant GMO seeds – and is then passed into the 'food products' that these seeds create, and which animals and humans eventually eat?

(4) How many animal enzymes … and human enzymes … does *glyphosate* inhibit?

The first question: What various chemicals did Monsanto insert into these seeds?

The partial answer is that Monsanto's genetically modified (GM) corn and cotton seeds are engineered to **contain** a poison from soil bacteria called *Bacillus thuringiensis* (*Bt* toxin). This toxin is one of the chemicals. The nature and quantity of other chemicals inserted into the food seeds are trade secrets of Monsanto. However, whatever combination of chemicals is inserted into these GMO seeds, the effect is toxic. When insects bite into these seeds the toxin ruptures their stomachs and they die.

Although many farmers use a variety of natural *Bt* sprays to deal with insects, the *Bt* toxin contained **inside** of the plants is specifically designed to be more toxic. Consequently, it is many times more powerful. When combined with additional chemicals, the synergy creates a toxicity which is even more potent!

All of this raises **another question**:

If the stomachs of insects rupture and the insects die when they bite into these GMO seeds, why would someone say it is safe for humans to eat the plants and 'food products' that are grown from these GMO toxins?

The answer is that many scientists around the world say it is NOT safe to eat them.

The second question, What natural chemicals and bacteria already inside of the plants are removed, displaced, or killed when Monsanto inserts its GMO genes and chemicals into the plants?

Answer: Again, no one knows ... except perhaps Monsanto. And Monsanto will not reveal the answer.

However, scientists know that:

> Whenever a 'foreign' gene is inserted into any organism, it disrupts the internal dynamics of that organism... and usually for the worse, because millions of years of evolution are being disturbed.

Since all organisms have defensive mechanisms to 'protect' themselves from any 'foreign body,' it is also not known if any of these potentially new 'protective' chemicals are harmful to humans – the people who consume the various 'food products' which are created from them these plants. Therefore,

> it is also not known what 'defensive' chemicals are generated by the seeds to 'protect' themselves from these 'foreign' chemicals which are being inserted.

Apart from the toxicity, what we know for sure is that the nutritional content of GMO plants is reduced; micronutrients such as iron, manganese, and zinc can be reduced as much as 80-90%! This creates malnutrition, and can lead to obesity. [2]

The third question, when these plants are sprayed with Roundup and other herbicides, how much *glyphosate* is absorbed into these genetically modified plants – which then become the GMO 'food products' that these seeds create, and which animals and humans eventually eat?

Answer: Research has revealed that there are many negative and serious repercussions to the human body, most of which cannot even be presently predicted.

Worse: Various medical and research studies around the world indicate that many of these toxins enter the body and the blood stream, even of fetuses.

If Monsanto knows the answer to this question, they will not disclose it. Monsanto regards its internal analyses as 'trade secrets' and protects them through the legal process.

Glyphosate's mode of action is to be absorbed by plants and weeds and translocated to growing points; there it inhibits an enzyme involved in the synthesis of various amino acids during the *process of growing.* Since *glyphosate* is absorbed by the GMO crops, the question one must ask is: *does this enzyme-inhibiting process continue inside of the human bodies which eat these GMO crops?*

Many dangers have been revealed in recent studies, including one published in May 2012 by the National Institutes of Health*(USA)* in the *Archives of Toxicology.* Entitled *"Cytotoxic and DNA-damaging properties of glyphosate and Roundup in human-derived buccal epithelial cells,"* it addresses part of this concern.

The study reveals how *glyphosate* damages epithelial cells, namely the tightly-packed protective cells which cover the internal and external surfaces of the body organs. If these cells are damaged, the organs which they are protecting can become damaged.

Cytotoxic means poisonous to cells. The study disclosed that "Since we found genotoxic effects after short exposure to concentrations that correspond to a 450-fold dilution of spraying in agriculture, our findings indicate that inhalation may cause DNA damage in exposed individuals." [3]

Genotoxic means poisonous to the genes!

A even more recent study, published in the January 2014 issue of the *International Journal of Toxicology*, entitled, *'Glyphosate Commercial Formulation Causes Cytotoxicity, Oxidative Effects, and Apoptosis on Human Cells: Difference With its Active Ingredient* was conducted by four (4) research scientists at the University of Buenos Aires in **Argentina**.

The research revealed the synergistic toxicity of combining chemicals. Even if *glyphosate* may not reveal its various toxic effects in isolation, the studies showed what when *glyphosate* was combined with the other chemicals in the insecticide [Roundup] it became increasingly toxic. "…G[glyphosate] formulation triggered caspase 3/7 activation and hence induced apoptosis pathway in this cell line." [Apoptosis is the body's programmed cell death.] "These results confirm that G formulations have adjuvants working together with the active ingredient and causing toxic effects that are not seen with acid glyphosate." [4]

The fourth question: How many animal enzymes, including human enzymes, does *glyphosate* inhibit?

Answer: In short-term studies it is clear that *glyphosate* is toxic to humans. It is known that animal and human enzymes are affected. However, when the GMO plants absorb *glyphosate,* which is then combined with other chemicals (in Roundup or others),

> GMO crops are known to be even more toxic to many organs in the body.

Since there have not been any long-term studies, and evolution is a slow process, the long-term consequences of these toxins are presently unknown. However, you will see that one of the most disturbing developments indicated in the following studies is that

> Scientists already know that these toxins can affect the genes themselves!

How are GMOs created? DNA is inserted into the food seeds.

The word 'insert' sounds surgical, but the process is far from gentle. There are variations on the 'insertion' methodology. However, it is all violent, creating unpredictable botanical disturbances inside the seeds.

All genetic engineering requires the manipulation of DNA. When a gene is transferred between

27

organisms that could be conventionally bred, like different kinds of fish, animals or plants, the process is known as *cisgenesis*. When a 'foreign gene' is taken from one species and inserted into another species, or if a 'foreign chemical' is inserted into a seed or species, it is called *transgenesis.* In that case, the result is referred to as '*transgenic.*'

One way the scientists at the chemical companies 'insert' the new genes into a seed is as follows: First, they coat thousands of miniscule pieces of gold or tungsten with the 'foreign' gene which is to be 'inserted.' Then, with a micro-syringe, a 22-caliber gene gun, they blast these 'foreign' genes into the nucleus of the host, namely the DNA of a dish of unsuspecting cells.

Of course, the scientists don't know if it is better for any 'inserted' DNA to have been 'inserted' at the top of a seed, at the bottom of a seed, on the right side, on the left side, or in the middle – because they don't know what the consequences are in any of those cases, or what the relative internal dynamics of the seeds are in any of those cases. They simply hope that many of these 'foreign' genes will end up in the 'right' place – inside of some of the DNA of the cells they are assaulting.

Shooting gene-coated metal at DNA, at a speed of hundreds of miles per hour, will inevitably create internal destruction within the target cells; such internal damage cannot even be effectively evaluated. Some of the target cells will be destroyed, and other parts will be damaged or dislocated.

> This entire process impacts the genetic blueprint of the entire organism which has taken millions of years to evolve.

The process of 'inserting' a foreign gene into the DNA of a host is called 'insertion mutation.' The word 'mutation' explains what we need to know: something has been changed!

> The results are also called 'insertion *carcinogenesis*'[1] because gene therapy studies have revealed that 'insertion mutation' can lead to leukemia in children.

[1] Carcinogenesis means 'the creation of cancer' (from Greek 'karkino' meaning cancer, and genesis meaning, 'to create').

––––––––––––

The final part of this 'food process' is that when these genes are blasted into the cells, it is hard to know exactly how many of them even end up inside of the target/host DNA. The GMO scientists estimate that only a small percentage actually makes it inside of the target/host DNA! So they needed to develop a method to track them. As a solution, these chemical scientists created an Antibiotic Resistant Marker, called an ARM, and attach it to the foreign gene.

Thus, at this point there are various pieces of metal and two 'foreign' genes being blasted into the DNA of a seed.

If the combined package of gold, tungsten and 'foreign' genes manages to be inserted into the host DNA, the ARM will neutralize that DNA's protective system – making it immune to certain antibiotics! Whichever gene does not successfully receive this 'package' (which includes the immunization gene) will die.

> Therefore: In a somewhat ghoulish development, only those genes which are immune to antibiotics will survive! This means that we will be ingesting GMO plants which resist antibiotics. Hence, we could be eating something which creates antibiotic-resistant diseases in our bodies!

This biological process is called 'horizontal gene transfer.' The Antibiotic Resistant Marker (ARM) genes which are inserted into the GMO food are transferred into the bacteria found in our digestive system. Since these are antibiotic-resistant, this could result in the accidental creation of new and dangerous antibiotic-resistant diseases.

N.B. One conclusive study already exists regarding Monsanto's 'Bt corn'; the research discovered that the corn contains an ARM gene which resists the antibiotic, ampicillin. The international medical community feared this would render ampicillin useless. So, this matter was addressed by the World Health Organization, and others, who are seeking a halt to the use of ARM genes.

These are only a few of the more   basic questions.

Some scientific commentary on a few of these issues:

In May 2013 Professor David Schubert of the Cellular Neurobiology Laboratory of the Salk Institute for Biological Sciences *(USA)* explained, "... the introduction of any gene, be it from a different or the same species, always significantly changes overall gene expression and therefore the phenotype of the recipient cell ... and the possibility that enzymatic pathways introduced to synthesize small molecules such as vitamins can interact with endogenous pathways to produce novel molecules...

"The potential consequences of all these perturbations could be the production of biomolecules that are either toxic or carcinogenic, and there is no a priori way of predicting the outcome." [5]

As Richard Lacey, Professor of Food Safety, Leeds University, in the *United Kingdom (England),* expressed it,

"The fact is, it is virtually impossible to even conceive of a testing procedure to assess the health effects of genetically engineered foods when introduced into the food chain, nor is there any nutritional or public interest reason for their introduction."

Dr. Peter Willis, theoretical biologist at Auckland University, *New Zealand,* noted,

"By transferring genes across species barriers which have existed for eons between species like human and sheep we risk breaching natural threshold against unexpected biological consequences. For example, an incorrectly folded form of an ordinary cellular protein can under certain circumstances be replicative and give rise to infectious neurological disease."

Dr. Joseph Cummins, Professor Emeritus of Genetics at the University of Western Ontario (*Canada*) warns,

"Probably the greatest threat from genetically altered crops is the insertion of modified virus and insect virus genes into crops. It has been shown in the laboratory that genetic recombination will create highly virulent new viruses from such constructions." [6]

"GMOs ARE INHERENTLY UNSAFE."

That was the official conclusion of a 2011 summary of GMO studies and research investigations from around the world, which was conducted by a group of medical doctors and scientists at several universities and research institutions in *India*. This scientific review was entitled, '*A Review of Impacts of Genetically Modified Food on Human Health.*'

The concluding remarks stated,

"There are several reasons why GMO plants present unique dangers. The first is that the process of genetic engineering itself creates unpredicted alterations, irrespective of which gene is transferred. This creates mutations in and around the insertion site and elsewhere…

"The biotech industry confidently asserted that gene transfer from GM foods was not possible; the only human feeding study of GM foods later proved that it does take place. The genetic material in soybeans that makes them herbicidal tolerant transferred into the DNA of human gut bacteria and continued to function…

"That means that long after we stop eating a GM crop, its foreign GM proteins may be produced inside our intestines." [7]

Thus, even if we stop eating GMO 'food products' the proteins and bacteria which they contain may develop a life of their own inside of our bodies.

There is no way to predict, or to quantify, the consequences of inserting this DNA into a seed.

As revealed in *Real Food Explained,* several things occur when a 'promoter gene' is spliced into another organism's DNA. Some of them include:

31

(1) The target gene does not merely produce the protein which the GMO company seeks to activate, but begins to activate all of the 1000 genes for which it is responsible;

(2) Since every organism has idle genes, there is no way to predict what these idle genes may produce if they are activated;

(3) The general nutritional content of a plant automatically diminishes, since the 'promoter gene' induces the host organism to invest a disproportionate percentage of its resources into the production of unnecessary proteins.

Because the 'survival' nature of organisms is to generate toxins to protect themselves from 'foreign' bodies, each step in the process provides an opportunity for these organisms to create possible poisons.

There is no way to determine if the plants are generating self-protecting toxins, what kinds of toxins, or how many toxins are being created. These unintended toxins will be consumed by the animals… and humans… who eat the resultant crops. [8]

Thus, by eating GMOs we are putting unknown toxins into our body, and there is no way to determine what 'survival toxins' our bodies are creating to protect themselves – or what effect those potential new toxins have on our health.

"…something else in the whole grain protects against death."

That was one of the conclusions of David R. Jacobs and Lyn M. Steffen, epidemiologists at the University of Minnesota *(USA)* in a 2003 study entitled, *'Nutrients, Foods, and Dietary Patterns as Exposures in Research: A Framework for Food Synergy '* published in the *American Journal of Clinical Nutrition.*

The study found that natural whole foods create a healthy diet, and part of the reason is the synergy and the internal dynamics of the various ingredients within the whole foods themselves. To disturb this natural internal synergy leads to unpredictable negative consequences.

"For example, findings of the strongly reduced risk of ischemic heart disease, diabetes, and some cancers among habitual consumers of whole-grain foods support the idea that food synergies play an important role in chronic disease prevention." [9]

SUMMARY: There is a reason why Monsanto and the chemical companies which produce GMO 'food products' hide or disguise their internal research: they don't want anyone to know the results. If they were proud of the results, they would advertise them – instead of concealing them.

There are several fundamental ... and unexplained... issues regarding the science of GMOs: (1) the various chemicals and toxins deliberately *injected* into the seeds; (2) the toxic chemicals *absorbed* by the GMO seeds from the insecticides sprayed on them which the seeds *are created to absorb*; (3) the *synergistic* effect of those toxic chemicals all working together; (4) the *internal dynamics* of the seeds which are disrupted by forcibly *injecting* chemicals into them; (5) the *internal dynamics* of the seeds once these chemicals and toxins are inside of them.

Currently, it is impossible for science to even observe and analyze the internal **process** inside of the seeds, and the **synergistic interactions and effects** of any of these chemicals. That's why it is particularly important to at least know what has been put into these seeds.

Monsanto and the other chemical companies which produce GMO 'food products' spend millions of dollars every year to *prevent* national and state governments from requiring that they label the content of their products (like ordinary producers of food are required to do).

Why do Monsanto and the other chemical companies fight to *prevent* any labeling of the chemical contents of their 'food products'? There is only one answer:

They don't want public consumers to know what chemicals they have put inside!

Introduction

The pages that follow illustrate a small sample of the reasons why Monsanto, Bayer, Syngenta, Dow, and DuPont want to keep consumers ignorant … and why these chemical companies pay corrupt politicians, lawyers, public relations companies, and academic 'consultants' millions of dollars a year to help them conceal the facts from the public about the toxicity of the GMO 'food products' that they produce.

In the following pages you will see that the chemical industry, which has taken control of the production of food, has been breeding crops for yield (profits), not for nutrition. Thus,

Chemical agriculture has achieved something never before accomplished in the history of mankind: humans who are simultaneously overfed and undernourished on a global scale.

It gets worse: Tobacco companies generate sales and profits by inserting chemical additives into cigarettes to create an addiction. Now, chemical companies generate profits by producing 'food products' which lack nutrition – thereby creating an addiction to eat more. Scientists around the world openly warn that the GMO companies are creating their own addicted customers – and slowly poisoning them! And, they have a captive market…

Nobody has to smoke. But, everyone has to eat!

[1] http://www.psr.org/chapters/oregon/assets/pdfs/powerpoints/gmo-and-rbgh-powerpoint.ppt
[2] http://articles.mercola.com/sites/articles/archive/2011/12/10/dr-don-huber-interview-part-1.aspx
[3] http://www.ncbi.nlm.nih.gov/pubmed/22331240
[4] http://www.researchgate.net/publication/259770098_Glyphosate_Commercial_Formulation_Causes_Cytotoxicity_Oxidative_Effects_and_Apoptosis_on_Human_Cells_Differences_With_its_Active_Ingredient
[5] http://www.thelibertybeacon.com/2013/05/08/the-risks-of-gm-food-by-prof-david-schubert/
[6] http://www.psrast.org/scicomm.htm
[7] http://www.academia.edu/542384/A_Review_on_Impacts_of_Genetically_Modified_Food_on_Human_Health
[8] http://www.realfoodexplained.com/process-making-gmo-safe/
[9] http://ajcn.nutrition.org/content/78/3/508S.long
NB A number of these issues are also discussed in the following links:
(A) *http://www.psrast.org/thoughtpolice.htm*

PART 1
SCIENTIFIC EVIDENCE
of
GMO HEALTH DANGERS

GLOBAL STUDIES
by
MEDICAL RESEARCH SCIENTISTS

DISEASES
and
MEDICAL MALADIES

ALLERGIES and the IMMUNE SYSTEM

*The word 'immune' (from the Latin 'immunis' meaning 'not affected')
means 'protected from.' The immune system is a complex system of
biological structures and processes within an organism which
protects it against diseases. A healthy immune system can detect a
wide variety of viruses and 'foreign' invaders of the organism, and
determine which are healthy for the organism's tissue and allowed
'in' and which are harmful to the organism's tissue and are to be kept
'out.'*

**A multi-generational diet modified the immune system of animals
– and may promote blood cancer (leukemia).**

———————

**"Several animal studies indicate serious health risks associated
with GM food, including infertility, immune problems,
accelerated aging, insulin regulation, and changes in major
organs and the gastrointestinal system."**

That was part of a 2010 summary report by five (5) research scientists
from separate research institutions in **India** which lists a variety of
allergy type issues that are triggered by exposure to GMO crops. The
review, entitled *'A Review on Impacts of Genetically Modified Food
on Human Health,'* was conducted by a team of scientists from
different research institutions and published by Dr. Sanjay Mishra in
2011 in *The Open Nutraceuticals Journal.*

The report explains that allergic reactions occur when the immune
system recognizes a 'foreign' object enters the body.

"All GM foods, by definition, have something foreign and
different…" [namely the *Bt* gene to resist pesticides]… and several
studies show that they provoke reactions."

Research has revealed that GM potatoes affect the immune system of
rats; GM peas create an inflammatory reaction in mice … "suggesting
that it might cause deadly allergic reactions in people."

In one paragraph, entitled, *'GMOs ARE INHERENTLY UNSAFE,'* the report cites

"The process of genetic-engineering itself creates unpredicted alterations, irrespective of which gene is transferred. This creates mutations in and around the insertion site and elsewhere."

Regarding the toxins put into the GMO seeds, the authors comment,

"The toxin creates holes in [insects'] stomachs and kills them... The fact that we consume that toxic pesticide in every bite of *Bt* corn is hardly appetizing. Studies verify, however, that natural *Bt*-toxin is not fully destroyed during digestion and does react with mammals."

The report then issued a stern warning of the long-term consequences of eating GM foods:

"The genetic material in soybeans that make them herbicide tolerant transferred into the DNA of human gut bacteria and continued to function. That means that long after we stop eating a GM crop, its foreign GM proteins may be produced inside our intestines...

"If *Bt* genes relocate to human gut bacteria, our intestinal flora may be converted into living pesticide factories, possibly producing *Bt* toxin inside of us year after year." [1]

Thus, the GMOs may be inflicting continual damage on our immune system – which is supposed to protect us from allergies. Even more alarming, the problem is *growing* inside of us!

"The F5 experimental animals showed enlarged inguinal and axillary lymph nodes, but not spleens, and increased WBC[1] counts in blood (but within the norm for Mus musculus)." Also, there was a "... significant decrease in the percentage of T cells[2] in spleen and lymph nodes and the B cells[2] in lymph nodes and

blood of the F5 experimental mice in comparison to the control F5 mice."

That was the conclusion of a 2010 study at the Division of Immunology, Department of Preclinical Sciences, Faculty of Veterinary Medicine, Warsaw University of Life Sciences, in Warsaw, *Poland*, conducted by seven (7) research scientists, led by Dr. M. Krzyzowska.

This study, entitled, '*The effect of multigenerational diet containing genetically modified triticale on immune system in mice,*' was also published in the U.S. National Library of Medicine of the National Institutes of Health.

In this research project five consecutive generations of mice were fed with pellets containing 20% of conventional triticale[3] grain (the control group) while the other group of rats (the experimental group) were fed pellets containing 20% of the transgenic triticale grain (GM grain) which was genetically designed to resist BASTA herbicide. [2]

What does this mean?

The lymphatic system is an essential component of the immune system which includes lymphatic fluid, lymphatic vessels, lymph nodes, spleen, tonsils, adenoids, Peyer patches, and the thymus. The fluid is transported slowly from the head and other extremities to larger vessels which then drain into the system of veins. Approximately 600 lymph nodes reside along these various channels, each of which encloses a sinus stuffed with macrophages which remove 99% of the antigens[4] that are delivered in this way. Through this process, infectious organisms are detected and removed. [3]

If the lymph nodes become enlarged, this process is interrupted. Allergies arise. Children are particularly sensitive to the development of large lymph nodes, and allergies.

Also, T-cells are the white blood cells in the immune system. A decline in the T-cells weakens the body's immune system, and can allow allergies to develop. B cells are white blood cells called 'lymphocytes' and are part of the   immune system.

40

The entire blood cell system was disturbed, which reduces its effectiveness in combating 'foreign' intrusions in the body.

[1] *'WBC' stands for White Blood Cell. A 'WBC count' measures the number of white blood cells – which are responsible for fighting infection*
[2] *'T cells' are white blood cells, called lymphocytes, that make up part of the immune system and combat diseases and harmful substances. 'B cells' are white blood cells called 'lymphocytes' and are part of the immune system.*
[3] *'Triticale' is a hybrid of wheat (Triticum) and rye (Secale)*
[4] *An 'antigen' is any substance which causes the immune system to produce antibodies against it.*

"The available evidence is sufficient to support a moratorium on the massive intake of GM crops by human populations until the genetic consequences are resolved in the laboratory."

That was one of the conclusions well over a decade ago, in a Toxicology Symposium at Guelf University in *Canada* in 2001, Dr. Joe Cummins, Emeritus Professor of Genetics, University of Western Ontario, *Canada*.

Professor Cummins added, "The bacterial genes used in constructing GM crops have a property that impacts on the immune system over and above the ability to produce antibodies...

"Apparently the CpG motif in DNA molecules and oligonucleotides[1] provides a signal that the immune system recognizes and initiates a primary sequence of reactions leading to activation of the immune system leading to inflammation (Manders and Thomas 2000 and Gurunathan et al 2000)...

"The oligonucleotide[1] acts as a promoter of lymphoma [blood cancer]."

In the symposium it was pointed out that DNA is not broken down inside the gastro-intestinal tract as was previously believed (and consistently claimed by the chemical companies). DNA sequences large enough to contain whole genes remained intact and entered the blood and tissues.

One of the papers that was reviewed focused on the subject of DNA and GMO feed on farm animals; the other focused on mice.

"These two studies show that food DNA is circulated to the tissues of animals and may even be transmitted from the mother to the fetal tissues."

The paper on mice (Shubbert et al, 1998) provided specific details, and

"showed that ingested DNA from a bacterial virus or from a plasmid transgene is incorporated in chromosomes and is passed from mother to fetus…"

"If food DNA sequences are randomly incorporated into coding sequences including introns, exons, or promoters, they will certainly act as mutagens[2]."

THE SUMMARY:

"In conclusion, the bacterial genes used in GM crops have been found to have significant impacts on the individuals ingesting GM crops. The impacts include inflammation, arthritis and lymphoma promotion.

"The consequences of GM genes being incorporated into the chromosomes of somatic[3] cells of those consuming GM food **and their unborn** has been ignored by those charged with evaluating the hazards of GM crops." [4]
[Emphasis added]

[1] *'Oligonucleotide' is a short nucleic acid polymer, a molecule whose structure is composed of multiple repeating units.*
[2] *A 'mutagen' is an agent that can increase the frequency of mutations in an orgamism.*
[3] *'Somatic' from Greek 'somatikos' (of the body) relates to the body and not to the psyche*

"… GM foods pose a serious health risk in the areas of toxicology, allergy and immune function, reproductive health, and metabolic, physiologic, and genetic health, and are without benefit… "

That was the conclusion in a May 2009 paper by the prestigious American Academy of Environmental Medicine (AAEM), in Wichita, Kansas *(USA)* which warned that eating "GM foods pose a serious health risk…" for the immune system, fertility and reproduction, the metabolism, the body's gastrointestinal system, and even the internal structure of our genes.

The AAEM summarized their findings, that,

"Several animal studies indicate serious health risks associated with genetically modified (GM) food…"

In short, a review by the AAEM warns that various parts of the human body are being systematically ravaged by the consumption of GMO 'food products.' [5]

———————

IN SUMMARY, GMO crops can create anti-biotic resistant genes in our bodies, can confuse the immune system, can disrupt the immune system, can cause food allergies, and can cause autoimmune diseases. Separate studies, by a multitude of medical professionals and research scientists, from various countries, over extended periods of time, were conducted:

All of the studies reveal disruptions of the immune systems when a GMO diet is consumed.

[1] http://www.academia.edu/542384/A_Review_on_Impacts_of_Geneticall y_Modified_Food_on_Human_Health
[2] http://www.ncbi.nlm.nih.gov/pubmed/21033555
[3] http://www.patient.co.uk/doctor/Generalised-Lymphadenopathy.htm
[4] http://www.saynotogmos.org/scientific_studies.htm
[5] http://www.aaemonline.org/gmopost.html

LIVER

The 'liver' (from Old English 'lifer') is a large meaty organ located on the right side of the belly. The liver's principal function is to filter the blood coming from the digestive tract before passing it on to the rest of the body. The liver also detoxifies chemicals, metabolizes drugs, creates proteins which are essential for blood clotting and other bodily function, and secrets bile that goes into the intestines to aid the digestion of lipids (naturally occurring molecules, including fats, fat-soluble vitamins such as A,D,E,K, monoglycerides, diglycerides, triglycerides, etc.) to help store energy.

GMOs produce granular degeneration in the liver.

––––––––––––

"The Roundup residues have been shown to be toxic to placental, embryonic, and umbilical cord cells. This was also the case for hepatic human cell lines in a comparable manner, inducing nuclei and membrane changes, apoptosis[1] and necrosis.[2]"

That was a conclusion in ***France*** in 2011 after reviewing 19 separate studies on GMO crops.

The review was conducted by a team of researcher scientists, Gilles-Eric Seralini, Robin Mesnage, Emilie Clair, Steeve Gress, Joel Spiroux de Vendomois, and Dominique Cellier. It was entitled, *'Genetically modified crops safety assessments: present limits and possible improvements.'*

The portion of this review referring to the liver states, "For one of the longest independent tests performed, a GM herbicide-tolerant soybean available on the market was used to feed mice. It caused the development of irregular hepatocyte[3] nuclei, more nuclear pores, numerous small fibrillar centers, and abundant dense fibrillar components, indicating increased metabolic rates... Anyway, these are specific parameters of ultrastructural dysfunction, and the relevance is clear. The liver is reacting."

Continuing, the report says, "The other major GMO trait has to do with the mutated (*mBt*) insecticidal peptidic toxins produced by transgenes in plants. In this case, some studies with maize confirmed histopathological[4] changes in the liver and kidneys of rats after GM feed consumption. Such changes consist in congestion, cell nucleus border changes, and severe granular degeneration in the liver."

It concludes,

"Taken together, the results indicate potential adverse effects in hepatic[5] metabolism… The liver together with the kidneys are the major reactive organs in case of food chronic intoxication." [1]

The liver's main responsibility is to filter the blood coming from the digestive tract, before passing it to the rest of the body. The liver also detoxifies chemicals and metabolizes drugs. It is on the 'front line' of becoming poisoned itself.

The toxins in the GMO crops, and the *glyphosate* sprayed on those crops (and absorbed into them), appear to be overwhelming the liver and contaminating the liver itself.

The liver and kidneys, detoxifying organs, are themselves being poisoned by GMO toxins.

[1] *'Apoptosis' is the programmed cell death (PCD) as part of normal cell changes and development*
[2] *'Necrosis' is a form of cell injury which results in the premature death of cells; it is caused by factors external to the cell or tissue, such as infection, toxins, or trauma.*
[3] *'Hepatocytes' are cells in the main tissue of the liver, and constitute 70-85% of the liver's cytoplasmic mass.*
[4] *'Histopathological' is the microscopic study of tissues in order to learn the nature and spread of disease.*
[5] *'Hepatic' (from Greek 'hepatikos' meaning 'liver') refers to the liver.*

[1] [*http://www.enveurope.com/content/23/1/10*

BIRTH DEFECTS/FEMALE INFERTILITY

A birth defect is a biological problem which occurs while the baby is in the mother's womb, and usually occurs during the first 3 months of the pregnancy. Currently, in the United States one out of every 33 babies is born with some form of birth defect.

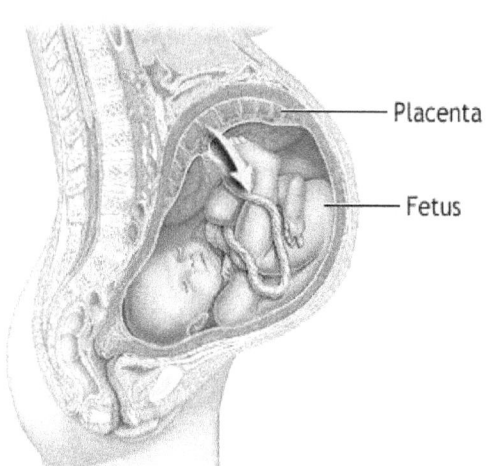

Placenta

Fetus

✲ADAM.

Image from:
http://www.nlm.nih.gov/medlineplus/ency/imagepages/17144.htm

Glyphosate leads to reproductive problems.
Toxins in GMOs found to have entered the fetal cords and fetuses of pregnant women.

"Glyphosate has endocrine[1] disrupting properties which create hormonal issues, which lead to reproductive problems such as infertility, birth defects, miscarriage, and sexual development."

A 2005 study with a team of five (5) research scientists was led by Dr. Gilles-Eric Seralini, the biochemist at the Institute of Biology of the University of Caen, in **France**. The results were published in *Environment Health Perspectives* by the National Institute of Environmental Health Sciences, at Research Triangle Park in North Carolina, **USA**.

Entitled, '*Differential Effects of Glyphosate and Roundup on Human Placenta Cells and Aromatase*,' the study reported that

"…glyphosate is toxic to human placenta JEG3 cells within 18 hours with concentrations lower than those found in agricultural use, and this effect increases with concentration and time or in the presence of Roundup adjuvants."

Dr. Seralini explained that: even weak doses of *glyphosate* showed toxic effects on human placental cell lines, emphasizing that "the effect is proportional to the dose, but also to the length of the exposure."

In referring to various epidemiological studies concerning female farmers using *glyphosate*, he further suggested this could explain the high levels of premature births and miscarriages.

He added that,

"… the effects of glyphosate are facilitated by the Roundup formulation in microsomes or in cell culture. We conclude that endocrine and toxic effects of Roundup, not just glyphosate, can be observed in mammals." [2]

[1] *The 'endocrine system' is the system of glands in the body, each of which secretes different types of hormones directly into the bloodstream.*

"This work clearly confirms that the adjuvants in Roundup formulations are not inert. Moreover, the proprietary mixtures available on the market could cause cell damage and even death."

That was one of the conclusions in a 2008 study by Dr. Nora Benachour and Dr. Gilles-Eric Seralini of the Institute of Biology, University of Caen, **France**. They entitled the report of their research *'Glyphosate Formulations Induce Apoptosis[1] and Necrosis[2] in Human Umbilical, Embryonic, and Placenta Cells.'*

The testing was done on HUVEC cells (Human Umbilical Vein Endothelial Cells), which are derived from the endothelium[3] of veins in the umbilical cord. "HUVED primary neonate umbilical cord vein cells have been tested with 293 embryonic kidney and JEG3 placenta cell lines."

The result: "All R[oundup/glyphosate] formulations cause total death within 24 h, through an inhibition of the mitochondrial succinate dehydrogenase activity[4], and necrosis, by release of cytosolic adenylate kinase[5] measuring membrane damage. They also induce apoptosis via activation of enzymatic caspases 3/7 activity[6]."

"In conclusion the R[oundup] adjuvants [chemical agents] change human cell permeability and amplify toxicity induced already by G[lyphosate], through apoptosis and necrosis."

The development of the cells themselves is affected, and the tests led to the early death of various cells. Because the embryo and fetus are particularly sensitive, the toxic effects on them are even more dangerous. [3]

IN SUMMARY, the *glyphosate* which is sprayed on GMO crops (and absorbed by them) disturbs the development of cells, and can kill the cells – especially in the embryo and fetus.

[1] *'Apoptosis' is the process of programmed cell death.*
[2] *'Necrosis' is the premature death of cells and other living tissues.*
[3] *'Endothelium' is the thin layer of cells that line the interior surface of blood vessels and other organs.*
[4] *The 'mitochondrial succinate dehydrogenase activity' is the activity of different enzymes and other actions in the mitochondrial cells and cell development. The mitochondria are the energy sources, i.e. 'the power houses', of the cells.*
[5] *'Adenylate kinase' is an enzyme which is involved in the 'homeostatis' (regularity, stability) of cellular energy.*
[6] *'Caspases 3/7 activity' is a protein activity in the development process. Unregulated natural activity of the caspases can lead to early cell death.*

'Glyphosate-based Herbicides Produce Teratogenic Effects on Vertebrates by Impairing Retinoic[1] Acid Signaling'

That was the name of a 2010 study conducted by Dr. Alejandra Paganelli and four (4) colleagues from **Paraguay** and **Argentina**, at the *Laboratorio de Embriologia Molecular* and the *Facultad de Medicina* at the University of Buenos Aires. In the research they injected low doses of *glyphosate* into amphibian embryos. The extremely sensitive cells of the   embryos are affected.

The effects included:

- increased death of cells which form the skull
- reduced head size
- genetic alterations in the central nervous system
- deformed cartilage
- undeveloped kidneys
- defects in the eyes.

One of the disturbing observations was that the *glyphosate* was **accumulating**: It was not being broken down by the cells. The *glyphosate* **accumulates** – and remains – in the body. It will continue to have its effects on these vital organs and tissues.

The scientists stated that these effects are:

"… completely comparable to what would happen in the development of the human embryo." [4]

[1] *'Retinoic acid' is a vitamin A-derived molecule. The 'retinoic acid signaling' is an essential component in the embryonic cell development.*

"… a glyphosate herbicide formulation and glyphosate alone caused malformations in the embryos of *Xenopus laevis* and chickens through disruption of the retinoic acid signaling pathway…"

That was one of the conclusions of a June 2012 study reported by the Gene Expression Group, Department of Medical and Molecular Genetics, King's College London School of Medicine, *United Kingdom*. The study was entitled, *'Teratogenic[1] Effects of Glyphosate-Based Herbicides: Divergence of Regulatory Decisions from Scientific Evidence.'*

The international team of eight (8) research scientists led by the Department Head, Dr. M. Antoniou *(United Kingdom)*, included MEM Habib *(Brazil)*, CV Howard *(Northern Ireland)*, RC Jennings *(United Kingdom)*, C Leifert *(United Kingdom)*, RO Nodari *(Brazil)*, CJ Robinson *(United Kingdom)*, and J Fagan *(United Kingdom).*

This study was published in the *Journal of Environmental & Analytical Toxicology.*

The authors reviewed a 2010 study which showed that "a glyphosate herbicide formulation and glyphosate alone caused malformations in the embryos of *Xenopus laevis* and chickens through disruption of the retinoic acid signaling pathway... However, examination of the German authorities' draft assessment report on the industry studies, which underlies glyphosate's EU authorization, revealed further evidence of glyphosate's teratogenicity[1]."

In short, *glyphosate* produced malformed embryos.

In the Introduction, the scientists also state, "An investigation (Paganelli et al) of the toxicity of a commercial Roundup herbicide formulation and its active ingredient glyphosate found that these substances caused severe malformations in the embryos of the South African clawed frog *Xenopus laevis* and chickens. In frogs, dilutions of 1/5000 of the formulation (equivalent to 430 mM of glyphosate) were sufficient to induce malformations, including shortening of the anterior-posterior axis, microcephaly[2], microphthalmia[3], cyclopia[4], and craniofacial malformations at tadpole stages.

"Embryos injected with pure glyphosate showed similar phenotypes, suggesting that glyphosate itself, rather than a surfactant or other adjuvant present in the formulation, was responsible for these development abnormalities. Roundup produced similar effects in chicken embryos, which showed a loss of rhombomere[5] remains, reduction of optic vesicles, and microcephaly."

The study also blasts the attempts "by Monsanto/Dow/Syngenta" to mislead the public by promoting their claims that *glyphosate* does not cause adverse reproductive effects. The study says that this claim by the chemical companies "does not stand up to scrutiny..." and

"The data clearly shows that glyphosate does cause adverse reproductive effects and malformations in laboratory animals."

"The study ... is relevant to human risk assessment because the retinoic acid[6] signaling pathway is a central signaling pathway in embryonic development that operates in virtually all vertebrates, whether amphibians, birds of mammals."

The study concludes with an ominous warning:

"A substantial body of evidence demonstrates that glyphosate and Roundup cause teratogenic effects and other toxic effects on reproduction, as well as genotoxic[7] effects." [5]

[1] *'Teratogenicity' is from the Greek word 'teratos' meaning 'monster' and is the potential to develop fetal malformation and to cause birth defects.*
[2] *'Microcephaly' is a birth abnormality which causes an abnormally small head.*
[3] *'Microphthalmia' is a birth abnormality in which one or both of the eyeballs are abnormally small.*
[4] *'Cyclopia' is a birth abnormality in which the embryo does not properly divide the orbits of the eyes into two cavities.*
[5] *'Rhombomere' is a segment of the developing neural tube in the evolving rhombencephalon (hind brain) region during the embryonic period. (The other two parts of the brain are called the 'midbrain' and 'forebrain.') Components of the hind brain transmit signals between the spinal cord and the higher parts of the brain, and control such autonomic functions as heartbeat and respiration.*
[6] *'Retinoic acid' is a metabolite (part of the metabolism) of vitamin A (retinol) which mediates the functions of vitamin A that are essential for growth and development.*
[7] *'Genotoxic' (meaning toxic to the genes) describes the property of chemical agents which damage the genetic information within a cell, causing mutations, which can also lead to cancer.*

IN SUMMARY, these studies are from medical practitioners and research scientists at various clinics, laboratories and universities **in ten (10) different countries!**

Each of these separate studies focused on different aspects of the reproductive process, whether in the body of the mother (human and animal), the embryo, or the fetus. All of the research concludes that there is damage to the reproductive process— which can lead to birth defects, or death.

The research confirms that GMO crops contain toxins. In addition, *glyphosate* is not only sprayed onto the GMO crops, and accumulates in the soil and water – it is also **absorbed** by the GMO plants themselves … which have been genetically engineered for the very specific purpose of allowing this poison to be sprayed on them.

Besides *glyphosate*, additional toxins and other chemicals have been inserted/blasted into these so-called 'GMO crops.' No one knows for sure what all of the chemicals are – except the chemical companies who produce them, and they refuse to allow any of their products to be labeled as to the contents.

Since the 'food products' from these GMO crops are eaten by humans, and by farm animals, there is no way to currently calculate what malformations and other birth defects the GMO crops and *glyphosate* may inflict upon human embryos and fetuses.

However, as the above studies show, there is now scientific evidence of the problems which are arising. And, the biological and medical problems are literally growing around the world… as the spread of GMO crops and the use of *glyphosate* and other toxins continue to grow and accumulate – not just in the fields, but also in our bodies!

[1] http://www.ncbi.nlm.nih.gov/pmc/articles/PMC1257596/
[2] http://pubs.acs.org/doi/abs/10.1021/tx800218n
[3] http://pubs.acs.org/doi/abs/10.1021/tx1001749
[4] http://www.omicsonline.org/2161-0525/2161-0525-S4-006.php

EMBRYO/FETUS

*An 'embryo' (from Greek 'embruon' meaning 'to be full to bursting')
is a multi-cellular diploid eukaryote in a female, which has been
fertilized by a male haploid, in its earliest stage of development from
the initial stage of the first cell division until germination (hatching or
birth). In humans it is regarded as an embryo until approximately
eight weeks after the fertilization, or approximately 10 weeks after the
last menstrual period, after which time it is called a 'fetus.'*

*'Fetus' (from the Latin word 'fetus' meaning 'newly-delivered' or
'fruitful' or 'offspring') is the unborn or un-hatched vertebrate after
attaining the basic structure of its kind. The fetal state climaxes at
birth; by the third month the arms and legs of the human fetus begin
to move and reflexive movements (such as sucking) begin; in four
months the fetus is about 5.3 inches (135 mm) long and weighs about
6 oz. (170 g.); during the fifth month downy hairs (lanugo) cover the
body and the skin becomes less transparent; in seven months a
protective greasy substance covers the now reddish and wrinkled
skin; in the eighth month fat deposits build up under the skin; in 266
days the fetus is regarded as 'full-term.'*

**A GMO diet leaves GMO toxins in the bloodstreams, fetal cords,
and fetuses of pregnant women.**

***Bt toxin (Cry1Ab protein) was found in the blood of pregnant
and non-pregnant women – and in the fetuses and umbilical
cords of the pregnant women.***

This was reported in a 2011 study conducted by a number of research
scientists let by Dr. Aziz Aris of the Department of Obstetrics and
Gynecology, Clinical Research Center, and the Faculty of Medicine
and Health Sciences at the University of Sherbrooke Hospital Center,
and Dr. Samuel Leblanc of the Faculty of Medicine and Health
Sciences at the University of Sherbrooke Hospital Center in ***Canada.***

The study was entitled, '*Maternal and fetal exposure to pesticides
associated to genetically modified foods in Eastern Townships of*

Quebec, Canada.' The results were published in the May 2011 issue of *Reproductive Toxicology* and *PubMed.gov* of the U.S. National Library of Medicine. [1]

The study consisted of women between the ages of 32 and 34 years of age, including 30 pregnant women with vaginal deliveries and their just-born babies and 39 healthy non-pregnant women having tubal ligations.[1] Blood samples were taken from these women and from the babies' umbilical cords at delivery.

The study points out the role of the placenta in the embryo's nutrition and growth, and in the regulation of the endocrine functions and in drug biotransformation. It is essential that the placenta have an optimum exchange of nutritious elements across the maternal-fetal unit (MFU) to have a successful pregnancy. However, the exchange from the placenta can also include substances "that represent a pathological risk for the fetus such as xenobiotics[3] that include drugs, food additives, pesticides, and environmental pollutants."

The study further elaborates that pathological conditions in the placenta "are important causes of intrauterine or perinatal death, congenital deformities, intrauterine growth retardation, maternal death, and a great deal of morbidity for both, mother and child."

At the conclusion of the study, the shocking results showed:

- **The blood of 93% (28 out of 30) of the pregnant women contained the Cry1Ab protein (the *Bt* toxin) from GM corn**

- **The blood of 80% (24 out of 30) of their babies contained the toxin**

- **Of the pregnant women who had the *Bt* toxin in their blood, 86% had passed it on to their babies while *in utero***

- **Sixty-nine percent (69%) of the non-pregnant women had this *Bt* toxin in their blood.**

- **A significantly higher proportion of pregnant women had this Cry1Ab protein (*Bt* toxin) in their blood compared to the non-pregnant women – and they passed it on to their fetuses. [2]**

[1] *'Tubal ligation' (often referred to as 'tying the tubes') is surgery to close a woman's fallopian tubes, which connect the ovaries to the uterus. Once a woman has this surgery she can no longer get pregnant.*
[2] *'Xenobiotics' (from Greek 'xeno' meaning 'foreign' and 'bio' meaning 'life') is any 'foreign' element which enters the body.*

"3-MPPA and Cry1Ab toxin are clearly detectable and appear to cross the placenta to the fetus."

That was one of the conclusions of the study. It emphasized the fact that the toxins were not destroyed by the mother's body, but *entered the fetus.*

> "Serum 3-MPPA[1] and CryAb1[2] were detected in PW [pregnant women], their fetuses, and NPW [non-pregnant women]."

"… Cry1Ab toxin was detected in 93% and 80% of maternal and fetal blood samples, respectively and in 69% of tested blood samples from non-pregnant women."

The researchers summed up the dangers by advising the need for more research: "This is the first study to reveal the presence of circulating PAGMF *[Pesticides Associates with Genetically Modified Food]* in women with and without pregnancy, paving the way for a new field in reproductive toxicology including nutrition and utero-placental toxicities."

For whatever reason, *glyphosate* and *gluphosinate* were found in non-pregnant women, but not in pregnant women. However, at the completion of the research, the toxins were discovered not only in the mothers, but also in the fetal cords… and in the fetuses.

The final conclusion:

"Given the potential toxicity of these environmental pollutants and the fragility of the fetus, more studies are needed, particularly those using the placenta transfer approach." [3]

The study also revealed that trace amounts of the CryAb1 toxins were detected in the gastrointestinal contents of livestock fed on GM corn, "raising concerns about this toxin in insect-resistant GM crops; that these toxins may not be effectively eliminated in humans, and there may be a high risk of exposure through consumption of contaminated meat."

It is assumed these toxins must have entered the bodies of the women and their fetuses through their diet of GMO foods. [4]

––––––––––––

"The consequence of GM food genes being incorporated into the chromosomes of somatic cells of those consuming GM food *and their unborn* [emphasis added] has been ignored by those charged with evaluating the hazards of GM crops."

As far back as 2001, in a *Toxicology Symposium* at the University of Guelph, ***Canada***, Dr. Joe Cummins, Emeritus Professor of Genetics of the University of Western Ontario, Canada provided a dire warning. His remarks, and a summary of them, were published in *SAY NO TO GMOS.org/ Scientific Studies*.

Dr. Cummins begins with an initial criticism, that

"the safety of genetically modified (GM) crops is hampered by the unwillingness of the regulators to recognize and to evaluate the impact of genetic effects that are outside simplistic models of genes and their behavior."

The research disclosed that a diet of GMO foods verifiably caused "inflammation, arthritis, and lymphoma promotion." He emphasized that the genes which are inserted into the GMO seeds contain something which "impacts on the immune system over and above the ability to produce antibodies." In other words, whatever is put into the GMO seeds does more than just allow these seeds to combat and kill insects. They cause consequences for whoever consumes them.

He summarizes two studies reviewed at the symposium, by Einspanier et al (2001) and Shubbert et al (1998), and warns mothers:

- "These two studies show that food DNA is circulated to the tissues of animals and may even be transmitted from the mother to the fetal tissues."

- "The available evidence is sufficient to support a moratorium on the massive intake of GM crops by human populations until the genetic consequences are resolved in the laboratory."

He states the final results of the symposium:

"In conclusion, the bacterial genes used in GM crops have been found to have significant impacts on the individuals ingesting GM crops."

[5]

[1] 3-MPPA (3-methylphosphinicopropionic acid) is one of the Bt toxins. It is a metabolite of gluphosinate, a broad-spectrum contact herbicide. (Gluphosinate and its metabolite methylphosphinicopropionic acid) Gluphosinate is one of the chemicals in GMO crops. It interferes with the biosynthetic pathway of the amino acid glutamine and with ammonia detoxification. Gluphosinate has been found to be toxic to reproduction. The Swedish Chemicals Agency and the European Parliament included it in a biocide ban in 2009.
[2] A Bt toxin. 'Cry1Ab' is one of the GMO toxins. It is an insecticidal protein produced by the soil bacterium Bacillus thuringiensis (Bt).

NB   Many mothers and women's groups are now addressing this issue of how GMO 'food products' are poisoning babies and children: through rBGH milk, through the GMO diet of women and expectant mothers, through the GMO soy products in baby foods, and through the school lunch programs which provide a GMO diet. Some of them are listed at the end of this book.

[1] http://www.sciencedirect.com/science/article/pii/S0890623811000566
[2] http://www.gmfreecymru.org/pivotal_papers/crucial24.htm
[3] http://www.ncbi.nlm.nih.gov/pubmed/21338670
[4] http://ddococktailhour.com/files/0/8/7/4/3/244299-234780/BTinpregnantwomen.pdf
[5] http://www.saynotogmos.org/scientific_studies.htm

UTERUS (WOMB)

The 'uterus' (from Latin 'uterus'), or womb ('wamb' from Old English, Old German, Norwegian)), is a hollow muscular organ

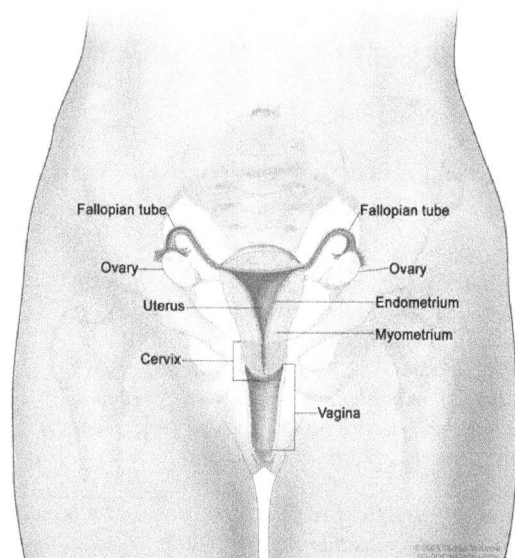

located in the pelvic cavity of female mammals in which the fertilized egg (ovum) implants and gestates. Within 5 to 7 days after the ovum is fertilized it becomes an embryo, attaches to the wall of the uterus (endometrium) where it is nourished by blood vessels developed for this purpose, creates a placenta, and develops into the fetus until childbirth.

The uterus is also essential for sexual responsiveness, since it directs the blood flow to the pelvis and the external genitalia, i.e. the ovaries, vagina, labia, and clitoris.

Image from: http://www.cancer.gov/cancertopics/pdq/treatment/unusual-cancers-childhood/Patient/page6

GMO diets disrupted reproductive cycles of rats and enlarged the uteri of both rats and pigs.

"Female rats fed genetically modified soybeans showed statistically-significant changes in their uterus and reproductive cycles."

In 2009 six (6) research scientists in ***Brazil*** cooperated in a study entitled, '*The Impact of Dietary Organic and Transgenic Soy on the Reproductive System of Female Adult Rat.*'

The scientists involved were from the Urogenital Research Unit, State University of Rio de Janeiro, and the Laboratory of Experimental Nutrition of the Fluminense Federal University in Rio de Janeiro.

The 'epithelium[1]' referred to above is a tissue which lines the cavities and surfaces of structures throughout the body, and also forms many glands. The glandular epithelium comprises only a minor part of the total endometrium[2] tissue, the mucous membrane tissue lining the uterine cavity. Although small, the glandular epithelium cells play an essential role in mammalian reproduction by secreting lumen products *(chemicals into the lumen, i.e. open spaces in the female)* into the uterus and serve as a substratum for blastocyst[3] attachment. The secreted uterine luminal fluids provide a method of transport for spermatozoa and the ovum.

In the research, female rats were fed genetically modified soybeans. After consuming this GMO diet, the rats showed statistically-significant changes in their uterus and reproductive cycles.

Groups of female rats which were fed non-GMO soy, or fed no soy at all, did not exhibit these effects.

The study concluded that "The volume density of endometrial glandular epithelium was greater in the GMSG [GM Soy Group] (29.5 +/- 7.17, P <0.001) when compared with the CG [Control Group] (18.5 +/- 7.4) and OSG [Organic Soy Group] (20.3 +/- 10.6) groups." [1]

IN SUMMARY: an unnatural expansion of the endometrial glandular epithelium signals unwarranted changes in the hormones involved in reproduction.

The conclusion of the study was that the internal structure of the uterus itself was 'disturbed and distorted' by the GMO diet.

[1] *'Epithelium' is a membranous tissue, composed of layers of cells, that covers most internal and external surfaces of the body and its organs.*
[2] *The 'endometrium' is the inner mucous membrane (wall) of the mammalian uterus.*

[3]*A 'blastocyst' (from Greek 'blastos' meaning 'bud' and Latin 'cystis' meaning 'bladder' or 'sac')is an embryo that has developed for five to six days after fertilization, and attaches to the endometrium, the inner mucous membrane (wall) of the uterus, where it will undergo the development process.*

"In this study, we found that female pigs fed the GM diet had median uterine weights that were 25% greater than non-GM fed pigs (p= 0.025)."

That was one of the disturbing conclusions of a joint 2013 study with six (6) farmers and research scientists from institutions in *Australia* and the *United States*, led by Dr. Judy Carman and the Institute of Health and Environmental Research in Australia. The study was published in the peer-reviewed *Journal of Organic Systems,* and was entitled, '*A Long-term toxicology study on pigs fed a combined genetically modified (GM) soy and GM maize diet.'*

The research, which focused largely on the uterus and the stomach, discovered that pigs fed a GMO experienced an enlargement of their uteri (uterus) by an astounding 25%.

In explaining the implications of these findings, Dr. Carman pointed out that "… pigs have a digestive system similar to people, so we need to investigate if people are getting digestive problems from eating GM crops."

The uteri of two pigs on the GMO diet were also full of fluid, which was not the case with pigs on the non-GMO diet.

She added another caution, "Pigs with these health problems end up in our food supply. We eat them." [2]

"… there are unexplained problems including spontaneous abortions, deformities of new-born animals, and overall listlessness and lack of contentment in the animals."

That was an observation by one of the farmers who participated in this study, Howard Vlieger, a farmer and livestock consultant in Iowa *(USA).*

He pointed out that when farmers feed their livestock GM crops they have experienced increased production costs – and increased usage of antibiotics. He said that for years there have been reports from veterinarians and farmers that the animals which are fed GM soy and corn in their diet end up with reproductive and digestive problems; sometimes the death rate of the livestock is high.

But most studies were not in the open fields. This research vindicated him. He went on to state,

"For as long as GM crops have been in the feed supply, we have seen increasing digestive and reproductive problems in animals. Now it is scientifically documented." [3]

IN SUMMARY, these research studies from scientists and experts in several countries all point to the same conclusion:

GMO crops cause disruptions in the uterus and in the reproductive process.

[1] http://onlinelibrary.wiley.com/doi/10.1002/ar.20878/full
[2] http://gmojudycarman.org/wp-content/uploads/2013/06/The-Full-Paper.pdf
[3] http://gmojudycarman.org/new-study-shows-that-animals-are-seriously-harmed-by-gm-feed/

CANCER

Cancer (from Latin 'cancer' meaning 'to decay') is not a single disease. It is a variety of diseases, more than 100 of them. Cancer is a term used to describe various diseases in which abnormal cells uncontrollably divide and invade other tissues. These cancerous cells spread throughout the body through the blood and

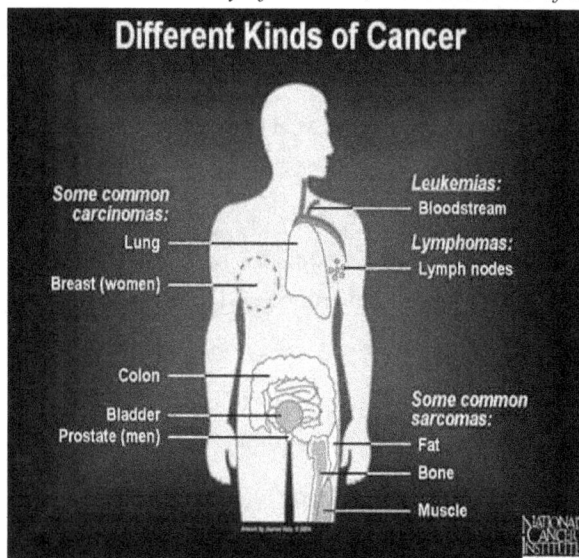

lymph systems. Each form of cancer is defined by the particular part of the body, or organ, which is affected, e.g. breast cancer, colon cancer, etc. Some of them are indicated below.

Image from:
http://www.cancer.gov/cancertopics/understandingcancer/cancer/AllPages

Toxins in GMO maize (corn) caused mammary tumors in female rats, tumors and cell deaths in male rats, and premature deaths in both male and female rats.

"Long term toxicity of a Roundup herbicide and a Roundup-tolerant genetically modified maize"

That's the title of a two-year study on rats and GMO crops and Roundup (the longest ever done to date). The joint research was conducted by eight (8) biological scientists, seven (7) from two universities in *France* and one (1) from a university in *Italy*. It was published in 2012 in *Food and Chemical Toxicology.*

The varieties of maize used in the study were the R[oundup]-tolerant NK603 (Monsanto Corp. USA). The result:

- "In females, all [GMO] treated groups died 2-3 times more than 'controls', and more rapidly. This difference was visible in 3 male groups fed GMOs"

- "Females developed large mammary tumors almost always more often than and before controls"

- "In treated males, liver congestions and necrosis were 2.5 - 5.5 times higher"

- "Males presented 4 times more large palpable tumors than controls which occurred up to 600 days earlier"

- "The maximum difference in males was 5 times more deaths occurring during the 17th month in the group consuming 11% GMO maize, and in females 6 times greater mortality during the 21st month on the 22% GM maize diet with and without R[oundup]."

The conclusion:

"These results can be explained by the non linear endocrine-disrupting effects of Roundup, but also by the overexpression of the transgene in the GMO and its metabolic consequences." [1]

[1] http://ac.els-cdn.com/S0278691512005637/1-s2.0-S0278691512005637-main.pdf?_tid=0549d47a-55fa-11e3-ac40-00000aab0f6b&acdnat=1385401987_e4f5298

BLOOD and BONES (Leukemia)

'Blood' (from Middle English 'blod') is a fluid which is constantly circulating through blood vessels (arteries and veins), and provides the various parts of the body nutrition and oxygen, and performs a cleansing action for waste removal. One-half of the content of the blood is plasma, which contains glucose and other dissolved nutrients, proteins that help the blood to clot, and helps transport substances through the blood. The other half of the blood is composed of blood cells: red cells to carry oxygen to the body's various tissues; white cells to fight infections; and platelets, smaller cells that help clot the blood.

'Bones' (from Middle English 'bon'), composed mainly of calcium phosphate and calcium carbonate, are the structures which form the skeletons of the various parts of the body, and play a major role in maintaining the calcium balance for the blood. The 206 bones in the body protect and support various internal organs, the skull being a protective armor for the brain and the ribs being a protective armor for the lungs. The bone marrow, the soft tissue in the center of the bone, creates and stores blood cells.

Toxins in GMOs damage red blood cells in animals, and poison the blood.

"Biopesticides which are genetically engineered into GMO crops, referred to as Bacillus Thuringensis (Bt) or Cry-toxins, may contribute to blood abnormalities like anemia and to hematological[1] malignancies, i.e. cancers such as leukemia."

That was the synopsis of a research study entitled, *'Hematotoxicity of Bacillus thuringiensis as Sprore-crystal Strains Cry1Aa, Cry1Ab, Cry1Ac, or Cry2Aa in Swiss Albino Mice.'*

The research was conducted by a team of seven (7) scientists at the Department of Genetics and Morphology, Institute of Biological Sciences, University of Brasilia, ***Brazil***. The study specifically addresses the various *Bt* poisons in the GMO crops, and their effects on the blood system.

Bt toxins are found within all GMO crops. The original intent of the study was to determine the environmental safety of GM crops. The investigation focused on the effects that the various *Bt* toxins have on non-insect and other animal species.

As they observed the results of their research, the Brazilian scientists noted that, "… our study demonstrated that *Bt* spore crystals genetically modified to express individually Cry1Aa, Cry1Ab, Cry1Ac, or Cry2A induced hematotoxicity [blood poison], particularly to the erythroid[2] lineage. This finding corroborates literature that demonstrated that alkali-solubilized *Bt* spore-crystals caused *in vitro hemolysis[3]* in cell lines of rat, mouse, sheep, horse, and human erythrocytes[1] and suggested that the plasma membrane of susceptible cells (erythrocytes, in this case) may be the primary target of these toxins."

In other words, these various GMO toxins introduced various poisons into the blood streams of the test animals.

The research revealed that the various combinations of CRY-toxins in the GMO seeds can target the red cell system, and that the *Bt* toxins suppressed bone marrow proliferation – which creates abnormal lymphocyte patterns consistent with certain types of leukemia.

The study concludes by issuing a stern warning of the dangers and poisons involved in 'microbiological control agents' (e.g. pesticides/herbicides):

"Thus, the Brazilian Collegiate Board of Directors of the National Sanitary Surveillance Agency (ANVISA) N° 194/02 advocates evaluations of toxicity and pathogenicity of microbiological control agents (MSA), given that little is known about their toxicological potential."

IN SUMMARY, as the Brazilian Collegiate Board of Directors of the National Sanitary Surveillance Agency concluded: "… little is known about the toxicological potential" of these GMO crops and their affect on the blood, bone, and marrow of people... and, of course, on embryos and fetuses. [1]

What we know for sure is that these GMO seeds are poisonous, because that's what they are scientifically designed to be.

---

[1] *'Hematology' from the Greek 'haima' meaning 'blood' is the study of blood.*
[2] *'Erythroid' from the Greek 'eruthros' meaning 'red' refers to the red blood cells. 'Erythrocytes' are the red blood cells, which are the principle way of delivering oxygen to the body in vertebrates.*
[3] *'In vitro hemolysis': 'hemolysis' from the Greek word 'hemo' (blood) and 'lusis' (loosening) refers to the rupturing of the red blood cells and the release of its contents into the surrounding fluids. 'In vitro' from Latin 'vitro' (under the glass) means these tissues are examined in a laboratory; whereas 'in vivo' from Latin 'vivo' (in the body) means that the experiments are done inside of the body.*

[1]   http://gmoevidence.com/wp-content/uploads/2013/05/JHTD-1-104.pdf

BREAST

*'Breast' (from the Old English word 'breost') is the area of the upper
ventral region on the left and right side of the torso of a primate,
which encloses the mammary gland which in the female can secrete*

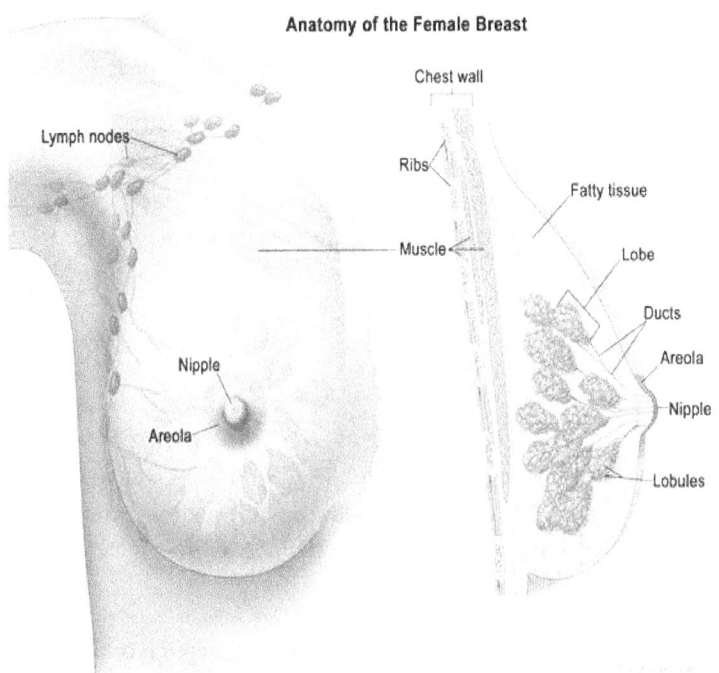

Anatomy of the Female Breast

*milk for feeding infants. Female sex hormones, principally estrogen,
promote breast development which makes the female breasts larger;
due to higher levels of testosterone in men, the male breasts do not
develop to be as large.*

Image from:
http://www.cancer.gov/cancertopics/pdq/treatment/breast/Patient/page1

**Toxins in GMOs caused mammary tumors and disturbed sex
hormonal balance in rats.**

**"Females developed large mammary tumors almost always
more often than and before controls, the pituitary was the**

second most disabled organ; the sex hormonal balance was modified by GMO and Roundup treatments."

This is a conclusion from a 2012 study conducted by a collaboration of eight (8) European scientists from research institutes in **France** and **Italy**. It was published in the November 2012 issue of *Food and Chemical Toxicology* and entitled, *'Long term toxicity of a Roundup herbicide and a Roundup-tolerant genetically modified maize.'*

The scientists "performed a 2-year detailed rat feeding study … using 10 rats per group … the highest number of rats regularly measured in a standard GMO diet study." The rats involved in the study were Sprague-Dawley rats, which are a multipurpose breed of albino rats used extensively in medical research because they are docile, i.e. calm and easy to handle.

The scientists reported,

"In female animals, the largest tumors were in total 5 times more frequent than in males after 2 years, with 93% being mammary tumors. Adenomas[1], fibroadenomas[2] and carcinomas[3] were deleterious to health due to a very large size, rather than the grade of the tumor itself.

"Large tumor size caused impediments to either breathing or nutrition and digestion because of their thoracic or abdominal location and also resulted in hemorrhaging. In addition, one metastatic ovarian cystadenocarcinoma[4] and two skin tumors were identified."

The research also stated, "Biochemistry data confirmed very significant kidney chronic deficiencies; for all treatments and both sexes, 76% of the altered parameters were kidney related…" and concluded,

"… These results can be explained by the non linear endocrine-disrupting effects of Roundup, but also by the overexpression of the transgene in the GMO and its metabolic consequences."

The authors state that this was the first long-term study of the effects of GMO crops and Roundup herbicides on bodily organs. "This report describes the first life-long rodent (rat) feeding study investigating possible toxic effects rising from an R-tolerant [Roundup-tolerant] GM maize (NK603) and a complete commercial formulation of R-herbicide [Roundup herbicide]," and the authors pointed out that the doses of the diet given to the rats "correspond to levels likely to arise from consumption or environmental exposure, such as either 11% GM maize in food, or 50 ng/L of glyphosate in R-formulation [Roundup formulation]as can be found in some contaminated drinking tap waters, and which fall within authorized limits."

"Altogether, the significant biochemical disturbances and physiological failures documented in this work confirm the pathological effects of these GMO and R[oundup] treatments in both sexes, with different amplitudes."

The authors provide a final warning, that this contamination from GMO crops and/or *glyphosate* from Roundup can even cause these medical issues from contaminated water "within authorized limits" provided by local governments. Thus, the study concludes by saying,

"The results of the study presented here clearly demonstrate that lower levels of complete agricultural *glyphosate* herbicide formulations, at concentrations well below officially set safety limits, induce severe hormone-dependent mammary, hepatic and kidney disturbances." [1]

[1] *'Adenomas' is a benign tumor of a gland ('adeno'= gland; 'oma' = tumor)*
[2] *'Fibroadenomas' is a non-cancerous breast tumor composed of fibrous and glandular tissue*
[3] *'Carcinomas' is a malignant cancer which arises from the epithelial cells*
[4] *'Metastatic ovarian cystadenocarcinoma' (also called 'epithelial ovarian cancer') is a form of cancer that occurs in the cells on the surface of the ovary*

"Glyphosate induces human breast cancer cells growth via estrogen receptors."

That's the title of a study by five (5) medical research scientists in **Thailand** and published September 2013 in *Food and Chemical Toxicology* and the US National Library of Medicine of the National Institutes of Health *(USA)*

In the study, "Glyphosate exerted proliferative effects only in human hormone-dependent breast cancer, T47D cells[1]... The proliferative concentrations of glyphosate that induced the activation of estrogen response element (ERE) transcription activity were 5-13 fold of control in T47D-KBluc cells and this activation was inhibited by an estrogen antagonist, ICI 182780, indicating that the estrogenic activity of glyphosate was mediated via ERs."

The study further points out, "Glyphosate-based herbicides are widely used for soybean cultivation, and our results also found that there was an additive estrogenic effect between glyphosate and genistein, a phytoestrogen in soybeans. However, these additive effects of glyphosate contamination in soybeans need further animal study." [2]

The disturbing conclusion is that not only does *glyphosate* induce cancer in human breasts, the other chemical additives in soybeans cause further maladies for the estrogen – and, of course, soy is a principal ingredient in infant milk and infant formula.

[1] *T47D is a general acronym for 'human breast cancer cells'*

[1]   http://www.sciencedirect.com/science/article/pii/S0278691512005637
[2]   http://www.ncbi.nlm.nih.gov/pubmed/23756170

———————

NB. Among the various reasons to breast feed new-born babies, are the reasons NOT to feed them formula. One of those reasons is that baby formula and other child-milk products often contain GMO chemicals, largely because cows have been injected with bovine growth hormones (rBGH). This chemical is intended to increase the milk production of the cow. However, this process has had numerous dangerous side effects which are toxic, and which can seep into the milk. (See MILK)

Also, soy products, including baby foods, are now largely GMO derived. *(See SOY.)* The scientific justification to breast-feed babies is overwhelming. The issue is to make sure the mother's milk itself is not contaminated by her own diet of GMO 'food products.'

INTESTINES

The 'intestines' (from Latin 'intestinus' meaning 'internal') are vital organs of the gastrointestinal tract (a 'tube' sometimes referred to as the alimentary canal, which extends from the mouth to the anus.) In

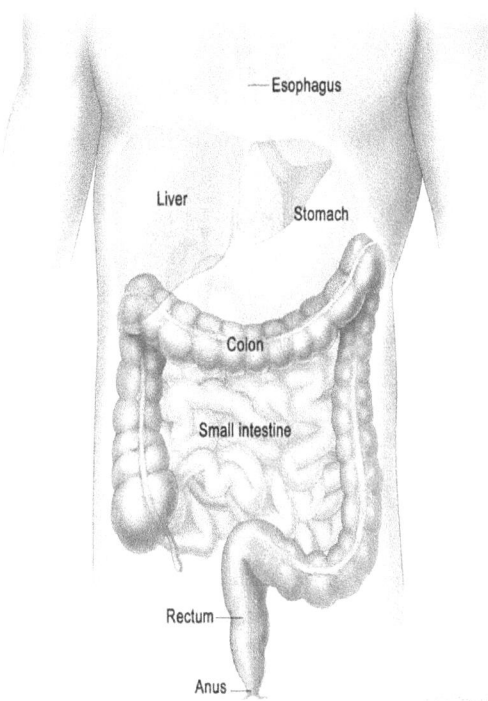

humans and other mammals there are two intestines, the small intestine (about 1 inch in diameter and 10 feet long) and the large intestine, also called the 'colon' (about 2 ½ inches in diameter and 5 feet long). The intestines extend to the anus from the lower part of the stomach, the pyloric sphincter, which is a valve that is a strong ring of smooth muscle which allows food to pass from the stomach to the first part of the small intestine.

Image from:
http://www.nlm.nih.gov/medlineplus/magazine/issues/spring09/articles/spring09pg7-8.html

GMO diet damages intestines, leads to cancer.

"Harvard Researchers Discover the Obvious About How Genetically Modified Foods Lead to Inflammatory Bowel Disease, Crohn's and Ulcerative Colitis."

That's the headline referring to a September 2010 study conducted by researchers at *Cell Host & Microbe,* Harvard School of Public Health *(USA).* [1]

The researchers discovered that "certain bacteria that inhabit the intestines provide the environmental trigger that initiates and perpetuates chronic intestinal inflammation in individuals who are genetically susceptible to inflammatory bowel disease (IBD)."

It was learned that,

"The genes of genetically modified foods are split with the E. coli bacteria, *Bt* toxin and other 'gene promoters' that leave the bacterium's residue in your gut that causes IBD[1], IBS[2], Crohn's and ulcerative colitis."

The report indicates that

"The statistical increase in digestive diseases and colorectal cancer can be directly traced to the creation of genetically modified foods and the addition of dangerous additive chemicals in packaged foods."

- One author was diagnosed with malignant colon cancer due to the effects of GMO foods and chemical additive such as MSG, high fructose corn syrup, maltodextrin and others.

- Another author's Crohn's, IBD and ulcerative colitis continued and worsened even after surgery, until halting the consumption of GMO foods and any product containing food additives – in food products which the manufacturers labeled as "healthy" foods. [1]

[1] *IBD is Inflammatory Bowel Disease, which involves chronic inflammation of all or part of the digestive tract. The major types are Crohn's disease and ulcerative colitis.*
[2] *IBS is Irritable Bowel Syndrome, a disorder which leads to abdominal pain, cramps, and changes in bowel movements.*

IN SUMMARY, our intestines and our entire digestive system are being poisoned by GMOs.

[1] http://howtoeliminatepain.com/crohns-disease/attention-crohn%E2%80%99s-and-ibd-sufferers-%E2%80%93-harvard-researchers-discover-the-obvious-about-how-genetically-modified-foods-lead-to-inflammatory-bowel-disease-crohn%E2%80%99s-and-ulcerative-c/

PROSTATE

*'Prostate' (from Greek 'prostates' meaning 'one who stands guard')
is a gland in the male reproductive system in most mammals,
generally described as the size of a walnut. The principal purpose of*

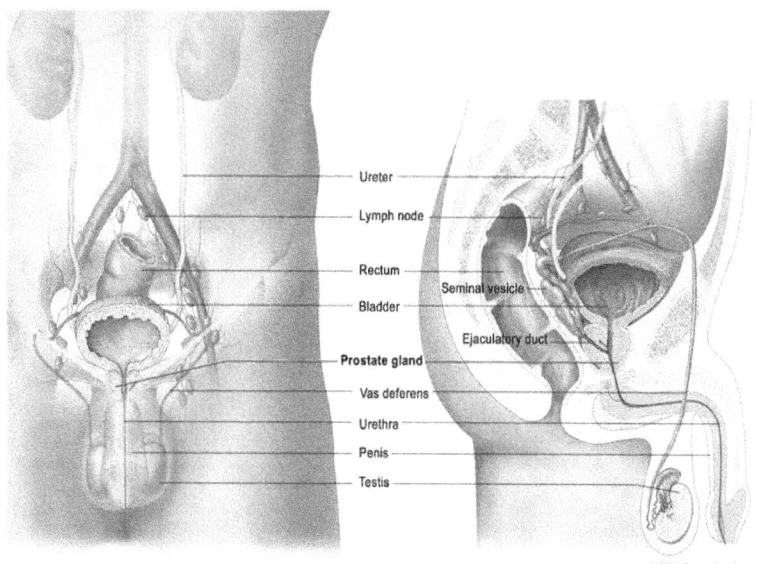

*the prostate is to secrete a fluid which becomes the majority of the
volume of the semen (along with spermatozoa and seminal vesicle
fluid).*

Image from:
http://www.nlm.nih.gov/medlineplus/magazine/issues/spring09/articles/s
pring09pg7-8.html

**GMO (rBGH) milk increases IGF-1 levels and the risk of prostate
cancer.**

**"Plasma levels of insulin-like growth factor 1 (IGF-1) have
been associated with risk of several cancers."**

Among the various studies on this subject is one published in *Cancer
Epidemiology, Biomarkers, and Prevention*, 2002. This research was
performed by four (4) medical research scientists at Harvard Medical
School and Brigham and Women's Hospital in Boston *(USA).* The

final paper was entitled *'Dietary Correlates of Plasma Insulin-like Growth Factor 1 and Insulin-like Growth Factor Binding Protein 3 Concentrations.'*

The program monitored "intakes of alcohol, energy, macronutrients, and specific foods…" Included were "increasing quartiles of milk intake." The objective was to see how the IGF-1 and the IGF-3 binding protein reacted.

The result saw a disturbance when there were increased IGF-1 levels. The study states,

> "We conclude that higher energy, protein, and milk intakes were associated with higher levels of IGF-1. These associations raise the possibility that diet could affect cancer risk through influencing IGF-1 level." [1]

Depending upon the levels of sensitivity of different organs in the body, susceptibility to cancer became an obvious concern. Thus the final warning:

> "Plasma levels of insulin-like growth factor 1 (IGF-1) have been associated with risk of several cancers."

Since the bovine growth hormone (rBGH) is specifically designed to increase IGF-1 levels in cows, the risks to humans who consume milk from these cows with higher IGF-1 levels has now become obvious.

———

"Plasma Insulin-Like Growth Factor-1 and Prostate Cancer Risk: A Prospective Study"

That's the title of a study, far back in 1998, which even then warned of the dangers of IGF-1 and prostate cancer.

The research was performed by eight (8) scientists, from the Harvard Medical Schools, the Northwestern University Medical School, *(USA)* and the Research Institute of the Jewish General Hospital and McGill University in Montreal, *Canada*. The study was reported in the 23 January 1998 issue of *Science*.

The study reported,

"Insulin-like Growth Factor-1 (IGF-1) is a mitogen[1] for prostate epithelial cells[2]...

"A strong positive association was observed between IGF-1 levels and prostate cancer...

"Men in the highest quartile of IGF-1 levels had a risk of 4.3 (95 percent confidence interval 1.8 to 10.6) compared with men in the lowest quartile."

Medical research confirmed that IGF-1 stimulates the division of the prostate cells, and can lead to cancer of the prostate. [2]

IN SUMMARY, stimulating the insulin growth factor 1 (IGF-1) in cows leads to an acceleration of the mitogen[1] process. IGF-1 in milk leads to the same process: a more rapid division of the prostate epithelial cells[2], leading to possible prostate cancer.

[1] *'Mitogen' is a chemical substance (usually some form of a protein) that encourages a cell to commence cell division.*
[2] *'Prostate epithelial cells' are the cells in the prostate's epithelium (the basic tissue which lines the cavities and surfaces of the organs).*

[1]   http://www.ncbi.nlm.nih.gov/pubmed/12223429
[2]   http://www.sciencemag.org/content/279/5350/563.short

STOMACH

The 'stomach' (from Greek 'stoma' meaning 'mouth') is a muscular organ on the left side of the upper abdomen which receives food from the esophagus. While the stomach muscles periodically contract in order to churn the food to enhance the digestion, the stomach secretes acid and enzymes which digest the food.

GMO diet causes disturbances with stomachs and uteri of pigs.

Pigs fed a GMO diet develop severe inflammation of stomach and stomach lining, and disturbing enlargement of the uterus.

This was the documented conclusion of a study published in June 2013 in the peer-reviewed *Journal of Organic Systems*.

Dr. Judy Carman, a biochemist and Director of the Institute of Health and Environmental Research (IHER), Flinders University, Adelaide, *Australia*, conducted research with seven (7) collaborators from two continents in a study entitled, '*A long-term toxicology study on pigs fed a combined genetically modified (GM) soy and GM maize diet.*'

The research, on the effects of a 'normal' diet of mixed GMO feeds for pigs, concluded that the GMO diet causes severe health issues with the digestive and reproductive systems, and an apparent strong involvement in the endocrine system.

The 22.7 week study (the current norm in today's pig industry) was conducted on 168 just-weaned pigs at a commercial piggery in the United States. Half of the pigs were fed a diet of widely-used GM soy and GM corn, and the other half were fed non-GMO feed. 'Blind autopsies' were performed in which the veterinarians did not know which pigs had been fed which feeds.

The study revealed a disturbing fact:

Once the pigs were weaned from their mothers and fed a GMO diet, "GM fed pigs showed severe stomach inflammation at a rate of 2.6 times that of non-GM-fed pigs (95% confidence interval = 1.29 –

77

5.21) … This occurred in both male (p = 0.041) and female (p = 0.034) pigs…

"We found severe stomach inflammation in 22% of male pigs fed the GM diet and in 41.7% of the female pigs fed the GM diet (compared to 5.6% and 18.9%, respectively, in pegs fed the non-GM diet."

The study concludes with the warning:

"Given the widespread use of GMO feed for livestock as well as humans, this is a cause for concern. The results indicate that it would be prudent for GM crops that are destined for human food and animal feed, including stacked GM crops, to undergo long-term animal feeding studies preferable before commercial planting, particularly for toxicological and reproductive effects." [1]

Another disturbing finding in the study is that the GMO diet caused the uteri (uterus) of the female pigs to become enlarged by an astounding 25%.] [2]

Professor Carman states,

"The new study lends scientific credibility to anecdotal evidence from farmers and veterinarians, who have for some years reported reproductive and digestive problems in pigs fed on a diet containing GM soy and corn."

"… we found these adverse effects when we fed the animals a mixture of crops containing these GM genes and the GM proteins that these genes produce."

An inflammation of this nature and degree can lead to long-term health maladies, including cancer.

[1] http://gmojudycarman.org/wp-content/uploads/2013/06/The-Full-Paper.pdf
[2] http://gmojudycarman.org/new-study-shows-that-animals-are-seriously-harmed-by-gm-feed/

MALE INFERTILITY

SPERM

'Sperm' (from the Greek word 'sperma' meaning 'seed') are the male

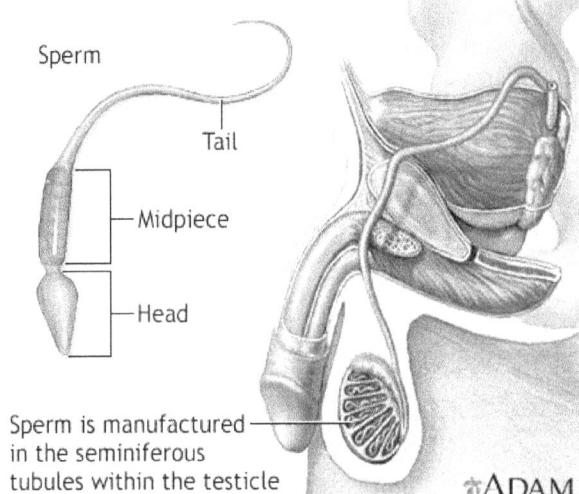

reproductive cells which are developed in the testicles. The cells are 'haploid' – each containing a single set of 23 chromosomes. They can join with the 23 chromosomes of the female egg to create a 'diploid' cell (containing two sets of chromosomes) which leads to the possibility of giving birth

'Spermatogenesis' is the process by which spermatozoa are produced from male primordial germ cells.

'Testosterone' is the principal sex hormone produced by the human body which is responsible for the normal growth and development of sexual desire and function, muscle growth, densification of bones, and hair growth. In men testosterone secrete it from the testes, the same reproductive glands which produce sperm. Females secrete it from their ovaries. Males produce about ten times as much testosterone as females, which is why they have the 'male' characteristics.

Image from:
http://www.nlm.nih.gov/medlineplus/ency/imagepages/19471.htm

Toxins in GMOs reduce the potency of sperm and sperm counts in rats.

———

"Pesticide treatment resulted in a decline in body weight, libido, ejaculate volume, sperm concentration, semen initial fructose, and semen osmolality.[1] This was accompanied with increases in the abnormal and dead sperm and semen methylene blue reduction time[2]."

This was revealed in a 1995 study by six (6) research scientists at the Department of Environmental Studies of the University of Alexandria in *Egypt*. The study entitled, *'Toxic effects of carbofuran and glyphosate on semen characteristics in rabbits,'* was published in the *Journal of Environmental Science and Health*, and reported by the National Center for Biotechnology Information in Maryland *(USA)*. The study concluded that,

"These effects on sperm quality may be due to the direct cytotoxic[3] effects of these pesticides on spermatogenesis and/or indirectly via hypothalami-pituitary-testis axis[4] which control the reproductive efficiency." [1]

IN SUMMARY, *glyphosate* damages both the process and the potency of semen and the related potency of the sperm which it transports.

[1] *'Osmolality' is a reflection on the concentration level of different types of chemicals in a substance, or the dilution level if chemicals have been merged into other chemicals, i.e. the potency and other issues regarding the chemicals in the semen.*
[2] *'Methylene blue solution' is a chemical applied to the sperm and is one measurement to monitor the quality of the sperm.*
[3] *'Cytotoxic' means being toxic to cells (in this case, sperm cells)*
[4] *'Hypothalami-pituitary-testis axis' refers to the relationship of these organs to each other, including the reproductive capabilities.*

———————

Glyphosate, **the herbicide used in Roundup, leaves a residue on Roundup Ready crops (GMO crops) which can affect testosterone levels and men's sperm counts.**

This was confirmed in a 2012 study by four (4) research scientists in *France* at the Institute of Biology of the *Universite de Caen Basse-Normandie* (E. Clair, R.

Mesnage, C. Travert, and G.E. Seralini).

The research, published in *Toxicology in Vitro* and *PubMed.gov* of the US National Library of Medicine *(USA)*, was entitled, *'A glyphosate-based herbicide induces necrosis[1] and apoptosis[2] in mature rat testicular cells in vitro, and testosterone decrease at lower levels.'*

The study revealed that *glyphosate* is actually toxic to testicle cells, and lowers testosterone synthesis (creation) significantly.

"At lower non-toxic concentrations of Roundup and glyphosate (1ppm), the main endocrine disruption is a testosterone decrease by 35%."

"The pesticide has thus an endocrine impact at very low environmental doses... This does not anticipate the chronic toxicity which is insufficiently tested ..." [2]

Hence, even the short-term results reveal that *glyphosate* is poisonous to the reproductive system... and the long-term "chronic toxicity" has not yet been tested.

When *glyphosate* is sprayed on the GMO crops (which are specifically created to combat this toxin), the amount of *glyphosate* and other chemicals absorbed by the GMO crops and passed into the 'food products' is unknown... (at least to the public, since Monsanto and the other chemical companies may know from their internal studies).

[1] *'Necrosis' is a form of cell injury which results in the premature death of cells; it is caused by factors external to the cell or tissue, such as infection, toxins, or trauma*
[2] *'Apoptosis' is the programmed cell death (PCD) as part of normal cell changes and development*

———

N.B. It should also be noted that although spermatogenesis, the process of sperm production, begins in male adolescence, the foundation is laid a few months before birth and immediately after birth. Therefore, there is much research to indicate that the lower sperm rate may begin in the womb – and may be attributable to the mothers. Much research seems to indicate that

81

'testicular dysgenesis syndrome' and the decline of male fertility originates in the womb.

Author's Note: There are numerous studies indicating that aspartame is a major cause of the decline in the sperm count. Aspartame is used in hundreds of diet drinks and foods. Other studies suggest that fluoride in the drinking water may also be a cause.

[1]   http://www.ncbi.nlm.nih.gov/pubmed/7797819
[2]   http://www.ncbi.nlm.nih.gov/pubmed/22200534

TESTICLES/TESTOSTERONE

The word 'testicles' is from the Latin word 'testiculus' meaning "witness" of virility [from which we derive the word 'testify'... 'witness']; the plural is "testes." The testicles are components of both the reproductive system and the endocrine system (the system of glands which secretes different types of hormones into the blood stream). The primary functions of the testicles are to produce sperm and to produce androgens, mainly testosterone.

'Testosterone', from the Latin word 'testis', is a white crystalline steroid hormone, the principal anabolic [building/development] and sex hormone in humans. It is responsible for sexual desire and

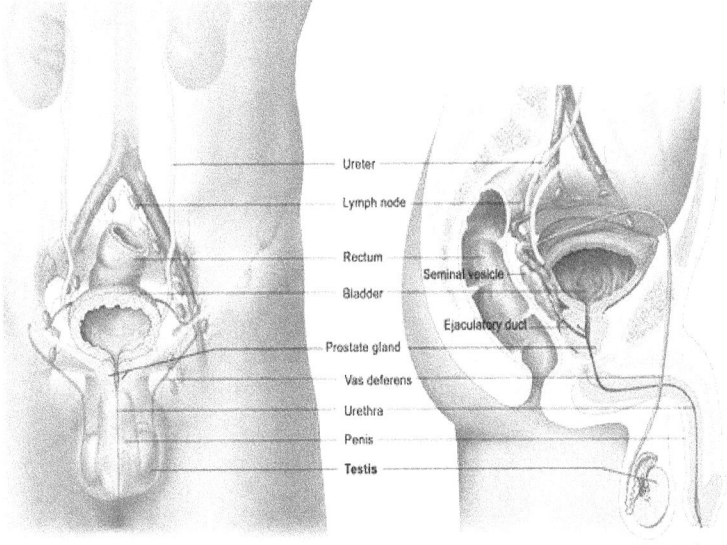

Image from:
http://www.cancer.gov/cancertopics/pdq/treatment/testicular/Patient/page1

function, muscular hyperthropy [muscle enlargement], densification of bones, and hair growth. Both sexes require it for normal sexual and physical development; however, males produce about 10 times as much, which gives rise to those traits traditionally referred to as 'masculine,' namely, physical strength, body hair, dominance and virility. Males secrete most of it from the testicles, and females secrete it from their ovaries. Both sexes produce minor amounts from their adrenal glands. Testosterone is partly responsible for the formation of the male genitalia, and stimulates the development of the prostrate and seminal vessels.

Toxins in GMOs disrupted reproductive cycles of rats

"Glyphosate has been described as an endocrine[1] disruptor affecting the male reproductive system; however, the molecular basis of its toxicity remains to be clarified."

That was the report of a June 2013 study conducted by ten (10) research scientists at the *Departamento de Bioquimica and Centro de Ciencias Biologicas at the Universidade Federal de Santa Catarina* in ***Brazil.*** The study was also published by the US National Library of Medicine of the National Institutes of Health (***USA***).

The title of the study was, '*Roundup disrupts male reproductive functions by triggering calcium-mediated cell deaths in rat testis and Sertoli cells'.*

The conclusion of the study was:

"We propose that Roundup toxicity, implicated in Ca2+ overload, cell signaling misregulation, stress response of the endoplasmic reticulum, and/or depleted antioxidant defenses, could contribute to Sertoli cell[2] disruption in spermatogenesis that could have an impact on male fertility." [1]

NOTE: If there is "Sertoli cell disruption" or "cell death," the process of male fertility and reproduction is inhibited or stopped.

---

[1] *The 'endocrine system' is a collection of tissues, glands, and cells of the organisms which secretes hormones into the bloodstream in order to direct the physiological and behavioral activities of the organisms.*
[2] *'Sertoli cells' are the somatic cells of the testes which are essential for the formation of the testes and for spermatogenesis. These cells facilitate the progression of germ cells to spermatozoa.*

"There was an alteration in testosterone levels and testicular morphology[1], when male rats were exposed to the commercial formulation of the herbicide *glyphosate*."

Those were the results of a 2010 study, entitled, *'Prepubertal exposure to commercial formulation of the herbicide glyphosate alters testosterone levels and testicular morphology,'* which was conducted by five (5) scientists at the Veterinary Medical School at the University of Sao Paulo, **Brazil**.

The study concluded,

"These results suggest that commercial formulation of glyphosate is a potent endocrine disruptor in vivo, causing disturbances in the reproductive development of rats when the exposure was performed during the puberty period." [2]

The conclusion:

The toxin *glyphosate* interferes with both the natural development and size of the testicles, and interferes with the testosterone levels which the testicles are able to produce.

[1] *'Morphology' is the form and structure of an organism, namely its specific structural pattern such as shape, size, and color (not its function, which is 'physiology')*

———————

The "severe oxidative stress" in the male testes from *glyphosate* inhibited testosterone production.

This was one of the conclusions from a 2013 study entitled, *'Pesticide-induced decrease in rat testicular steroidogenesis is differentially prevented by lipoate and tocopherol.'*

The study was performed by seven (7) researcher scienetists at the *Instituto de Investigaciones Bioquimicas de la Plata, at the Catedra de Bioquimica y Biologia Molecular* in **Argentina**.

The study "… demonstrated that the sub-chronic administration of low doses of Toc or a-Toc, glyphosate and zineb to rats (i.p. 1/250

LD50, three times a week for 5 weeks) provoked severe oxidative stress (OS) in testicles. These effects were also reflected in plasma."

The "severe oxidative stress" in the male testes created by *glyphosate* inhibited testosterone production, and it disrupted gonadotropin[1] levels. [3]

This development interferes with the entire male reproductive process.

[1] *'Gonadotropins' are protein hormones secreted by the gonadtrope cells, and are central to the endocrine system which regulates normal growth, sexual development, and reproductive functions. The 'gonad' (from Greek 'gonos' meaning 'procreation' or 'genitals') is the organ which creates the 'gametes' ('husband' and 'wife' genitals), namely the testes in the male and the ovaries in the female.*

Mice fed on GMO soy experienced changes in their testicles and damage to their young sperm cells.

A study as far back as 2004 by five (5) international researchers in **Italy** entitled, *'Ultrastructural analysis of testes from mice fed on genetically modified soybean'* revealed that mice fed on GMO soy experienced changes in their testicles and damage to their young sperm cells.

"In GM-fed mice of all ages considered, the number of perichromatin granules[1] is higher and nuclear pore density lower. Moreover, we found enlargements in the smooth endoplasmic reticulum[2] in GM-fed mice Sertoli cells." [4]

Both issues affect the reproductive process: disturbing the number of granules, and nuclear pore density,

[1] *'Perichromatin granules' are the granules which 'surround' the 'chromatin-fiber', which is a nucleo-protein complex that contains human cells into which is packed 3 Billion base pairs of DNA. The perichromatin region also has an RNA content whose vital role in genes is also affected by the number of granules.*
[2] *The 'endoplasmic reticulum' is a network of flattened sacs and branching tubules inside of the cells. It manufactures, processes, and transports a wide variety of chemical compounds for use inside and outside of the cell. Among*

other things, this network is essential for protein development and distribution.

IN SUMMARY, there have now been a plethora of studies … for over a decade … with research scientists from across the globe … who have demonstrated the toxicity of *glyphosate* and GMO 'food products' disturbing the reproductive system in males.

[1]   http://www.ncbi.nlm.nih.gov/pubmed/23820267
[2]   http://www.ncbi.nlm.nih.gov/pubmed/20012598
[3]   http://www.ncbi.nlm.nih.gov/pubmed/23465731
[4]   http://www.ncbi.nlm.nih.gov/pubmed/15718213

OBESITY/DIABETES
(MICRONUTRIENT-MALNUTRITION)

'Obesity' (from Latin 'obedere' meaning 'to eat away' or 'keep eating') is a medical condition in which excess body fat has accumulated to a degree that it has an adverse effect on the body's health. Obesity is defined as that point when a person's weight in kilograms is divided by the square of his/her height in meters, and the result is a body mass index (BMI) which is more than 30 kg/m2. [In inches and pounds it is calculated by weight (in pounds) divided by the square of height (in inches) x 703] Obesity increases the likelihood of heart disease, type 2 diabetes, obstructive sleep apnea, osteoarthritis, and some forms of cancer.

The nutritional deficiency of GMO crops leads to over-eating, causing obesity and diabetes.

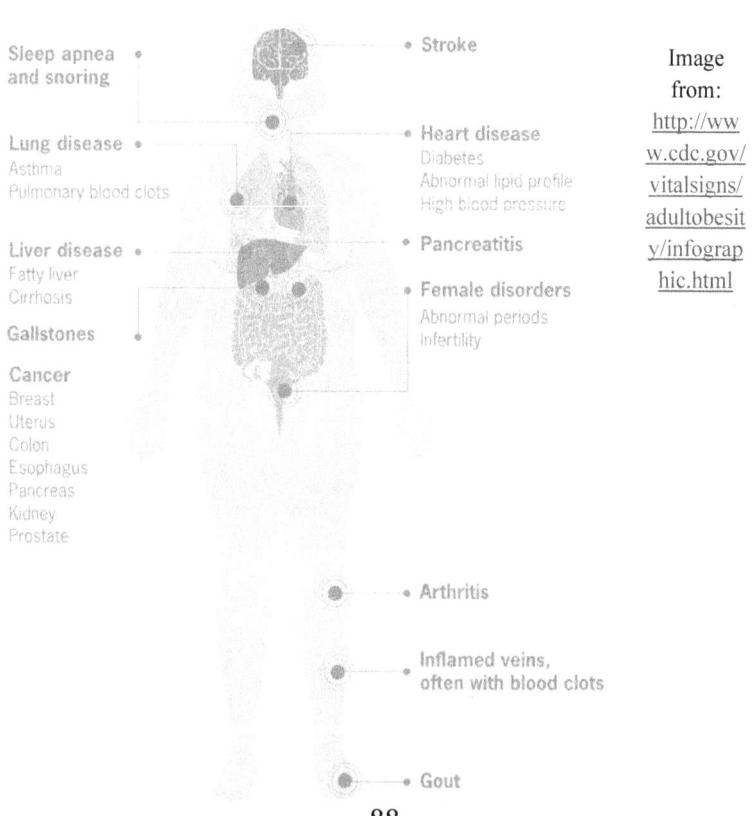

Sleep apnea and snoring

Lung disease
Asthma
Pulmonary blood clots

Liver disease
Fatty liver
Cirrhosis

Gallstones

Cancer
Breast
Uterus
Colon
Esophagus
Pancreas
Kidney
Prostate

Stroke

Heart disease
Diabetes
Abnormal lipid profile
High blood pressure

Pancreatitis

Female disorders
Abnormal periods
Infertility

Arthritis

Inflamed veins, often with blood clots

Gout

Image from:
http://www.cdc.gov/vitalsigns/adultobesity/infographic.html

88

"If you want to avoid obesity, then avoid eating genetically engineered (GE) corn, corn-based products, and animals that are fed a diet of GE grain."

That's the opening line from of a July 24, 2012 article by Anthony Samsel of The Cornucopia Institute in Wisconsin *(USA)* entitled, *'Obesity, Corn, GMOs.'*

Animals which consumed GMO grains experienced changes their digestive system, including liver, kidneys and pancreas, as well as in their genitals.

That was part of the conclusion of this July 2012 study of The Cornucopia Institute. The report, authored by Anthony Samsel, described a 10 year multi-national collaboration conducted at the Norwegian Veterinary College in *Norway.* Led by Professor Ashild Krogdahl, with collaborators from *Austria, Hungary, Ireland, Turkey, and Australia,* the general purpose of the study was to determine if consuming genetically modified grains had any adverse effects on animals, notably rats, mice, pigs, and fish. The more specific focus was on weight gain and any organ changes in the animals.

The research disclosed numerous effects on the intestines of the animals who consumed the GMO grains, as compared to those animals fed non-GMO grains. The animals which consumed GMO grains experienced changes to their digestive system, including liver, kidneys and pancreas, as well as in their genitals.

Dr. Krogdahl reported that the animals who consumed the GMO grains

- were slightly larger,
- ate more,
- developed a different micro-structure in their intestines,
- were less able to digest proteins,
- and experienced changes in their immune systems.

When the body's ability to digest proteins is diminished, it affects the biochemistry of amino acids. This has a direct relationship to the rise of obesity.

The Cornucopia Institute report discussed the additional implications of a diminished ability to digest proteins:

"… diabetes, digestive disorders, inflammatory bowel disease, colitis, autism spectrum disorders (ASD) (ADD), autoimmune diseases, sexual dysfunction, sterility, asthma, COPD, and many more."

The article summarizes,

"Translated to humans, the study suggests: if you dine on meat from an animal which was fed GE grains or consume products made from GE grains like corn, you could get the same life altering effects… These GE foods transfer their effects to you." [1]

Eating GMO foods leads to undernourishment, what scientists call 'micronutrient-malnutrition,' or 'hidden hunger.'

Many nutrients are physically forced out of the food seeds in order to make room for the GM toxins (*Bt* bacteria and herbicides) implanted in those seeds. This reduces the nutritional value of the 'food products' created from those GMO seeds.

Glyphosate resistance in GM corn and soybeans reduce manganese uptake and efficiency by 10% to 50%, and iron and other nutrients are also reduced.

This was the conclusion of Dr. Don Huber, professor of botany and plant pathology at Purdue University in Indiana *(USA)*.

In discussing Roundup and the *glyphosate* which it imbeds in the soil itself, Dr. Huber said,

"As little as 2.5 percent of the recommended rate of glyphosate can greatly inhibit uptake and translocation of Fe (iron) and Mn (manganese) by non-target plants." *[Emphasis added]*

Despite this small amount, the consequences were dramatic:

The manganese uptake was reduced by 80%, and the iron uptake was reduced by 50%.

Soy beans are another area. Dr. Huber explained that *glyphosate* resistance in GM corn and soybeans reduces manganese uptake and efficiency by 10 to 50%, and that iron and other nutrients can also be reduced.

Dr. Huber summarized the issue by saying,

"[Glyphosate]… is an economical and effective broad-spectrum systemic herbicide that can have extensive non-target effects on nutrient availability, soil environment, and agricultural sustainability."
[2]

It is essential to understand the interrelationships between the plants, the soil, and the soil microbes themselves. Food quality is directly related to the quality of the soil and the microorganisms that live there. These organisms help the plants to absorb and use the soil's nutrients, and add to the basic nutrition of the plants.

Glyphosate kills these natural microbes, thereby depriving plants of what the microbes will bring to the plant. So,

a) in addition to the toxic gene implanted into the food seed, applying *glyphosate* externally further destroys the nutrition of the food seeds by poisoning the weeds whose compost is a source of nutrition for the soil, and by poisoning the entire micro-ecosystem, i.e. the earthworms, caterpillars, insects, and bacteria.

b) the plant absorbs the *glyphosate* and passes this poison into the food crop itself – and eventually to those who eat it.

In a December 10, 2011 interview with Dr. Joseph Mercola, Dr. Huber said,

"You have to realize what an herbicide, or a pesticide, is. They are metal chelators. In other words, they immobilize specific nutrients…

[I]t's a compound that can grab onto another element and change either its solubility or its availability for the critical function it has physiologically. Glyphosate is very unique...If you look at the essential minerals for plants, you see calcium, magnesium, potassium, copper, iron, manganese, zinc, and all of those other critical transition elements, as well as structural components for some of them...If you can chelate and, in that chelation process, essentially immobilize that essential nutrient, you have provided an opportunity to either kill a weed or damage and kill an organism – any organism... Those nutrients aren't just required by the weed, but they're required by microorganisms. They're required by us for our own physiologic functions..." [3]

———————

One of the most insidious issues regarding diabetes is that the medical industry, the pharmaceutical industry, and the advertising industry all see diabetes as a source of huge profits for the future. More gadgets are produced, people are told to buy the equipment and prick their fingers every day even if they are only 'near diabetic,' more drugs are created, more advertising every day in magazines and in the media, more surgeries are recommended for various parts of the body, more pills are routinely prescribed, and insulin sales increase.

Genetic Engineering & Biotechnology News estimates that within the next 10 years the industry will reach $70 Billion. They describe it by saying, *Epidemiology Drives Opportunity* and explain that the aging population is one source of revenue, but "Eating and exercise habits in the industrialized world and particularly in the U.S. are likely to make the markets for type 2 diabetes products among younger individuals more robust than even population demographic figures suggest." [4]

"This is a global pandemic in the making."

As Pollan summarizes it, "Apparently it is easier, or at least more profitable, to change a disease of civilization into a lifestyle than it is to change the way that civilization eats." [5]

———————

IN SUMMARY,

GMOs lack the nutrition of natural foods that our bodies require, especially younger bodies. Processed foods have already removed much of the fiber, which is what makes us feel full so we stop eating. The lack of nutrition in the GMOs adds to the body's craving.

In addition, the seeds of GMO 'food products' are *designed to contain toxins*, many of which have consequences to our health which no one is able to predict. Further, because GMO crops are genetically engineered to resist the toxins sprayed on them, the tendency for the past decade or more has been to use MORE *glyphosate* and its component herbicides and pesticides. This kills even more microorganisms, systematically depleting the soil itself of more and more nutrients … leading to even less nutrition in the crops.

So, after growing GMO crops and absorbing *glyphosate*, the soil lacks nutrients to provide to the plants. In addition to the dynamic dislocation of proteins within the seeds themselves, this is another reason why the plants lack the nutrients to provide to those who eat them… animals and humans.

Glyphosate, particularly when combined with the other chemicals in the GMO crops, deprives the soil and the plants of nutrients which our bodies need. Since the plants themselves are deprived of nutrition, they have less to pass on to those who eat them. Thus, those who consume GMO 'food products' develop the condition called 'micronutrient-malnutrition.'

[1]   http://www.cornucopia.org/2012/07/obesity-corn-gmos/
[2]   http://www.agweb.com/assets/import/files/58P20-22.pdf
[3]   http://articles.mercola.com/sites/articles/archive/2011/12/10/dr-don-huber-interview-part-1.aspx
[4]   http://www.genengnews.com/gen-articles/biomarket-trends-diabetes-market-opportunities-soaring/2117/
[5]   Pollan, Michael, *In Defense of Food* [The Penguin Press, 2003, p136]

DIGESTIVE SYSTEM

The word 'digest' is from the Latin word 'digerere' meaning 'to separate.'

"The digestive system breaks down food and fluids into much smaller nutrients. In this complex process, blood carries the nutrients throughout the body to nourish cells and provide energy. The GI tract [gastrointestinal tract, i.e. the alimentary canal] is divided into two main sections: the upper GI tract [which includes the mouth, pharynx, esophagus, and stomach, which leads to the small intestine] and the lower GI tract [which includes the intestines (bowel) and the anus.] The bowel is made up of two sections: Small intestine – the duodenum, jejunum, and ileum, and the Large intestine – the cecum (where the appendix is attached), colon, and rectum.

"The digestive tract is a twisting tube about 30 feet long. It starts at the mouth and ends at the anus. In between are the esophagus, stomach, and bowels (intestines). The liver and pancreas aid digestion by producing bile and pancreatic juices which travel to the intestines. The gallbladder stores bile until the body needs it for digestion.

"In addition, the liver, pancreas and gallbladder produce digestive juices to aid the digestion of food." [The Medical College of Wisconsin] [1]

GMO toxins interfere with digestive process and inhibit nutrition.

———————

"Genetically modified food (GMF) creates evident threat to consumers' health... DNA of transgenic plants is instable... Due to high trypsin[1] inhibitor content the GMF is digested more slowly what, alike Bt toxin presence, increased probability of alimentary canal[2] diseases."

This was the conclusion of a study, published in May 2012 *PubMed.gov* of the National Institutes of Health *(USA),* by two (2) research scientists Dr. G. Cichosz and Dr. S. K. Wiackowski of the University of Warmia and Mazury in ***Poland.***

The study was entitled, *'Genetically modified food – great unknown'.*

According to this study, because genetically modified 'food products' (GMOs; GMF) have a trypsin inhibitor effect which interfere with the digestion process, more time is required for the digestive system to digest them – and to be absorbed into the body. This interferes with the entire process of absorbing nutrients into the body itself.

It also raises the issue of whether the toxins in the GMO 'food products' have been destroyed by the acids and other chemicals in the digestive process – or if those toxins have survived and been passed into the blood stream and the body.

The slowing of the digestive process, including the continued "*Bt* toxin presence" also "increases the probability of alimentary canal diseases" since the chemical processes have been interrupted.

Other studies indicate similar issues with the digestive system. They continue,

"Next threats are bound to be the presence of fitoestrogens and residues of Roundup pesticide that can diminish reproductiveness..."

'Fitoestrogens,' or more commonly *'phytoestrogens,'* are *'xenoestrogens'* (meaning 'outside of the body'), namely 'plant-derived estrogens.' These can interfere with the entire estrogen process, by either mimicking natural estrogen or creating anti-estrogenic effects. In either case, these *phytosetrogens* evaluated in the study can interfere with the female reproductive processes.

Finally,

"the presence of fitoestrogens and residues of Roundup pesticide... can... even lead to cancerogenic transformation through disturbance of human hormonal metabolism."

The entire hormonal metabolism of the body is at risk.

As seen in other studies, this research raises serious health issues with the chemicals in the GMO seeds and the chemicals in Roundup, including *glyphosate.*

The general conclusion is that

> "Genetically modified food (GMF) creates evident threat to consumers' health", leads to an "increased probability of alimentary canal diseases," can "diminish" the reproductive systems, and can lead to cancer. [2]

[1] *'Trypsin' is a chemical in the digestive system and is a part of the process to hydrolyze (to break down the chemicals with water) proteins, ultimately into amino acids, in order to reduce them for absorption into the blood stream.*
[2] *'Alimentary canal' refers to the entire 'tube' of the digestive tract, i.e. the gastrointestinal tract (so-called 'GI tract').*

"The inclusion of genetically modified (GM) plants in the human diet has raised concerns about the transfer of transgenes from GM plants to intestinal microflora[1] and enterocytes[2]."

That was one of the conclusions of a 2004 study entitled, *'Assessing the survival of transgenic plant DNA in the human gastrointestinal tract.'* The research was a collaborative project by seven (7) research scientists from the biology, bioscience, and medical science departments of the University of Newcastle upon Tyne in the **United Kingdom**, and published in the US National Library of Medicine of the National Institutes of Health *(USA)*.

The research states that, "The amount of transgene that survived passage through the small bowel varied among individuals…" and that, "The persistence in the human gut of DNA from dietary GM plants is unknown…"

The 'transgenes' are those inserted/blasted into the GMO seeds. As indicated in previous studies, these toxic 'transgenes' survived the digestive process, and remained inside of the body. *There, these toxins can reproduce all by themselves, by the millions!*

After discussing the details of the study, the researchers stated, "… we conclude that gene transfer did not occur during the feeding experiment." [3]

In other words, these bacteria were not an immediate result of currently eating. They remained in the body from previous exposure to GMOs.

Once they linger in the body, they can begin to multiply themselves inside of our system! There, they *compete* with the natural bacteria in our bodies, the microflora[1] and enterocytes[2]. This interferes with our digestive system – and, by implication, our nutrition. Obviously, this can lead to unpredictable health and medical issues which have never been encountered before.

[1] *'Microflora' are the bacteria population in the intestine.*
[2] *'Enterocytes' are the predominant cells in the small intestinal mucosa and are responsible for the final digestion and absorption of nutrients, electrolytes, and water.*

IN SUMMARY, studies by a multitude of research scientists in different countries have now revealed that GMO 'food products' are putting foreign bacteria into our digestive tract.

These bacteria are now growing and multiplying all by themselves – even after we stop eating GMO 'food products'!

[1]   http://www.froedtert.com/SpecialtyAreas/Gastroenterology/DiseasesofDigestiveTract.htm
[2]   http://www.ncbi.nlm.nih.gov/pubmed/23009001
[3]   http://www.ncbi.nlm.nih.gov/pubmed/14730317

PANCREAS

The 'pancreas,' from Greek 'pankreas' meaning 'all plant,' is a long tube-like organ behind the stomach. It produces juices which aid in breaking down food and hormones, to help control blood sugar levels. It plays a role in digestion and in diabetes.

Toxins in GMOs cannot be properly digested by human intestines...leading to overeating, i.e. obesity and diabetes.

"Therefore, this study further supports the idea that a diet containing significant amounts of GM soybean can influence the pancreatic metabolism in mouse."

That was the conclusion of a study in ***Italy*** in 2003 entitled, *'Fine structural analyses of pancreatic acinar cell nuclei from mice fed on genetically modified soybean.'* The research was published in the *European Journal of Histochemistry.*

This collaborative study was performed by six (6) medical scientists from research institutes and universities, including the University of Urbino, University of Pavia, the *Istituto di Genetica Molecolare del CNR,* and *Istituto Zooprofilattico Sperimentale dell'Umbria e delle Marche,* Perugia, Italy.

The study points out that there is a limited amount of information to draw a direct connection to specific metabolic issues. Based on what the scientists were able to discover, "We found a significant lowering of nucleoplasmic[1] and nucleolar splicing[2] factors as well as a perichromatin granule accumulation[3] in GM-fed mice, suggestive of reduced post-transcriptional hnRNA processing and/or nuclear export."

This means the splicing process and the digestive process were not functioning properly,

> "... a diet containing significant amounts of GM food seems to influence the zymogen synthesis[4] and processing."

As the authors state,

"Therefore, taken together, our data suggest a decrease in nucleolar[2]
activity in mice fed on GM soybean."

The report concludes that much further study is required to understand
the consequences of eating GMO food. However, it is clear that there
are issues regarding the metabolism and digestive process. "The
modifications observed in pancreatic acinar cell nuclei of GM-fed
mice could be related to the reduction in digestive enzyme synthesis
and secretion previously described in the same animals. (Malatesta et
al, 2002b).

"Therefore, this study further supports the idea that a diet containing
significant amounts of GM soybean can influence the pancreatic
metabolism in mouse." [1]

IN SUMMARY, GMO soybeans cannot be effectively digested,
thereby affecting the body's entire process of metabolism.

[1] 'Nucleoplasm' is one of the types of protoplasm (the living contents) in a
cell.
[2] *'Nucleolar splicing' is part of the internal structural process in the cells*
[3] *The accumulation of granules on the chromatin, which is a long fiber thread
of DNA and protein.*
[4] *'Zymogen synthesis' is the synthesis of digestive enzymes, some coagulation
factors, and various proteins, all of which are part of the digestive process.*

[1]   www.ejh.it/index.php/ejh/article/download/851/971

GMO-CAUSED ABNORMALITIES
to
OTHER
BIOLOGICAL ORGANS

BRAIN

The 'brain' (from the Old English word 'braegen') is an organ in the center of the nervous system in all vertebrate and most invertebrate animals, and exercises central control over the other organs of the body by generating patterns of muscle activity and by driving the secretion of chemicals called hormones. The brain is located in the head, near the primary sense organs for vision, smell, hearing, balance, and taste.

Glyphosate causes cell death and neruo-degenerative disorders, such as Parkinson's disease.

"Furthermore, the results showed that glyphosate induced cell death via autophagy[1] pathways, in addition to activating apoptotic pathways."

This was the conclusion of a study by a team of five (5) doctors and research scientists at the Department of Neurology & Institute of Neurology, Ruijin Hospital, affiliated with Shanghai Jiao Tong University School of Medicine in Shanghai, *China*.

The study, published in the May-June 2012 issue of the journal *Neurotoxicol Teratol,* was entitled, *'Glyphosate induced cell death through apoptotic and autophagic mechanisms.'* It was also published in the US National Library of Medicine of the National Institutes of Health (*USA*).

The researchers reported,

"Previous studies indicated that the exposure to glyphosate, a widely used herbicide, is possibly linked to Parkinsonism, however the underlying mechanism remains unclear…

"We investigated the neurotoxic effects of glyphosate in differentiated PC12 cells and discovered that it inhibited viability of differentiated PC12 cells in dose-and-time dependent manners. Furthermore, the results showed that glyphosate induced cell death via autophagy[1] pathways in addition to activating   apoptotic[2] pathways."

The study indicated that *glyphosate* may be linked to Parkinson Disease, a degenerative disorder of the central nervous system, leading to uncontrollable body movements. The motor symptoms of Parkinson Disease are the consequence of the death of dopamine[3]-generating cells in the mid-brain, i.e. the *substantia nigra[4]*. The initial symptoms of the disease are shaking and slowness of movement; later, however, thinking and behavioral problems arise, commonly leading to dementia.

The study confirms that "Herbicides have been recognized as the main environmental factor associated with neurodegenerative[5] disorders, such as Parkinson's disease."

The research states specifically,

"We investigated the neurotoxic effects of glyphosate in differentiated PC12 cells[6] and discovered that it inhibited viability of differentiated PC12 cells in dose-and-time-dependent manners."   [1]

Many scientists suggest that since the brain is connected directly or indirectly to virtually every organ in the body, the brain is not likely to escape any and all of the chemical contaminations which *glyphosate* causes to the other organs in the body.

Of particular interest is the relationship of the brain to the intestines, since recent science illustrates how many chemicals in the brain are produced in the intestines. There is now an increasing amount of evidence of how the GMO 'food products' and *glyphosate* affect the other organs of the human body… and, therefore, affect the brain.

So what we eat – and don't eat – is now seen to be an essential part of the brain's health, physical and mental.

---

[1] *'Autophagy' is the normal catabolic mechanism by which cells deliberately degrade their unnecessary or dysfunctional components in order to conserve the energy for the other cell functions.*

[2] *'Apoptosis' is the normal process of programmed cell death (PCD) that occurs in multi-cellular organisms. Hence, the artificial and unintended activation of these processes, by an injury or 'foreign' chemicals, leads to the premature degradation or death of the cells.*

[3] *'Dopamine' is a neurotransmitter that helps control the brain's reward and pleasure centers, and aids in the regulation of movement and emotional responses.*

[4] *'Substantia nigra' (Latin for 'black substance' since it is darker than other parts of the brain) is part of the brain structure, and is located in the mid-brain where it is an important motor center and plays a role in the production of dopamine and in regulating movements.*

[5] *'Neurodegenerative disease' is an umbrella term for a range of conditions which primarily affect the neurons in the human brain. The neurons are the essential components of the nervous system, which includes the brain and spinal cord. Neurons cannot replace themselves; so when they are destroyed, or degenerate, they lead to the 'neurodegenerative diseases' such as Parkinson's disease, Alzheimer's, Huntington's, and other incurable diseases.*

[6] *PC12 cells are one of the lines of cells used in neurotoxicology (the study of the effects of chemicals and other matter which may be toxic to the brain) to monitor and measure various reactions, including nerve growth factors.*

[1]   http://www.ncbi.nlm.nih.gov/pubmed/22504123

GENES

A 'gene' (from the Greek 'genos' meaning 'offspring') is a molecular unit of heredity consisting of a sequence of DNA that occupies a specific location on a chromosome and determines a particular characteristic in a living organism.

GMO molecules can "silence" human genes.

―――――――

"What we found is that the molecules created in this wheat, intended to silence wheat genes, can match human genes, and through ingestion, these molecules can enter human beings and potentially silence our genes."

This was the conclusion of a study published in the October 9, 2012 issue of the *Digital Journal.* The article by Elliott Freeman was entitled, *'Scientists: New GMO wheat may 'silence' vital human genes.'*

The research was done by Professor Jack Heinemann of the University of Canterbury (***Australia***), who announced the results of his research into GMO wheat by saying,

He stated, "The findings are absolutely assured. There is no doubt that these matches exist."

The conclusions and analysis of the study were supported by Director Scott Kinnear of the Safe Food Foundation and Institute, set up to investigate issues of food safety and quality, and Professor Judy Carman of Flinders University, both in ***Australia***.

Dr. Carman added,

"If this silences the same gene in us that it silences in the wheat – well, children who are born with this enzyme not working tend to die by the age of five." [1]

―――――――

"Therefore, a gene that has been transferred might be incorporated in an unpredictable place in the genome (Godfrey, 2000)"

That's a conclusion of one of the research authors in *"Toxicity Studies of Genetically Modified Plants: A Review of the Published Literature"* by Dr. Jose L. Domingo of the Laboratory of Toxicology and Environmental Health, School of Medicine, "Rovira I Virgili" University in **Spain**. The particular section of the 'review' is entitled, *'Genetically Modified DNA in Food'* and discusses how this 'foreign' toxic DNA in the GM diet might enter the human intestines and blood systems.

Although long-term studies have yet to be done, another of the authors concluded,

"DNA fragments, after passing through the intestinal wall, might be actively removed by cells of the gut immune system or they might enter the circulation." (Jonas et al, 2001)

Thus, the toxic DNA inside of the GMO 'food products' could enter the intestines and blood stream of those who eat it.

Another author reported that,

"… material that had not been subjected to such treatments ["temperatures of 95°C or above for more than a few minutes"] not only had non-fragmented DNA but also retained specific polymerase chain reaction (PCR)[1]-detectable sequences suggesting that DNA was intact." (Chiter et al., 2000).

In another words, even after being digested by the body the toxic DNA which had been inserted into the GMO seeds was still capable of reproducing itself – millions of times!

The formal review itself concludes,

"… experimental studies carried out by independent researchers do not underrate the possibility that a transgene could be itself toxic of be transferred to the genome of the consumer." [2]
[Typo in original]

106

The toxic DNA in the GMO seeds can even be transferred into the genome itself!

————————

IN SUMMARY, when the toxic DNA inserted/blasted into the GMO seeds are eventually eaten and digested:

- The toxic DNA may enter the bloodstream and circulatory system

- The toxic DNA may enter the genome itself – and uncontrollably multiply millions of times within our bodies

- Each human cell has a minimum of 20,000 genes, any number of which can be altered by the toxins in the GMO crops… with unknown and unpredictable consequences.

[1] A 'polymerase chain reaction' (from Greek 'poly' meaning 'many' and 'meres', meaning 'parts') is a biochemical process in molecular biology in which a single piece of DNA can amplify and generated millions of copies of a particular DNA sequence.

[1]   http://www.digitaljournal.com/article/332822
[2]   http://www.biosafety.ru/ftp/domingo.pdf

HAIR

'Hair' (from Old English 'haer') is a biomaterial, primarily composed of the protein keratin, and made from dead cells (which is why it does not hurt to cut it). It is a bio-material that is part of the waste removal process of blood vessels, which provide both nourishment and waste removal for both dermal and epidermal cells. Hair grows (or is pushed out) from follicles found in the dermis, the layer of skin under the epidermis.

A multi-generational GMO diet causes hair to grow in abnormal locations in the bodies of hamsters.

In April 2010 the biologist Alexey V. Surov with the 'Russian Academy of Sciences' reported on a joint study by the 'National Association for Gene Security' and the 'Institute of Ecological and Evolutionary Problems,' both in ***Russia***. In the study three generations of hamsters were fed varying diets, including GMO soy. The third generation experienced a growth of hair in their mouths. [1]

Some of the hair was in clumps, and extended over the teeth of the rats. This was part of related 2009 research entitled, '*A New Example of Ectopia[1]: Oral Hair in Some Rodent Species,*' which revealed that the animals fed GMO-soy grew pouches of hair in their mouths:

"The number and size differed… Some were as deep as the tooth roots…and the teeth became loose…. Some of these pouches contained single hairs; others, thick bundles of colorless or pigmented hairs reaching as high as the chewing surface of the teeth. Sometimes the tooth row was surrounded with a regular brush of hair bundles on both sides." [2]

---

[1] *'Ectopia' is the abnormal location or position of a body part or organ, which can occur congenitally or as part of an injury or experiment. (From the Greek 'ektopos' which means 'out of place')*

[1]   http://voiceofrussia.com/2010/04/16/6524765.html/
[2]   http://www.truefoodfoundation.org/ectopia-from-gmo.pdf

KIDNEYS

The kidneys (name is of unknown origin) are a pair of organs, each 4 to 5 inches long, located behind the abdomen. Their function is to filter the blood – which passes through the kidneys several times a day. The kidneys regulate the body's balance of fluids, regulate the balance of electrolytes, and remove wastes. As they filter the blood, the kidneys create urine which drains town tubes (ureters) to the bladder which holds the urine until it is expelled.

Toxins in GMOs damage kidneys in animals.

Years of research reveal that GMOs create kidney damage.

A 2009 study in **France** by four (4) research scientists, Joel Spiroux de Vendomois, Francois Roullier, Dominique Cellier, and Giles-Eric Seralini, was published in the *International Journal of Biological Sciences.* It was entitled, *'A Comparison of the Effects of Three GM Corn Varieties on Mammalian Health.'*

In the study the researchers state, "We present for the first time a comparative analysis of blood and organ system data from trials with rats fed three main commercialized genetically modified (GM) maize (NK 603, MON 810, MON 863), which are present in food and feed in the world."

The study was detailed and "Approximately 60 different biochemical parameters were classified per organ and measured in serum and urine after 5 and 14 weeks of feeding..." The conclusion was:

- "Our analysis clearly reveals for the 3 GMOs new side effects linked with GM maize consumption, which were sex- and often dose-dependent.

- Effects were mostly associated with the kidney and liver, the dietary detoxifying organs, although different between the 3 GMOs.

- Effects were also noticed in the heart, adrenal glands, spleen, and haematopoietic system.[1]

109

- We conclude that these highlight signs of hepatorenal toxicity[2], possibly due to the new pesticides specific to each GM corn.

- In addition, unintended direct or indirect metabolic consequences[3] of the genetic modification cannot be excluded." [1]

It should be noted: The final sentence indicates that in addition to damage to the kidneys, liver, heart, and other organs, there was also possible damage to genes.

[1] *The 'haematopoietic system' is the bodily system of organs and tissues, primarily the bone marrow, spleen, tonsils, and lymph nodes, involved in the production of blood.*
[2] *'Hepatorenal toxicity' refers to the poisoning of the liver*
[3] *'Metabolic consequences' can have effects on hormonal release, glucose regulation, cardiovascular function, blood pressure, an inhibition of the stress hormone cortisol, reduced leptin and increased ghrelin levels (which produce subjective hunger, and can lead to diabetes and obesity).*

[Author's note: these various issues are discussed more specifically throughout this Handbook.]

The following refers to *19* separate studies regarding GMO crops and their effects on kidneys.

In 2011, Environmental Science Europe reported a summary of 19 studies involving GMO crops entitled, *'Genetically modified crops safety assessments: present limits and possible improvements.'*

Led by Dr. Gilles-Eric Seralini, the report included the scientists Robin Mesnage, Emilie Clair, Steeve Guess, Joel Spiroux de Vendomois, and Dominique Cellier, with the affiliated institutions of the University of Caen, the University of Rouen, and the Committee for Research and Independent Information on Genetic Engineering (CRIIGEN), all in *France*.

The summary commences,

"We reviewed 19 studies of mammals fed with commercialized genetically-modified soybean and maize which represent, per trait and plant, more than 80% of all environmental genetically modified organisms (GMOs) cultivated on a large scale, after they were modified to tolerate of produce a pesticide."

"In the NK603 study, statistically significant strong urine ionic disturbances and kidney markets could be explained by renal leakage which is well-correlated with the effects of glyphosate-based herbicides (like Roundup) observed on embryonic kidney cells…. Kidney dysfunctions are observed with mBt maize producing mutated insecticides such as in MON863."

It continues, "…we quote the initial EFSA report: 'Individual kidney weights of male rats fed with the 33% MON863 diet were statistically significantly lower compared to animals on control diets,' 'small increases in the incidences of focal inflammation and tubular regenerative changes in the kidneys of 33% MON863 males.' This was confirmed by the company tests, and another counter analysis revealed disrupted biochemical markers typical of kidney filtration or function problems."

The review concludes, "Last but not least, a total of around 9% of parameters were disrupted in a meta-analysis… Surprisingly, 43.5% of significant different parameters were concentrated in male kidneys for all commercialized GMOs, even if only around 25% of the total parameters measured were kidney-related… Even if our own counter analysis is removed from the calculation, showing numerous kidney dysfunctions, around 32% of disturbances are still noticed in kidneys." [2]

IN SUMMARY, the conclusions from a multitude of studies document that there is damage to the kidneys (and other organs) from eating GMO crops.

[1] http://www.ijbs.com/v05p0706.htm
[2] http://www.enveurope.com/content/23/1/10

GMO CROPS
and the
RESULTING
'FOOD PRODUCTS'

CORN (MAIZE)

'Maize' (from the indigenous Mesoamerican Taino people's word 'maiz') was domesticated by the indigenous people in Mesoamerica in prehistoric times, where thousands of varieties developed. Because of its ability to grow in diverse climates, in the 15th and 16th centuries traders began to spread maize around the world. In English it is now generally referred to as 'corn' (from the Old Slavic word 'kurnoni' meaning 'grain' – OED).

GMO corn produces tumors and organ damage in rats.

After two years of eating a GMO diet, rats developed massive mammary tumors, and damage to kidneys, the liver, and other organs.

That was the result of a two-year study done by a group of eight (8) European scientists from **France** and **Italy**. The study revealed that rats which were fed a diet of genetically engineered corn for two years developed massive mammary tumors, kidney and liver damage, and other biological and health problems.

The study was published in the November 2012 issue of the peer-reviewed journal *Food and Chemical Toxicology,* and entitled, *'Long term toxicity of a Roundup herbicide and a Roundup-tolerant genetically modified maize.'* The study provides photos as well as graphs.

One of the disturbing aspects of the study is that:

The level of Roundup used in the study is actually permitted by the US government in drinking water and GMO crops.

The authors pointed out that the study concerned, "The health effects of a Roundup-tolerant genetically modified maize (from 11% in the diet), **cultivated with or without Roundup**, and Roundup alone… *[Emphasis added]*

- "All results were hormone and sex dependent … Females developed large mammary tumors almost always more often than and before controls …

- The pituitary was the second most disabled organ… the sex hormonal balance was modified by GMO and Roundup treatments.

- "In treated males, liver congestions and necrosis were 2.5-5.5 times higher…

- Marked and severe kidney nephropathies[1] were also generally 1.3-2.3 greater.

- Males presented 4 times more large palpable tumors than controls, which occurred up to 600 days earlier. "

The authors also reported that the biochemistry results confirmed "very significant kidney chronic deficiencies."

The research scientists concluded that,

"These results can be explained by the non linear endocrine-disrupting effects of Roundup, but also by the over expression of the transgene in the GMO and its metabolic consequences." [1]

[1] *'Neuropathy' is from Greek 'neuron' meaning 'nerve' and 'pathos' meaning 'disease'. Hence, neuropathy is a disease of the nerves, generally an inflammation or degeneration of the peripheral nerves, i.e. the outer nerves of an organ.*

———————

"… these deficiencies are …exactly the deficiencies in a human being that lead to a susceptibility to sickness, disorders, and cancer."

That how the "Moms Across America" *(USA)* summarize the general results of a research project entitled, *'2012 Nutritional Analysis: Comparison of GMO Corn versus non-GMO corn.'*

The owners of the blog *Moms Across America.com* explain that they received a copy of the report from De Dell Seed Company in ***Canada,*** which, in turn, had obtained it from ProfitPro, an agriculture company based in Minnesota *(USA)*.

The report summarizes the shocking deficiencies of GMO corn compared to regular corn:

- large amounts of vital nutrients have been removed, and

- the GMO corn contains high levels of *glyphosate* (the weed-killing herbicide).

In their on-line article *'Stunning Corn Comparison: GMO versus NONGMO,'* the "Moms Across America" provided some graphs and highlights from the study to reveal that:

- Real corn has **7 times** more manganese than GMO corn! (Organic corn has 14 ppm of manganese, compared with 2 ppm in GMO corn.)

- Real corn has **437 times** more calcium! (Organic corn has 6,130 ppm, compared to GMO corn of 14 ppm.)

- Real corn has **56 times** more magnesium! (Organic corn has 113 ppm, compared to GMO corn of 2 ppm.)

The lack of nutrition in GMO 'food products' reveals the inevitable consequences. One of the by-products of this 'hidden hunger' is the body's continual craving for more nutrition, which inevitably leads to more eating. And, if more and more nutrient-deficient GMO 'food products' are consumed, this leads to obesity.

In addition to the nutrient deficiency, there are actual poisons in the GMO corn, namely *glyphosate* and formaldehyde:

Animal tests in Europe reveal that liver damage occurs at *glyphosate* levels of .0001ppm. Yet, American EPA standards permit up to .7ppm *glyphosate* levels in water.

Combining these two factors, the mathematical conclusion is that:

- The EPA standards allow *glyphosate* in America's water levels to be **7000 times** greater than what European tests show is even safe for animals to consume without causing cause liver damage... let alone humans.

- Even more disturbing: since GMO corn contains 13 ppm of *glyphosate*, the toxicity level in GMO corn is **130,000 times** more toxic than water standards in Europe! [2]

In addition to the health issues of GMO maize, there are serious environmental issues!

"Recently, three of Monsanto's GM maize varieties (MON 810, NK 603 and MON 810x NK603) failed to form cobs, leaving 200,000 [494,200 acres] hectares of GM maize barren."

This is one of the conclusions in a May 2009 African Centre for Biosafety Report in *South Africa*.

Although farmland in South Africa has been destroyed, the article continues,

"Undeterred, Monsanto is now pushing its flop GM maize onto the rest of the continent... The defective maize is set to be approved for commercial growing by 2015."

The tool which is being used to promote the GMO maize onto the rest of the continent is an organization called 'Water Efficient Maize for Africa.'

"WEMA was first touted for a good number of years, with much fanfare, as a charitable project intent on bringing drought tolerant maize varieties to resource poor African small farmers. However, with a sleight of hand and stony silence, WEMA included MON810[1] into the mix."

There is another 'sleight of hand' to make Monsanto and WEMA look charitable – while making huge profits, and polluting the environment. When Monsanto says it is "giving" the seeds "royalty free," it does not mean the seeds are free to the small farmers in Africa. On the contrary, as this GM Watch article indicates,

"The patents on the gene sequences still reside with Monsanto, and farmers will have to pay a premium price for the GM seeds." [3][4]

There is another toxic danger from GMO corn: GMO corn is also used as the bio-fuel, ethanol, which infects the lungs.

[1] http://www.sciencedirect.com/science/article/pii/S0278691512005637
[2] http://www.momsacrossamerica.com/stunning_corn_comparison_gmo_v ersus_non_gmo
[3] http://www.biosafety-info.net/file_dir/14859528524a1b5798b3c82.pdf
[4] http://www.acbio.org.za/index.php/media/64-media-releases/448-monsantos-failed-sa-gm-maize-pushed-into-rest-of-africa

---

GMO CORN PRODUCT: High Fructose Corn Syrup

"High doses of free fructose have been proven to literally punch holes in the intestinal lining allowing nasty products of toxic gut bacteria and partially digested food proteins to enter your blood stream..." The resultant "inflammation .... is at the root of obesity, diabetes, cancer, heart disease, dementia, and accelerated aging."

That is one of the warnings by Dr. Mark Hyman, Chairman of the Institute for Functional Medicine and six times New York Times best-selling author *(USA)*. [1]

High Fructose Corn Syrup (HFCS) is an inexpensive genetically engineered sweetener. In Canada HFCS is called 'glucose/fructose.'

HFCS is a group of corn syrups that have undergone various forms of chemical 'processing,' largely altering the enzymes, to convert much of the cornstarch (a polymer of interlinked chains of glucose molecules) into fructose in order to enhance the sweetness.

HFCS has been shown to contribute to obesity, cardiovascular (heart) disease, diabetes, and hyperlipidemia[1].

Due to its low cost, there are thousands of 'food products' which contain HFCS. Hundreds of them are 'food products' which appear to be "natural" (and are deceitfully mislabeled as "natural").

Consuming too much sugar in any form leads to various diseases, particularly obesity and diabetes. However, because of the existence of the genetically engineered HFCS in thousands of 'food products' the annual consumption of sugar has accelerated, contributing to the wide spread problem of obesity.

[1] 'Hyperlipidemia' is a term meaning high lipid (fat) levels in the blood. It usually means high cholesterol and high triglyceride levels, and can accelerate the process of atherosclerosis (hardening of the arteries).

NB Unlike glucose which stimulates the production of insulin and leads to the creation of energy, fructose is metabolized in the liver, which turns it into glucose or triglycerides – fat.

[1] http://drhyman.com/blog/2011/05/13/5-reasons-high-fructose-corn-syrup-will-kill-you/#close

MILK

The word 'milk' derives from many sources, perhaps dating back to the Old Saxon 'miluk.' Milk is a white liquid produced by the mammary glands of mammals. The early lactation milk of mothers provides the new-born offspring with antibodies to protect it against diseases, and provides various nutrients. Through human evolution adults eventually developed the ability to produce lactase, and thereby to digest milk. This led to the production, and sale, of milk to adults, and eventually to children.

GMO (rBGH) milk increases risk of breast and prostate cancer.

Numerous studies have shown links between increased IGF-1 levels and increased risk of cancer, especially breast cancer and prostate cancer.

Monsanto created another GMO product, specifically for cows.

Humans have a growth hormone created by the pituitary gland, called *somatrtropin*, which promotes growth and cell replication.

The natural form of this hormone in cows is a bovine growth hormone (BGH), also known as *bovine somatotropin (BST)*. This hormone increases the levels of another hormone, known as Insulin-like Growth Factor 1 (IGF-1), which stimulates milk production.

Through genetic engineering Monsanto created a synthetic growth hormone, called the 'recombinant bovine growth hormone' (rBGH), sometimes referred to as rBST.

This chemical is marketed to dairy farmers, to inject into cows. When the rBGH is injected into cows, it increases the secretion of the IGF-1. This increases milk production by between 15% and 20%.

However, IGF-1 is a hormone that does not simply stimulate the growth of normal cells: it also stimulates the growth of *cancer* cells.

Even more concerning, IGF-1 in cows has an identical amino acid sequence to human IGF-1. This raises the question:

If humans drink milk which has been produced by genetically engineering an increase in IGF-1 in the cows, could this increase the IGF-1 in humans?

Bovine growth hormones (rBGH) are *scientifically designed* to increase IGF-1!

—————

"Avoidance of rBGH dairy products in favor of natural products would thus appear to be the most practical and immediate 'dietary intervention to … [achieve] the goal of preventing cancer."

That was part of the correspondence between Oxford University *(United Kingdom)* and Dr. Samuel Epstein of the University of Illinois, School of Public Health *(USA)*, reported in *JNCI Journal of the National Cancer Institute* in a February 2001 article entitled, *'Re: Role of the Insulin-Like Growth Factors in Cancer Development and Progression.'*

As far back as 1996 Dr. Epstein published an article in the renowned *International Journal of Health Sciences* clearly warning of the dangers of high levels of IGF-1 contained in milk containing the synthetic bovine growth hormone (rBGH).

Dr. Epstein expressed his concern that IGF-1 in rBGH milk could be a potential risk factor for breast and gastrointestinal cancers, explaining "… a substantial portion of IGF in milk from rBGH-injected cows is in a more bioactive, unbound, protein-free form than is IGF in milk from untreated cows." He added,

"Furthermore, converging lines of experimental and epidemiological evidence have incriminated excess IGF levels in rBGH milk as risks for breast and colon cancers." [1]

—————

Over 15 years ago a study by The European Commission – Food Safety, *(Italy)* in a March 1999 *"Report on Public Health Aspects of the Use of Bovine Somatotropin,"* confirmed "rBST [rBGH] is known to increase the levels of insulin-like growth factor 1 (IGF-1) in cows, which can lead to increased IFG-1 in milk."

The study warned, "IGFs possess endocrine[1], paracrine[1] and autocrine[1] activities. IGF-1 acts as a progression factor in the cell cycle and has mitogenic[2] and anti-apoptotic[3] properties…

"Numerous medical reports…describe the detrimental role of IGF-1 as cellular growth regulator and tumour promoter."

The study also warned of health dangers to the cows and to the milk itself: "In identifying the potential hazards, secondary risks related to the use of rBST in dairy cows need to be considered as well. These arise from possible changes in milk composition of treated animals and impairment of animal health, in particular the increased incidence of mastitis[4] resulting in a more frequent use of antimicrobial substances…"

The report also raised other issues related directly to the cows:

"Studies of animals exposed to rBST [rBGH] raise concerns about potential changes in milk protein that could lead to allergies."

The European Commission – Food Safety points out the obvious: this not only adds to the suffering and health issues of the animals, but

"The increased incidences of infections could lead to increased use of antibiotics and an increased risk of antimicrobial residues in milk and to antibiotic resistant bacteria." [2]

Such "antibiotic resistant bacteria" could end up in the milk. Thus, another study validates the dangers:

If certain medical issues occur in humans due to rGBH milk, antibiotics may not be effective.

"Use of rBST increased the risk of a cow failing to conceive by 40%."

"Cows treated with rBST had an estimated 55% chance of developing clinical signs of lameness."

Those are some of the conclusions seven (7) research scientists in **Canada** reported in the *Canadian Journal of Veterinary Research*, 2003, entitled *A meta-analysis review of the effects of recombinant bovine somatotropin* which was published in the US National Library of Medicine of the National Institutes of Health *(USA)* in October 2003.

"This manuscript presents the results of a review of the effects of recombinant bovine somatotropin (rBST) on dairy cattle, reproductive performance, and culling that was carried out by an expert panel established by the Canadian Veterinary Medical Association (CVMA)… in a response to a request from Health Canada [Government of Canada]…"

"A series of meta-analyses was used to combine data on health-related parameters that were extracted from all randomized clinical trials that had been published in peer-reviewed journals or which were provided by Health Canada from the submission by Monsanto for registration of rBST in Canada."

In addition to the conclusions indicated above, the study discovered that "Recombinant bovine somatotropin was found to increase the risk of mastitis by approximately 25% during the treatment period…"

The study also "… concluded that the use of rBST would likely reduce the lifespan of dairy cattle." [3]

"The role of IGFs in cancer is supported by epidemiological studies…"

That's according to another article, published in *oxford.journals.org*, entitled, *'Role of the Insulin-like Growth Factor Family in Cancer*

Development and Progression,' in the *Journal of the National Cancer Institute*, 92:1472-89, 2000.

"The role of IGFs in cancer is supported by epidemiological studies, which have found that high levels of circulating IGF-1 and low levels of IGFBP-3 are associated with increased risk of several common cancers, including those of the prostrate, breast, colorectum, and the lung."

The research was conducted by Professor Herbert Yu, Director of the Cancer Epidemiology Program at the University of Hawaii, *USA,* and Professor Thomas E. Rohan, Chairman of the Department of Epidemiology & Population Health at the Albert Einstein College of Medicine *(USA).*

In the formal Conclusion of the study, the authors state,

"Laboratory experiments demonstrate that IGFs are able to stimulate the growth of a wide variety of cancer cells and to suppress apoptosis[3]."

"In addition to their direct affect on cancer cells, IGFs also interact synergistically with other mitogenic[2] molecules and counteract antiproliferative molecules that are involved in cancer development and progression." [4]

"… high circulating levels of IGF-1 are associated with elevated risk of breast cancer."

This is the conclusion of another study, a collaborative effort led by the Department of Epidemiology and Public Health and Yale Cancer Center at Yale University *(USA)*, which included research scientists from the *USA* and *China.* It was published in the US National Library of Medicine, entitled, *'Insulin-like growth factors and breast cancer risk in Chinese women.'*

The research confirmed,

"Insulin-like growth Factor (IGF)-1 has mitogenic[2] and antiapoptotic[3] effects on breast cancer cells.

High-circulating IGF-1 was found to be associated with increased risk of breast cancer in several previous epidemiological studies, mostly with Caucasian populations."

"The study confirms that high circulating levels of IGF-1 are associated with elevated risk of breast cancer." [5]

[1] *(a) 'Endocrine' refers to the system of cells, glands, and tissues of an organism that secrete hormones into the blood stream. (b) 'Paracrine' signaling is a method of cell-to-cell communication to induce changes or alter the behavior of nearby cells. (c) 'Autocrine' is a mode of hormone action in which a cell secretes a hormone which binds to receptors and affects the function of the cell type that produced it.*

[2] *'Mitogen' is a chemical substance which prompts a cello commence cell division, triggering mitosis (the process by which a cell creates two identical daughter cells, instead of simply replicating each of its chromosomes)*

[3] *'Apoptosis' is the programmed cell death (PCD) that occurs in multi-cellular organisms. ('Anti-apoptotic' effect inhibits the normal process)*

[4] *'Mastitis' is an infection and inflammation of breast tissue.*

———————

As far back as 1998 a study entitled, *Plasma Insulin-Like Growth Factor-1 and Prostate Cancer Risk: A Prospective Study,* published in *Science* on 23 January 1998, was done by eight (8) researcher scientists led by Harvard, and currently at various universities in the United States *(USA).*

The researchers concluded then that, "Insulin-Like Growth Factor-1 (IGF-1) is a mitogen for prostate epithelial cells… A strong positive association was observed between IGF-1 levels and prostate cancer risk. Men in the highest quartile of IGF-1 levels had a relative risk of 4.3 (95 percent confidence interval 1.8 to 10.6) compared with men in the lowest quartile."

The conclusion was that, "Identification of IGF-1 as a predictor of prostate cancer risk may have implications for risk reduction and treatment." [6]

[1] *S.aureus is 'Staphylococcus aureus', a type of bacteria which generally cause skin infection, but can also cause pneumonia, food poisoning, toxic shock syndrome, and blood poisoning (bacteremia). It is often referred to as 'staph infection.'*

IN SUMMARY,

- High levels of IGF-1 created by rBGH can create severe biological and medical problems in humans.

- If cows develop allergies and/or udder infections (mastitis), these cows could pass these bacteria into the milk which people (and children) drink.

- If antibiotics are put into the milk to create bacteria-resistant milk in order to combat these bacteria, these newly-created antibiotic-resistant-bacteria in the milk will get into the human body.

- When these newly-created antibiotic-resistant bacteria from rBGH milk get into the human body, various antibiotics will not be effective on the humans who develop diseases from these bacteria

---

NOTE: Use of bovine growth hormones (rBGH) is not permitted in Australia, New Zealand, Japan, Canada... and the 27 countries of the European Union. However, it was approved for use in the United States by the FDA in 1993 – after only a 90-day study – on rats, not on cows!

[1] http://jnci.oxfordjournals.org/content/93/3/238.1.full
[2] http://ec.europa.eu/food/fs/sc/scv/out19_en.html
[3] http://www.ncbi.nlm.nih.gov/pmc/articles/PMC280709/
[4] http://jnci.oxfordjournals.org/content/92/18/1472.full.pdf
[5] http://www.ncbi.nlm.nih.gov/pubmed/12163322
[6] http://www.sciencemag.org/content/279/5350/563

NB To see images of cows injected with rBGH view the following link:
https://www.google.com/search?q=bovine+growth+hormone+cows&rlz=1C
1CHFX_enUS460US460&espv=210&es_sm=93&source=lnms&tbm=isch&
sa=X&ei=nLdqUuX-A9W-
4APB8IDYDw&ved=0CAkQ_AUoAQ&biw=1280&bih=709

POTATOES

'Potatoes' (from the 16th century Spanish word 'patata') were originally from the Andes region, and are now one of the four main crops of the world (behind rice, wheat, maize).

GMO potatoes: The Beginning of the GMO Health Scandals.

"We are putting new things into food which have not been eaten before. The effects on the immune system are not easily predictable…"

That was one of the conclusions of Dr. Arpad Pusztai, former research scientist with the Rowett Institute in **Scotland,** and one of the first scientists to expose the dangers of eating GMO 'food products.' This occurred in 1998, when Dr. Pusztai's research indicated that GMO potatoes are toxic.

When Dr. Pusztai fed GMO potatoes to rats, the adverse effects on their bodies became immediately evident. The rats' brains, livers, and testicles grew smaller, and their pancreases and intestines became enlarged. There were also changes in their immune system. [1]

Dr. Pusztai released some of the information from his research, and a political firestorm erupted. Monsanto began an immediate campaign to discredit Dr. Pusztai, and he was terminated from his decades-long position at the Rowett Institute (to which Monsanto had previously given substantial donations).

When his scientific results were publicly exposed, it led to an international scandal involving the Prime Minister of Great Britain and the then-president of the United States. Monsanto was supported by the current British Prime Minister Tony Blair and the US President Bill Clinton – both of whom wanted the economic benefits and tax revenues arising from the sales of these 'food products.'

However, after years of suffering public abuse and attacks on his character and reputation, Dr. Pusztai was vindicated and the results of his research were verified and   validated.

Among the discoveries was that when the chemical lectin was inserted directly into the rats, or inserted into 'natural' potatoes fed to the rats, the animals apparently had no side effects. However, when the lectin *was added to the GMO potatoes* which were fed to the rats, the internal damage to the rats was pronounced. The conclusion was that:

> The *process of genetic engineering* itself contributed to this development.

When a seed is genetically engineered, the genes which are 'inserted' (blasted) into the seed of a plant disturb the internal dynamics of the seed, destroy some parts of the seed, and set in motion the natural 'protective instinct' of the seeds. Inserting a DNA construct into a seed creates botanical alterations in the internal structure and functionality of the plant's genes... and it is done in a violent manner. This is called 'insertional mutagenesis,' namely the internal organs of the seeds are altered. The consequences of these various internal dynamics are unpredictable ... and uncontrollable!

This revelation by Dr. Pusztai, followed by Monsanto's international effort to discredit him, began the global war on GMO seeds. The resultant publicity of Monsanto attacking a renowned scientist brought the GMO matter to the attention of the public. Governments and the scientific community began to realize that research was necessary to see how much damage GMO seeds, and the resultant 'food products', were causing to human health. A brief history of Dr. Pusztai's discoveries and Monsanto's attempt to destroy him are recounted by Organic Consumers Association. [2]

As a result of the publicity, and the consequent pressure from the public, various scientific and government organizations in Europe eventually took action to ban GMO crops from the European Union.

The global battle over how Monsanto and other chemical companies got into the business of producing 'food products' – and endangering human health – all began with the potato.

[1] http://stopogm.net/files/Ewen.pdf
[2] http://www.organicconsumers.org/articles/article_18101.cfm

SOY

'Soy,' or soy beans, (from Chinese word 'shi-yu' from 'shi' meaning 'fermented soybeans' and 'yu' meaning 'oil') originated in Asia before recorded history. Soy beans are legumes, namely plants grown primarily for their food grain seeds. Through traders, the soy bean reached Australia, Europe, and North America in the 18th century, and Africa in the 19th century. Soy is now used in a multitude of food products, including milk and baby formula.

A variety of different animals on a GMO soy diet experienced:
- **cellular changes in liver, pancreas, and testes;**
- **functional disturbances in hearts and kidneys;**
- **changes in ovaries and uteri;**
- **loss of reproductive capability**

"The findings suggest that GM RR soy could pose serious health risks to humans. The fact that differences were found between GM-fed and non-GM-fed animals contradicts the FDA's assumption that GM soy is substantially equivalent to non-GM soy." *[Emphasis added]*

This is one of the conclusions of a 2010 report entitled, *"GM Soy: Sustainable? Responsible?"* co-authored by a group of international scientists.

The report summarizes more than 100 independent studies – performed on a variety of animals – which demonstrate the serious health and environmental dangers of GM [genetically modified] Roundup Ready soy and from Monsanto's *glyphosate* herbicide.

The principal participants in the study were Michael Antoniou (***United Kingdom***), Paulo Brack (***Brazil***), Andres Carrasco (***Argentina***), John Fagan (***USA***), Mohammed Ezz El-Din Mostafa Habib (***Brazil***), Paolo Yoshio Kageyama (***Brazil***), Carlo Leifert (***United Kingdom***), Rubens Onofre Nodari (***Brazil***), and Walter A. Pengue (***Argentina***). [1]

(The report was also published by *earthopensource.org*, which made the study available in 5 languages. [2])

The report cited various research studies which revealed that:

- "In a rare long-term feeding study, mice fed GM RR soy showed cellular changes in the liver, pancreas, and testes."

- "Mice fed GM soy over their entire lifetime showed more acute signs of aging in their liver."

- "Rabbits fed GM soy showed enzyme function disturbances in kidney and heart."

- "Female rats fed GM soy showed changes in their uterus and ovaries compared with controls fed non-GMO soy or a non-soy diet."

- "In a multigenerational study of hamsters, most of the GM soy-fed hamsters had lost the ability to produce by the third generation. The GM-fed hamsters had slower growth and higher mortality among pups."

Another conclusion was that,

> "Since GM RR [Roundup Ready] soy was approved for commercialization, studies have found ill effects in laboratory animals fed on GM RR soy…"

The various studies also report that when animals are fed a GM diet, the genetically-modified DNA can be found in the milk and body tissues (namely, the meat) of the animals. The research indicated that:

- GM DNA from GM maize and GM soy were found in milk from animals raised on GM crops. The GM DNA was not destroyed by pasteurization.

- GM DNA from soy was found in the blood, organs, and milk of goats. An enzyme, lactic dehydrogenase, was found at significantly raised levels in the heart, muscle, and kidneys of kids fed GM RR soy. This enzyme leaks from damaged cells and can indicate cellular injury.

The studies addressed the claims made by Monsanto and other chemical companies that GM DNA does not survive digestive process. It refuted these false claims, and concluded, "… these assumptions are false."

The GM toxins are in the soy eaten by humans, and these toxins **remain** in the milk and meat of animals which are fed a diet of GM soy.

The final conclusion of the study was clear:

"The FDA's ruling was widely recognized as an expedient political decision with no basis in science. More controversially, the FDA ignored the warnings of its own scientists that GM is different from traditional breeding and poses unique risks to human and animal health." [2]
(A summary is also available in the link [3] below).

IN SUMMARY, GM (GMO) crops are containers of poison, both for humans and animals. Whether people consume GMO crops, or eat GMO-contaminated meat and milk, the GMO toxins accumulate inside of the human bodies – and they grow inside.

[1] http://www.nongmoproject.org/wp-content/uploads/2011/02/GM-Soy-Report.pdf
[2] http://earthopensource.org/files/pdfs/GM-Soy-Sustainable/gm_full_eng_v15.pdf
[3] http://earthopensource.org/files/pdfs/GM-Soy-Sustainable/gm_sum_eng_v12.pdf

LABELING the CONTENTS
of
GMO 'FOOD PRODUCTS'

Concealing the Chemical Contents of GMO 'Food Products'

"WE HAVE A RIGHT TO KNOW … IF OUR FOOD HAS BEEN GENETICALLY ENGINEERED."

That's the on-line headline of *justlabelit.org* which discusses the startling fact that

"Most Americans haven't been told about some of the ingredients that are in the food they eat." [1]

Despite (or because of) all of these medical studies which reveal health problems with GMO 'food products,' Monsanto and the other chemical companies have fought vigorously to **prevent** *any* attempt to label the contents of *any* of their GMO 'food products.'

Indeed, Monsanto and the other chemical companies are being assisted by many food distribution companies in an effort to **prevent** *any* labeling of these products – *on the national, state, and local levels!* Together they spend millions of dollars every year to block the attempts of voters in different states from creating "Labeling Laws." Such examples include the recent (2012-2013) attempts in California and the State of Washington which had such issues in their public voting process. [2]

In addition, the massive legal departments of Monsanto and their allies even initiate litigation against local and state governments that *have passed* legislation – and against companies which *support* any law or policy requiring that these GMO 'food products' be labeled.

For example, when the State of Vermont enacted a law (1994) requiring products to be labeled if they contained the 'bovine growth hormone' (rBGH), Monsanto and a number of organizations went to court to block the implementation of the law (with the bizarre and cynical legal claim that it violated the First Amendment by forcing milk producers to label their products…?). Some of the other organizations involved (then and in later GMO-labeling battles) were The Grocery Manufacturers of

134

America, the National Food Processors Association, The Milk Industry Foundation, the Ice Cream Association, and a variety of trade and lobbying groups that financially benefit from the sale of rBGH milk and 'rBGH milk products' which contain the bovine growth hormone. [3]

In 2002 the state of Oregon attempted to pass a law entitled '*Oregon Labeling of Genetically-Engineered Foods Act*, called 'Measure 27,' to label GMO food products so that the citizens/consumers could see what these products contained. The measure was severely defeated. Why? The opponents outspent the supporters of the law by $5.5 Million to $200,000, with the

> "...vast majority of the opposition funding from corporations headquartered outside the state: Monsanto, Dupont, Syngenta, Dow Agro Sciences, BASF, Aventis, Hoechst, and Bayer Crop Science."

"These opponents' other activities include:
- Chemical Weapons: Monsanto (Agent Orange, PCBs, dioxins), Dow (napalm), Hoechst (mustard gas)
- Pesticides: Monsanto (DDT), Dow (dioxins, PCBs, Dursban)"
  [4]

Of course, in addition to its other chemical activities, Monsanto also produces Roundup (*glyphosate*). It is projected that by 2017 the global *glyphosate* market will reach 1.35 Million metric tons! [5]

In a similar initiative in the state of Washington in November 2013, the proponents of labeling also lost -- but by a smaller margin, 54.8% to 45.2%. Proponents of the labeling bill raised a little more than $7 Million; while opponents, led again by the biotech companies and agribusiness from outside of the state, poured in over $22 Million. The top five contributors were Monsanto, DuPont Pioneer, Dow Agro Sciences, Bayer CropScience, and the Grocery Manufacturers Association. [6]

For the past 20 years Monsanto, the other chemical companies, and their 'food' distributors have fought *any* attempt to label the contents of their GMO 'food products' – on local, state, and national levels. Now they are attempting to pass legislation in the U.S. on the national level to prevent any individual state from passing labeling laws.

(NB: Unlike the U.S. and Canada, 64 countries either label or ban various GMO 'products') [7]

On April 16, 2014 by a vote of 28-2, the Senate of the State of Vermont passed a bill requiring mandatory labeling of foods sold in Vermont that contain genetically modified organisms (GMOs). On April 23, 2014 the Vermont House of Representatives voted 114-30 to concur with the Senate version of the bill.

The significance of this legislation is that it will have the national impact of a federal law in the market place. That's because food distributors will create a firestorm among consumers if these distributors have separate labels in different states for the same 'food products' – some labels disclosing that their 'food products' contain GMO chemicals and toxins, while other labels claim these same 'foods' are "natural" or "all natural."

The passage of this legislation in Vermont also leads other states closer to their own implementation of labeling laws. For example, Connecticut and Maine have similar laws, but contain 'trigger' provisions which prevent them from being implemented until other states have similar laws.

Ronnie Cummins, founder and Director of the Organic Consumers Association, which has been one of the leaders in the effort to label GMO foods, commented, "With the passage of the Vermont GMO labeling law, after 20 years of struggle, it's time to celebrate our common victory. But, as we all know, the battle for a new food and farming system, and a sustainable future, has just begun." [8]

It is expected that Monsanto and other GMO companies will seek to create legislation to block the law, which doesn't go into effect until July 1, 2016. In the past, Monsanto and their distributors have also spent millions of dollars on legal fees to prevent labeling of the contents of their 'food products' by initiating various kinds of litigation. It is expected they will   continue to do so.

Food distributors already provide detailed labeling of the contents of their foods, including the vitamins, minerals, fats, sodium, potassium, sugars, and the calorie counts. Yet, they work with Monsanto to ban any labeling of the chemical contents of GMO 'food products' which are on most grocery store shelves!

In addition, "political friends" of the GMO industry are seeking to override state laws requiring full disclosure, and to deny states the right to enact their own laws to protect food health. Various Members of the U.S. Congress of both Democrat and Republican parties are now attempting to pass national legislation banning labeling. This effort is led by Rep. Mike Pompeo who introduced a bill in April 2014, misleadingly entitled "Safe and Accurate Food and Labeling Act of 2014" – which even allows the continued use of "natural" or "all natural" product labels on a wide variety of chemically treated foods and beverages. Critics call it the Dark (Denying Americans the Right to Know) Act since it seeks to deny American citizens the right to know what's in their food. President Obama, a major supporter of Monsanto who even created a new and powerful position at the FDA for the Monsanto vice president Michael Taylor, is expected to support this legislation.

On the other hand, the organic food industry and those who support non-GMO foods are mobilizing to promote the labeling of contents in foods, state by state like in Vermont, and by lobbying Members of the U.S. Congress who seek to deny the public the right to know what's in their foods and beverages.

Oregon voters are expected to have a ballot initiative on this subject in November 2014. The effort is being led by Scott Bates and GMO Free Oregon. It is supported by people and organizations around the country, as well as organic food groups, including the Organic Consumers Association.

Other states have various initiatives in these efforts to label foods – so that people can actually know what they are eating.

[1] http://justlabelit.org/
[2] http://www.organicconsumers.org/articles/article_28699.cfm
[3] http://www.ratical.org/corporations/rBSTlabeling.html

[4]   http://www.psr.org/chapters/oregon/assets/pdfs/powerpoints/gmo-and-rbgh-powerpoint.ppt

[5]   http://www.prweb.com/releases/glyphosate_agrochemical/technical_glyphosate/prweb8857231.htm

[6]   http://www.usatoday.com/story/news/nation/2013/11/06/washington-state-voters-reject-gmo-labeing/3450705/

[7]   http://www.labelgmos.org/the_science_genetically_modified_foods_gmo

[8]   http://www.organicconsumers.org/articles/article_29781.cfm

'DOOMSDAY VAULT'
for
NON-GMO SEEDS

Preserving Non-GMO Seeds for the Wealthy

"Doomsday Vault Opens in Norway"

That's the title of a CNN.com/Europe report on a "Doomsday Seed Vault" hidden in an island in Spitzbergen, Norway, where millions of 'natural' seeds are being stored. [1]

Who are the people behind setting up this once-secret vault of 'natural' seeds? The answer:

"Bill Gates and GMO Cronies Plan $30 Million Seed Vault While Poisoning the Planet"

That's the title of an article by Christina Sarich in a July 3, 2013 issue of the *Waking Times.* The author writes,

> "Along with him [Bill Gates], pals from the Rockefeller Foundation, the Monsanto corporation, the Government of Norway, the Syngenta Foundation, and others are building a 'doomsday seed bank' officially named the 'Svalbard Global Seed Vault' on the Norwegian Island of Spitsbergen..."

Who are the players? Monsanto, the leading chemical company and producer of GMOs; Bill Gates and the Bill and Melinda Gates Foundation (owners of 500,000 shares of Monsanto and major promoters of GMOs worldwide); Syngenta, producer of chemicals and GMOs; DuPont/Pioneer, chemical company giants which also produce GMO seeds; the Rockefeller Foundation, which began the 'Green Revolution' and participated in the original research and financing of GMO crops; CGIAR, a global network of Rockefeller supporters.

Quoting the website of the group, the purpose of the seed vault is for "Ensuring that the genetic diversity of the world's crops is preserved for future generations..."— while, of course, this group is promoting GMO crops which are systematically destroying agricultural diversity around the globe! [2]

Among the obvious questions are:

(1) Why are all of these people who are making a fortune selling GMO seeds creating a 'Doomsday Vault' of 'natural' seeds?

(2) Who is entitled to the use of these seeds?

(3) Are they also storing GMO seeds, or just 'natural' seeds?

Since all of those involved in this 'Doomsday Seed Vault' are aware of the toxic science of GMO crops, one can draw one's own conclusion as to their motives.

[1] http://www.cnn.com/2008/WORLD/europe/02/26/norway.seeds/
[2] http://www.wakingtimes.com/2013/07/03/bill-gates-and-gmo-cronies-plan-million-dollar-seed-vault-while-poisoning-the-planet/

ANIMALS
and
OTHER LIVING CREATURES

BEES

A 'bee' (from Old English 'beo' or 'bee' back to Middle Dutch 'bie'...?) is a flying insect, closely related to ants and wasps, and producers of honey and beeswax.

Glyphosate (Roundup) is poisoning the bee population.

"Pollination is critical for food production and human livelihoods, and directly links wild ecosystems with agricultural production systems... In fact, pollinators such as bees, birds, and bats affect 35 percent of the world's crop production, increasing outputs of 87 of the leading food crops worldwide, as well as many plant-derived medicines."

This was part of a report called *'Biodiversity...for a world without hunger'* by the Food and Agriculture Organization of the United Nations (FAO) in *Italy*. [1]

Bees are the most important pollinating insects on earth.

There are about 20,000 species of bees in the world, and they are essential to the food supply. Their interdependence with plants as part of the mutual life cycle creates a symbiosis known as 'mutualism,' a mutually beneficial relationship between unlike organisms.

Bees depend upon pollen as a source of protein, and on flower nectar or oils as a source of energy. They have feathery body hairs that help them collect pollen, some of which they lose when they move from flower to flower. When this pollen falls off onto different flowers and plants, some of it lands on the pistils (the reproductive structures), resulting in cross-pollination, one of nature's ways to procreate.

Cross-pollination is so important to food production that beekeepers in many countries now regard it as more important than the production of honey!

"Bee colony collapse disorder (CCD) is a growing threat to the efficient production of fruits, vegetables, and nut crops, in addition to the critical role of bees as pollinators for numerous seed crops."

This was part of the Introduction in a paper by Dr. Don Huber, Professor of Plant Pathology at Purdue University, *(USA)*, published on-line in August 2013 by *GMOEvidence* entitled,

'Is glyphosate a contributing cause of bee colony collapse disorder (CCD)?'

Dr. Huber says that,

"Perhaps a more problematic cause of CCD has been overlooked even though it is the most indiscriminately and extensively used chemical in agriculture and the environment."

"This organic *phosphonate* chemical that has been over looked is the estimated 880 million pounds of the popular, broad-spectrum, systemic herbicide glyphosate (also marketed as Roundup)... "

Dr. Huber points out how widespread the use of *glyphosate* has become, including crop production on millions of acres of 'GMO Roundup Ready' food crops such as alfalfa, canola, corn, cotton, soybeans, and sugar beets, and ... in addition... is now being used as a desiccant (drying agent) prior to harvest for barley, beans, peas, peanuts, sugar cane, wheat, and other crops.

He warns that although *glyphosate* is used year-round, there are "especially high concentrations in plants, air, water and soil during primary bee foraging periods," and that,

"The exposure, physiological damage, and biological impact of glyphosate are consistent with all of the known conditions related to CCD..."

In his concluding remarks Dr. Huber warns:

"New studies refer to this compound as the most biologically disruptive chemical in our environment (Samsel and Senoff, 2013)."

[2]

"The widespread use of honey substitutes, including high fructose corn syrup, may thus compromise the ability of honey bees to cope with pesticides and pathogens and contribute to colony losses."

This was a conclusion reached by entomologists at the University of Illinois *(USA)* in a research paper published in the Proceedings of the National Academy of Sciences on March 21, 2013 entitled, *'Honey constituents up-regulate detoxification and immunity genes in the western honey bee Apis mellifera.'* [3]

This raises another issue, which is even more insidious. To maximize profits, many beekeepers are putting high fructose corn syrup (HFCS) in the diet of bees in their colonies.

Bees ingest pollen and nectar, and create honey as their food supply. They store up the honey during the warm months of the year. During the winter they gather together to keep warm, and eat the then-dried honey.

Beekeepers take as much of the honey as they can to sell, and leave as much as they think the bees need to survive. However, to remove more of the honey and still not allow the bees to starve, they often leave a substitute food for the bees to eat: *high fructose corn syrup!* And HFCS is made from GMOs!

The research discovered a possible link between providing bees a diet of high fructose corn syrup (HFCS) and the collapse of bee colonies. The findings were also reported on April 30, 2013 by Bob Yirka in *phys.org* in an article entitled,

'Researchers find high-fructose corn syrup may be tied to worldwide collapse of bee colonies.'

146

It should be noted that the researchers did not claim that HFCS was directly toxic to the bees. Instead,

"Their findings indicate that by eating the replacement food instead of honey, the bees are not being exposed to other chemicals that help the bees fight off toxins, such as those found in pesticides."

The specific enzyme is 'p-coumaric,' which increases the power of their immune system and turns on detoxification genes.

"Taking away the honey to sell it, and feeding the bees high fructose corn syrup instead, they claim, compromises their immune systems, making them vulnerable to the toxins that are meant to kill other bugs." [4]

GMO corn has less nutritional value than organic corn. Eating GMO products seems to deprive the body of nutrients and prevents the body from fighting off toxins, leading to the development of allergies and other medical maladies. Disturbing research now seems to indicate that this may be affecting the bees as well.

IN SUMMARY, a combination of poisonous practices may be decimating bee colonies around the world. Spreading the toxin-filled GMO crops and *glyphosate* in the environment, AND, at the same time, *feeding bees a diet of high fructose corn syrup* (a GMO 'food product'), appears to be fatal for the bee population.

THUS, since bees are responsible for pollinating a major percentage of the food we eat, this could also become devastating for food production.

[1] http://www.fao.org/biodiversity/components/pollinators/en/
[2] http://gmoevidence.com/dr-huber-glyphosate-and-bee-colony-collapse-disorder-ccd/
[3] http://www.pnas.org/content/early/2013/04/26/1303884110.abstract?sid=4c54022c-69aa-4377-b174-d4111047a0f5
[4] http://phys.org/news/2013-04-high-fructose-corn-syrup-tied-worldwide.html

BUTTERFLIES/CATERPILLARS

A 'butterfly' (according to Oxford English Dictionary speculation) comes from Old Dutch 'botervlieg' and 'boterschijte' meaning 'butter-shit' because butterfly excrement may have thought to resemble butter. Butterflies are pollinators, who travel great distances, and date back to the Eocene period, 40-50 million years ago.

Caterpillars (possibly from Late Latin 'catta pilosa' meaning 'hairy cat') are the larvae of the Lepidoptera order, moths and butterflies. Voracious eaters, most are herbivorous and are regarded as pests by farmers; others are insectivorous and eat pests which attack plants.

Glyphosate (Roundup) is poisoning the butterfly habitat.

"Milkweed loss in agricultural fields because of herbicide use: effect on the monarch butterfly population"

That's the title of a January 2012 research article in the journal *Insect Conservation and Diversity* authored by John M. Pleasants of Iowa State University *(USA)* and Karen S. Oberhauser of the University of Minnesota *(USA)*.

Like bees and bats, Monarch butterflies are migrating pollinators that travel great distances. During their travels, and at their destination, they pollinate flowers and plants. Although they do not have the impact that bees and bats wield, they are still a major component of the pollination process.

The study dealt with the 'overwintering' seasons, when the North American Monarch butterflies go south to the warmer weather in Mexico. The study revealed that over the past decade the size of the Mexican overwintering population of monarch butterflies has decreased. Approximately 50% of the butterflies are from the Midwest in the U.S. where the larvae feed on a diet of common milkweed.

However, there has been a significant decline in the milkweed over the past decade.

"This loss is coincident with the increased use of glyphosate herbicide in conjunction with increased planting of genetically modified (GM) glyphosate-tolerant corn (maize) and soybeans (soya)."

The annual procreation of Monarch butterflies in the Midwest is positively correlated with the size of the subsequent overwintering population in Mexico. So if that population declines, it means the procreation in the Midwest has declined. The researchers reported,

"We estimate that there has been a 58% decline in milkweeds on the Midwest landscape and an 81% decline in monarch production in the Midwest from 1999 to 2010."

The authors concluded that the loss of the milkweed is due to the use of GMO corn and maize, and that this

"is a major contributor to the decline of the monarch population." [1]

The implications are obvious. Since the milkweed is the only plant on which Monarch larvae can feed, if the milkweed is destroyed then the Monarch population will also disappear.

If Monarch butterflies become extinct, along with the bees and bats, without these indispensible and irreplaceable pollinators it will become impossible to grow food.

[1] http://www.mlmp.org/results/findings/Pleasants_and_Oberhauser_2012_milkweed_loss_in_ag_fields.pdf

COWS (and other farm animals)

'Cows' (from Old English 'cu' meaning 'cow' and from a variety of other derivations in Dutch, German, Danish, Swedish, and other languages) are the most common domesticated ungulates (hoofed animals) classified as 'Bos primigenis' and the subfamily 'Bovinae.' It is believed they were first domesticated over 10,000 years ago in Mesopotamia, near southern Turkey and northern Iraq.

Bovine Growth Hormone (rBGH) damages the reproductive process in cows.

"BST [rBGH] usage increases the incidence of several disease conditions..."

That's one of the conclusions, as far back as 1999, by the 'Scientific Committee on Animal Health and Animal Welfare of the European Commission' *(Belgium)* which issued an analysis entitled, *'Report on Animal Welfare Aspects of the Use of Bovine Somatotrophin.'*

The study also concluded:

- "Pregnancy rate dropped from 82 to 73% in multiparous[1] cows and from 90 to 63% in primiparous[2] cows...

- "The frequency of multiple births, which can cause welfare problems, was substantially increased by BST..."

- "There is evidence that BST treatment can adversely affect reproduction..."

- "IGF-1 increases approximately five fold."

- "Use of BST increases:

    ** the risk of clinical and sub-clinical mastitis
    ** the number of cases of mastitis
    ** milk somatic cell counts [cell deaths] in some herds." [1]

"Use of rBST increased the clinical risk of mastitis by approximately 25%."

That's according to the *'Report of the Canadian Veterinary Medical Association Expert Panel on rBST'* published in **Canada** in 1999.

The study reported other findings:

- "There were a number of effects on reproductive performance that were associated with the use of rBST…"

- There was also inconclusive evidence of increased risk of cystic ovaries[3] and twinning,"[4]

The study concluded:

"There were four specific conditions (risk of cystic ovaries, twinning, retained placenta, and abortion/fetal loss) for which there appeared to be an effect associated with the use of the drug [rBST]." [2]

"The usually required long-term toxicology studies to ascertain human studies were not conducted. Hence, such possibilities and potential as sterility, infertility, birth defects, cancer and immunological derangements were not addressed."

That's according to the 1998 "Gaps Analysis Report" produced by the Health Protection Branch of the government of **Canada**.

"The reason for this report is to determine whether the required human safety review and evaluation for this drug were adequately addressed and, if not, to provide a critical 'gaps analysis' of same."

The ultimate conclusion:

"Both procedural and data gaps were found which fail to properly address the human safety requirements of this drug under the Food and Drugs Act and Regulations."

The Report revealed an increased risk of mastitis (inflammation of the udder) that may be associated with rBST. This has resulted in an increase in different bacteria, as well as pus and blood secretions – all

151

of which could be passed along in the milk. This could have health implications for humans, and create an antibiotic resistance in farm-borne human pathogens.

The Report says, "The BST-induced mastitis is harder to treat than naturally occurring mastitis and duration of treatment is longer due to high incidence of infection with S.aureus...[5]

"There is a one-third higher incidence of antibiotic-resistant bacteria. BST use increases the amounts of drugs in general to treat the various adverse effects it causes in cattle." [3]

[1] *'Multiparous' means giving birth to more than one offspring at a time.*
[2] *'Primiparous' means being pregnant for the first time*
[3] *Ovarian cysts can interfere with a female's ability to ovulate*
[4] *Twinning, i.e. having twins frequently, can become detrimental to health*
[5] *S.aureus is 'Staphylococcus aureus', a type of bacteria which generally cause skin infection, but can also cause pneumonia, food poisoning, toxic shock syndrome, and blood poisoning (bacteremia). It is often referred to as 'staph infection.'*

"rBGH Research at University of Vermont (UVM) Raised Concerns"

As far back as 1991 research by the University of Vermont *(USA)* was reported by *Rural Vermont (USA)* in the on-line journal *Mindfully.org,* in an article by Andrew Christiansen entitled, *Recombinant Bovine Growth Hormone: Alarming Tests, Unfounded Approval – The Story Behind the Rush to Bring rBGH to Market'*

For questionable reasons, the University of Vermont delayed releasing the results of its study in a timely manner. But *Rural Vermont* did, both in a written disclosure, as well as in testimony before the Vermont legislature. The University was then compelled to disclose its findings.

"Our 1991 report exposed many animal health problems, including an alarming number of dead and severely deformed calves. Subsequent controversy exposed additional problems, both in the UVM test herd **and in the FDA's review process.**"
[Emphasis added]

152

The report described how:

- "… the FDA illegally leaked proprietary information…"

- the FDA lied to the press, saying the cows did not have ID numbers

- in order to distort the statistics, the FDA lied about which cows were in the 'control' group

- "the FDA employed Monsanto researchers to review Monsanto research"

- the FDA ignored its own findings which indicated that by using rBGH there was a 79% greater risk of mastitis

- in an unprecedented approval technique the FDA approved the use and sale of rBGH by allowing the manufacturer to list 21 different health risks on the warning label

Like the cows and the milk, the corrupt FDA itself was contaminated from the beginning! [4]

"While the FDA was lax in its review of rBGH, Monsanto aggressively attempted to suppress reports about the health risks involved in the use of the drug."

That's part of the analysis of the GRACE Communications Foundation *(USA)* in an on-line review on *sustainabletable.org.* The analysis reveals a multitude of techniques employed by Monsanto to "suppress reports about the health risks" in rBGH.

The alleged techniques include intimating members of the press and news media, threatening politicians, initiating legal actions against farmers who are not compliant with Monsanto's policies, co-opting academicians, use of political pressure on government officials, and co-opting politicians. The details of these allegations are in the article, with the link below.

In addition to the FDA's lies, distortions, and unethical behavior, the shocking display of FDA corruption was exposed when it was revealed that the entire clinical   investigation was a fraud:

"The FDA's approval was based solely on one study administered by Monsanto in which rBGH was tested for 90 days on 30 rats... The study was never published."

[5]

[Note: Monsanto later sold this business to Eli Lilly and Company in 2008]

[1]   http://ec.europa.eu/food/fs/sc/scah/out21_en.pdf
[2]   http://www.gov.mb.ca/agriculture//livestock/nutrition/bza08s04.html
[3]   http://ucbiotech.org/biotech_info/PDFs/Chopra_rBST_Nutrilac_Gaps_A
      nalysis_Report.pdf
[4]   http://www.mindfully.org/GE/RBGH-Alarming-TestsJul95.htm
[5]   http://www.sustainabletable.org/797/rbgh

NB To see images of cows injected with rBGH view the following link:
https://www.google.com/search?q=bovine+growth+hormone+cows&rlz=1C
1CHFX_enUS460US460&espv=210&es_sm=93&source=lnms&tbm=isch&
sa=X&ei=nLdqUuX-A9W-
4APB8IDYDw&ved=0CAkQ_AUoAQ&biw=1280&bih=709

FISH

'Fish' (from Old English 'fisc' and derived from other more ancient variations in Old German, Old Norse, and Latin) are not part of any monophyletic group of organisms, but represent the evolution of many species… which are still evolving.

GMOs are creating 'Franken-fish'.

"Interspecific hybridization is a route for transgenes from genetically modified (GM) animals to invade wild populations, yet the ecological effects and potential risks that emerge from such hybridization are unknown."

The above quote was one of the conclusions of a February 2012 research study which examined the consequences of mating a genetically-modified Atlantic salmon with a brown trout. The study was entitled, *'Hybridization between genetically modified Atlantic salmon and wild brown trout reveals novel ecological interactions'* and published in the *Proceedings of the Royal Society B* in ***Canada.***

The issue is that by genetically engineering some fish, those fish can contaminate the entire fish population as well as create a new species of fish with unpredictable characteristics… and dominate and destroy the natural fish population.

"Transgenic hybrids were viable and grew more rapidly than transgenic salmon … transgenic hybrids appeared to express competitive dominance and suppressed the growth of transgenic and non-transgenic (wild-type) salmon by 82 and 54 percent, respectively."

One repercussion was obvious: the more powerful hybrid fish were out-competing the other fish for food, resulting in stunting the growth of the natural fish. [1] [2]

NB All genetic engineering requires the manipulation of DNA. When a gene is transferred between organisms that could be conventionally bred, like different kinds of plants, animals or fish, the process is known as cisgenesis. When a 'foreign gene' is taken from one species and implanted or inserted into another species, it is called transgenesis. With fish, both are done.

Genetically engineering is targeted on those fish which lend themselves to aqua-farming, including salmon, trout, carp, cod, turbot, halibut, and tilapia. The objective is to accelerate the growth process in order to create larger fish for sale in a smaller amount of time.

Another objective is to have the fish develop a resistance to pathogens, such as bacteria and viruses, in order to maximize the quantity of fish that survive the fish-farming experience. The genetic engineering can be an insertion of different DNA, or by introducing various "additives" into the feed that is put into the diet of the fish – to resist pathogens, or to alter their growth patterns, or make them look tastier, or to find other ways to maximize the profits of fish farms.

Depending upon what the genetically-modified objective is, no one knows for sure what chemicals will be injected into the fish – or how those various chemicals will synergistically interact with each other inside their new 'host.'

And, of course, we have the standard danger which exists with all GMO 'food products':

the *genetically engineering process* itself disturbs the internal dynamics of the organs into which the 'foreign' DNA are inserted or blasted – with unknown, and unpredictable, consequences for those who eat whatever the final product(s) come to be.

[1] http://rspb.royalsocietypublishing.org/content/280/1763/20131047.abstract
[2] http://rspb.royalsocietypublishing.org/content/280/1763/20131047.full#sec-13

INSECTS

'Insects' (from Latin 'insectum' and Greek 'entomon' meaning 'cut into sections') are invertebrates with three pairs of jointed legs, compound eyes, and a pair of antennae. Insects are the main pollinators on earth.

GMO toxins are creating new breeds of insects and pests.

"Monsanto got the science completely wrong on this one. Independent biosafety scientists have discovered that the inheritance of resistance in African stem borers is a dominant, not recessive, trait as erroneously assumed. Hence, the insect resistance management strategies that Monsanto developed, and accepted by our regulators, based on these erroneous assumptions, were utterly ineffective."

This was a conclusion of Mariam Mayet, Director of the African Centre for Biosafety Report *(South Africa)*, released on October 24, 2013.

The Report continues: "Independent scientists have shown that Monsanto's GM maize variety, MON810[1] – which has been growing in SA [South Africa] for 15 years – has completely failed due to the development of massive insect resistance, leading to the GM maize being withdrawn from the SA market."

"Monsanto has compensated farmers who were forced to spray their crops with pesticides to control the pests, calling into question the very rationale for GM crops."

Now that Monsanto's GMO maize has been found to increase the insect problem in South Africa, it will be forced onto continental Africa where it will increase the insect population there, and increase the use of insecticides and herbicides, further polluting the African farmlands. [1]

[1] *MON810 is Monsanto's genetically-modified maize.*

"African Caterpillars Resistant to GM Maize"

That's the title of a September 2013 report by *'Institut de recherché pour le développement (IRD)'* [Institute of Research and Development] *(France)* explaining how one of the major agricultural pests in Africa has developed a resistance to the *Bt* toxin which is inserted into the GMO corn.

> The *Buessola fusca* caterpillar has not only developed a resistance to the toxins in the GMO crops; the resistance has become a *dominant trait* which can now be passed down.

This is the first time that resistance to *Bt* maize can be inherited as a 'dominant' characteristic rather than as a 'recessive' one. Thus, the caterpillar and their offspring became resistant to the *Bt* in the GMO crops.

To address this issue, the scientists crossed the *Bt*-resistant moths of South Africa with non-*Bt*-resistant moths from Kenya. The result backfired: the offspring were also *Bt*-resistant.

This means that the toxins which are central to GMO crops to combat the pest are no longer effective. Therefore, the justification for GMO crops to even exist has been destroyed. But… Monsanto keeps selling its seeds! And, now it can sell even more pesticides!

In explaining how this non-anticipated resistance to the *Bt* toxins was developed, the article quoted the researchers,

"The moth* does not seem to have followed the expected pattern of adaptation."

> "… sooner or later, insect species may be able to develop a mechanism of resistance against pesticides."

The biological complexity of the seeds, the internal dynamics of the seeds, the organisms in the crops which evolve, the insects and bacteria in the soil and in the water – and the entire biosphere in which the seeds develop: all of these 'natural' inter-relationships seem to combat the scientifically-created GMO seeds.

158

Despite the claims of the GMO companies, the researchers say,

"...it is very likely that the Busseola fussa [caterpillar] has developed
an unconventional resistance mechanism yet to be identified."

Therefore, a dramatic and dangerous increase in both the types and
the amounts of pesticides is now occurring, to create

**"a more diverse array of toxins for the control of pest
populations..."** [2]

** Moths and butterflies are relatives in the order of Lepidoptera, both
evolving from caterpillars. The present estimate is that there are 160,000
species of moth and 15,000 types of butterflies. Caterpillars are often
regarded as pests which feed on the seeds of plants. (Because many species
eat fiber, when they 'grow up' they eat clothing.)*

**Monsanto's GMO crops are actually strengthening the
immune system of pests.**

The principal author of a 2013 University of Arizona *(USA)* study,
Visiting Professor Yves Carriere from the Center for Agricultural
Research for Development (CIRAD) in *France,* explained the
underlying assumption of Monsanto's multi-toxin GMO crop:

"Redundant killing can be achieved by plants producing two toxins
that act in different ways to kill the same pest; so if an individual pest
has resistance to one toxin, the other will kill it."

According to the theory, if pests (caterpillars in this case) are resistant
to the first toxin, then the second toxin will kill them. But apparently,
not true! In the agricultural fields, the empirical reality did not
conform to the theories of Monsanto's scientists.   Pointing to the
results of the research,

"The findings show that the crucial assumption of redundant killing
does not apply in this case and may also explain the reports indicating
some field populations of cotton bollworm rapidly evolving resistance
to both toxins."

In addition, the research team analyzed published data from eight different species of pests. They discovered that in 19 out of 21 experiments some degree of cross-resistance occurred between the two toxins, Cry1 and Cry2.

The conclusion was obvious:

> "Contradicting the concept of redundant killing, cross resistance means that selection of one toxin increases resistance to the other toxin."

Monsanto's theory was that using more than one toxin would definitely kill the agricultural pests. However, rather than killing these insects, *Monsanto's GMO poisons are actually helping the agricultural pests develop a resistance to the various toxins involved.*

CIRAD is specifically interested in various issues regarding pest resistance to *Bt* crops in Africa. The University of Arizona's own March 28, 2013 press release was entitled, *'Multi-Toxin Biotech Crops Not Silver Bullets, UA Scientists Warn.'* In it they concluded,

> "These findings show that the crucial assumption of redundant killing does not apply in this case and may also explain the reports indicating some field populations of cotton bollworm rapidly evolved resistance to both toxins."

The report includes a warning,

> "... if inheritance of resistance is dominant, as seen with the bollworm, matings between a resistant moth and a susceptible moth can produce resistant offspring, which hastens resistance."

In short, instead of killing these agricultural pests, the GMO crops may actually be "hastening" the development of resistance to toxins by these pests – around the world! [3]

160

IN SUMMARY:

After years of planting GMO crops, global research consistently reveals that GMO crops actually *help pests develop a* resistance to pesticides.

The implications are:

- more costs for the farmers for different types and amounts of pesticides

- more and stronger toxins put into the food supply

- more environmental pollution for soil, air, water, animals and people

[1] http://www.acbio.org.za/index.php/media/64-media-releases/448-monsantos-failed-sa-gm-maize-pushed-into-rest-of-africa
[2] http://en.ird.fr/the-media-centre/scientific-newssheets/438-african-caterpillars-resistant-to-gm-maize
[3] http://uanews.org/story/multi-toxin-biotech-crops-not-silver-bullets-ua-scientists-warn

DRAMATIC INCREASE
in USAGE of
HERBICIDES/PESTICIDES

Dramatic Growth in Use of Pesticides – as GMO Crops Develop Increased Resistance

---

"Herbicide-resistant crop technology has led to a 239 million kilogram (527 million pound) increase in herbicide use in the United States between 1996 and 2011... Overall, pesticide use increased by an estimated 183 million kgs (404 million pounds)..."

That's one of the discoveries of a study by Dr. Charles Benbrook, a research professor at the Center for Sustaining Agriculture and Natural Resources, at Washington State University (*USA*). The paper is entitled *'Impacts of genetically engineered crops on pesticide use in the U.S. – the first sixteen years.'*

Although the GMO industry has consistently claimed that GM crops reduce the use of pesticides (which include herbicides, insecticides, and fungicides... i.e. herbicides are, in fact, pesticides). These claims have now been proven to be false. Pesticide usage has dramatically increased!

Dr. Benbrook's research revealed that in North America farmers applied 318 million more pounds of pesticides alone, as a result of planting GM seeds over the first 13 years of commercial use. In studying the specific year of 2008, he learned that fields of GM crops required an *increase* of 26 pounds of pesticides per acre than fields which had non-GM varieties of crops.

In addition more herbicides were required to deal with weeds:

"Weed management costs per hectare increase by 50% to 100% or more in fields infested with glyphosate-resistant weeds..."

"In Illinois soybean production, the increase in herbicide costs is estimated at 64%... while in Iowa corn production, the increase is 67%."

Then, when adding the increased costs of the GMO seeds themselves, and the pesticides, and the herbicides, "The markedly higher cost/hectare of herbicide-resistant seeds must be added to the higher herbicide costs noted above to more fully reflect the added costs associated with HR [Herbicide Resistant] technology."

- For example: "… the cost of GE soybean seed in 2010 was 47% higher per bushel than non-GE seed."

- "In the case of corn, conventional seed prices rose … to $58.13 in 2010… The average cost of GE corn seed per acre in 2010 was $108.50, with some GE cultivars selling for over $120 per planted acre."

Of the three principal GM crops in the US, namely soy, maize, and cotton, GM RR [Roundup Ready] soy accounted for 92% of the total increase in herbicide use.

Dr. Benbrook also discovered dramatic increases in the use of herbicides in Argentina because of the planting of GM soy (GM soy constitutes 98% of all soy crops in Argentina).

The new HR [Herbicide Resistant] weeds have become a major problem for many farmers who plant GE [genetically engineered] crops, since the eradication of these weeks is now driving up the volume of herbicide needed each year by about 25 percent.

The study found that although initially there was a 64.2 million pound reduction in chemical insecticides use attributed to *Bt* (GMO) corn and cotton, GM herbicide-tolerant crops have now actually increased herbicide use by a total of 382.6 million pounds over 13 years.

Dr. Benbrook's analysis shows use of GMO crops has caused shifts in weed communities and the evolution of stronger weeds. This spread of resistant weeds has now forced farmers to increase herbicide application rates (especially *glyphosate*), spray more often or in greater amounts, and add different kinds of herbicides that work through alternate modes of action. [1]

Contrary to the claims of GMO companies:
- As insects develop a greater resistance, the GMO crops require ever-increasing amounts of insecticides and pesticides

- As weeds develop a greater resistance, the GMO crops require ever-increasing amounts of herbicides;
- Apart from the health aspects of increased usage of toxins, the cost of producing the food products themselves are dramatically increasing and surpassing the costs of regular farming.

"Evolution of resistance in pests can reduce the effectiveness of insecticidal proteins from *Bacillus thuringiensis* (*Bt*) produced by transgenic crops."

This was further confirmation from another study, entitled, *'Insect resistance to Bt crops: lessons from the first billion acres'* authored by Bruce E Tabashnik, PhD, Head of the Department of Entomology, University of Michigan *(USA)*; Thierry Brevault, PhD, entomologist at CIRAD (French Agriculture Research Center for International Development), *France*; and, Yves Carriere, PhD, Department of Entomology, University of Arizona *(USA)*. It was published on June 10, 2013 in the on-line journal *nature biotechnology*.

The article states, "We analyzed results of 77 studies from five continents reporting field monitoring data for resistance to *Bt* crops, empirical evaluation of factors affecting resistance or both:

"Although most pest populations remained susceptible, reduced efficacy of *Bt* crops caused by field-evolved resistance has been reported now for some populations of 5 or 13 major pest species examined, compared with resistant populations of only one pest species in 2005." [2]

Research around the globe reveals that insects and pests are developing an **increasing** resistance to GMO crops, requiring more and more usage of herbicides and pesticides.

166

'Africa bullied to grow defective Bt maize: the failure of Monsanto's MON810 maize in South Africa'

That's the title of an October 23, 2013 research report from the African Centre for Biosafety (ACB) in *South Africa.* The report shows how Monsanto's GM maize failed in South Africa – and is now being forced into other African countries.

Under "KEY FINDINGS" the report states:

"Monsanto's *Bt* Maize, MON810, has failed hopelessly in South Africa as a result of massive insect resistance after only 15 years of its introduction into commercial agriculture."

The study pointed out that, "…IRM strategies were based on the false assumption that the inheritance of resistance to MON810 was a recessive, not a dominant trait…However, recent research has shown that the inheritance of resistance is a dominant trait and that in order to stem rapid and large-scale resistance, **farmers will need to plant 50% non-*Bt* maize as a refuge where non-resistant individuals can breed."** In other words, in order to plant GMO crops without destroying the biological insect environment, the farmers will have to plant at least 50% non-GMO crops!

So what is Monsanto going to do now?

The report spells it out: "In 2008, The Bill Gates and Warren Buffet Foundations announced a pledge of US$47 million towards the development of the Water Efficient Maize for Africa (WEMA) project… Monsanto has pledged to contribute four drought resistant varieties from its research and development pipeline to the project. The project is being rolled out in five countries – South Africa, Uganda, Kenya, Tanzania, and Mozambique."

But despite the appearance of generosity, "Through a sleight of hand MON810 was incorporated into the WEMA project plans in 2011."

In addition, the report indicates that Monsanto has genetically engineered this defective trait into a local maize in Egypt called *'Ajeeb Yieldgard,'* has now patented it, and has gotten it "approved" for "commercial growing through circumvention of the Egyptian biosafety law." Monsanto will now profit from this defective crop. [3]

Now that Monsanto's GMO maize has been found to increase the insect problem in South Africa, it is moving onto continental Africa where it will increase the insect population, increase the use of insecticides and herbicides, and further pollute the African farmlands.

———————

IN SUMMARY,

* GMO crops have come to require an INCREASE in the use of pesticides, especially *glyphosate*. This means ever-increasing amounts of toxins are being absorbed by these crops that go into the food supply, whether consumed directly by humans or by the animals that we eat and whose milk we drink

* Ever-increasing amounts of toxins are being pumped into the environment, so that more soil, water, and air, are being systematically poisoned every year!

* The toxin-filled GMO crops and the toxic sprays being put on them are INCREASING the size, strength, and proliferation of weeds and insects.

* Many countries are now banning the GMO crops and pesticides and herbicides. With the help of wealthy investors and world leaders, Monsanto is expanding into new, unsophisticated markets to sell its pesticides and herbicides.

Worldwide research has now demonstrated that the longer the GMO crops are being planted, the less effective the pesticides and herbicides become. In fact, they *contribute* to the evolution of stronger insects and weeds. Therefore, more and more pesticides and herbicides are required – in higher volumes, increased usage, and greater varieties.

[1]   http://www.enveurope.com/content/pdf/2190-4715-24-24.pdf
[2]   http://www.nature.com/nbt/journal/v31/n6/full/nbt.2597.html
[3]   http://www.acbio.org.za/images/stories/dmdocuments/BT-Maize-Report-Oct2013.pdf

ENVIRONMENTAL
CONTAMINATION

AIR and WIND CONTAMINATION

Ethanol – Loaded with GMO Toxins – is a Major Air Pollutant.

"Ethanol vehicles pose a significant risk to human health, study finds."

That's the title of an April 18, 2007 article by Mark Shwartz in *STANFORD News Service*, reporting on a study done by Dr. Mark Z. Jacobson, an atmospheric scientist at Stanford University *(USA)*.

GMO corn is used in the bio-fuel, ethanol. Many drivers use E10 'gasohol' which is a blend of 10% ethanol and 90% gasoline; other drivers use E85 which is a blend of 85% ethanol and 15% gasoline (the fuel used in the Stanford study).

Using a computer model to forecast the future if E85 replaced gasoline, Dr. Jacobson discovered a disturbing fact:

"If every vehicle in the United States ran on fuel made primarily from ethanol instead of pure gasoline, the number of respiratory-related deaths and hospitalizations would likely increase…"

Although levels of the cancer-causing agents benzene and butadiene were lowered by using ethanol, the levels of formaldehyde and acetaldehyde rose!

This is due to "the chemicals that come out of a tailpipe are affected by a variety of other factors…" – with whatever is in the air, including "… sunlight, clouds, wind, and precipitation."

As a result, it was projected that

"… E85 is likely to increase the annual number of asthma-related emergency room visits… and the number of respiratory-related hospitalizations."

170

Dr. Jacobson concludes by stating,

> **"… using E85 will cause at least as much health damage as gasoline…"**

While Dr. Jacobson identifies the danger, he confirms the potency of "the chemicals that come out of the tailpipe" – which should be lessened and ameliorated by the "sunlight, clouds, wind, and precipitation," not toxically intensified by them! If there is one thing we learn from 'the cleansing power of nature' it is that the environment dilates, diminishes, and reduces the toxic elements to which it is exposed. Therefore, these toxic chemicals that came "out of a tailpipe" must have been extremely potent.

What chemicals come "out of a tailpipe" with ethanol? The chemicals in GMO corn!

Since GMO corn contains a variety of toxins, AND the GMO corn absorbs the poison *glyphosate*, the question is:

How many potent toxins are put into the atmosphere by automobiles from this GMO fuel source which contains a 'combination' of poisonous chemicals?

Obviously many! And, according to Dr. Jacobson's research, unlike other substances in nature, they are NOT reduced by "sunlight, clouds, wind, and precipitation"! [1]

———————

IN SUMMARY, the GMO crops and their companion-poison *glyphosate* are polluting the air around the world! This affects any living creature where the wind blows! It includes other crops, soil bacteria, insects, flowers, birds, bees, animals, and people.

Ethanol in automobiles is a major pollutant and is spreading the GMO toxins to homes and schools in cities.

[1] http://news.stanford.edu/pr/2007/pr-ethanol-041807.html

SOIL CONTAMINATION

Toxins in GMO Crops Kill Soil Bacteria and Destroy Top Soil.

"… decades of unsustainable industrial agricultural practices have resulted in massive loss of top soil and land degradation. Worldwide, the 1.5 billion ha of land now under cultivation are almost equal in area to the amount that has been abandoned by humans since farming began."

This was a conclusion in a September 18, 2013 on-line article of The Permaculture Research Institute of *Australia* entitled, *'Paradigm Shift Urgently Needed in Agriculture – UN Agencies Call for an End to Industrial Agriculture & Food System.'*

The article provided some hope to counteract the poisoning of the planet by the toxin-filled GMO crops.

"Rehabilitation of degraded land has the potential to double the amount of agricultural land globally."

"The successes of small agro-farms are well-known. Study after study has documented improvements in yield and income…There is evidence of improved nutritional value in organically grown food, not just from reduction or elimination of pesticide residues, but from increased content of vitamins and micronutrients." [1]

However, to continue to destroy the farmland and fields by the continuous planting of toxin-filled GMO seeds makes the future bleak. The gene for *Bt* (*Bacillus thuringiensis*) inserted/blasted into GMO seeds not only kills insects. Understandably, it also kills ladybugs, moths, lacewings, butterflies… and bees. Furthermore, *Bt* toxins become imbedded into the soil from the *Bt* plant roots, and are poisonous to earthworms, caterpillars, and other fauna in the soil.

Some of the major areas of concern include:

- Genetic contamination of the soil and the associated micro-organisms resulting from   horizontal gene transfer[1]

- Disruption of the soil ecosystem through the modified characteristics of the toxin-filled GMO crops and their roots

- Continual contamination of the soil due to the residue of toxin-filled GMO seeds that remain in the soil after cultivation and harvesting

- Unknown contamination of the soil via the billions of dead insects that died from ingesting the toxic GMO seeds, and the resultant poison that their decaying, poisoned bodies put into the soil

- The unknown and unquantifiable spread of toxic *Bt* pollen onto other plants through the wind, and the resultant contamination of the soil when these plants die and infect the soil

- The unknown impact on the soil organisms which have not yet been identified by scientists, and the life cycles and involvement of these organisms in the ecosystem

Among the many issues with 'horizontal gene transfer' is:

- How do the internal dynamics of the recipient organism 'adjust' to the new (toxic) genes it acquires?

- How will these new genetically modified organisms affect the soil bacteria, as well as the overall environment, whether soil, water, or air?

- What new effects will these organisms, and their decaying residue, have on plants?

Just as the internal dynamics of the GMO seeds cannot be predicted once a new gene is blasted into it; so too, one cannot predict the internal dynamics occurring within the trillions of bacteria involved in the soil through 'horizontal gene transfer' – all of which organisms are now being affected by the *Bt* crops!

[1] 'Horizontal gene transfer' is the transfer of genetic materials between bacteria from living, decaying, or dead micro-organisms into other organisms. During this process new genetic 'information' travels through the generations as the cells continually divide.

In addition to the *Bt* contamination of GMO crops, the increasing use of *glyphosate* (Roundup) on the GMO 'Roundup Ready' crops expands the spread of *glyphosate* in the environment. When *glyphosate* is sprayed on the weeds it poisons and kills the weeds – which for millions of years have died and become a part of the nutrition of the soil. *Glyphosate* also poisons the soil directly, killing the complex underground ecosystem of earthworms, microbes, mycorrhizal fungi, and various bacteria. In addition:

- The rain washes the *glyphosate* residue off the fields, and into the streams, rivers, and groundwater which becomes the drinking water for animals, birds, and humans

- Animals eat the *Bt* crops, and crops that were sprayed with *glyphosate* – then these animals are eaten by other animals … or people

- The *glyphosate* is blown by the wind into adjacent areas and fields, and the contamination process begins again in new areas

- Butterflies, moths, and flying insects fly into fields sprayed with *glyphosate* and imbibe it, or get it on their wings or feet, and spread it wherever they go

- The poison is continuously spread by birds, rodents, fish, and others in the food chain that eat the toxin-filled GMO seeds, and by GMO-contaminated insects –and by their predators who eat them

- When weeds die from being sprayed with *glyphosate*, they become part of nature's compost and are absorbed by the soil. The toxins contained in this compost enter the roots of the next generation of weeds and plants

[1] http://permaculturenews.org/2013/09/18/paradigm-shift-urgently-needed-in-agriculture-un-agencies-call-for-an-end-to-industrial-agriculture-food-system/

WATER CONTAMINATION

Glyphosate (Roundup) is Polluting Global Groundwater and Potable Water Supply.

"Glyphosate was present above limit of quantification levels in 41% of the samples... This is one of the few works related to the analysis of glyphosate in real groundwater samples and the presented data confirm that, although it has low mobility in soils, glyphosate is capable or reaching groundwater."

That was a conclusion in a unique study of the toxic effects of *glyphosate* on our water supply by eight (8) research scientists in **Spain**, entitled *'Determination of glyphosate in groundwater samples using an ultrasensitive immunoassay and confirmation by on-line solid-phase extraction followed by liquid chromatography coupled to tandem mass spectrometry.'*

The study was conducted by the Institute of Environmental Assessment and Water Research (IDAEA—CSIC) in Barcelona and published in 2012 in the journal *Analytical and Bioanalytical Chemistry* and by the US National Library of Medicine *(USA).*

Explaining why there is so much confusing research on the subject, the authors state, "...glyphosate is still a challenging compound from an analytical point of view because of its physicochemical properties: relatively low molecular weight, high polarity, high water solubility, low organic solvent solubility, amphoteric behavior and ease to form metal complexes."

Yet, after analysis the conclusions are clear: "glyphosate was present above limit of quantification levels in 41% of the samples with concentrations as high as 2.5 mg/L and a mean concentration of 200 ng/L." [1]

The groundwater is being poisoned by *glyphosate*.

Of course, the run-off of rain water from fields into the rivers and streams carries the residue of *glyphosate* from the herbicide-sprayed farmlands, as well as the dead, toxin-filled bodies of the insects which were poisoned by the toxin-filled GMO crops.

It is also known that, in addition to killing the essential soil bacteria, *glyphosate* inhibits the photosynthesis in freshwater cyanobacteria.[1] Naturally, the streams and rivers flow into the lakes, oceans and seas, spreading this toxic contamination even further... to the fish of the sea.

---

[1] *'Cyanobacteria' (from Greek 'kyanos' meaning 'blue' and 'bakterion' meaning 'small staff') are the tiny aquatic bacteria which create energy through photosynthesis.*

---

[1]   http://www.ncbi.nlm.nih.gov/pubmed/22101424

WEEDS (SUPER WEEDS)

Toxins in GMO Crops are Creating Pesticide-Resistant Super Weeds.

"Resistant weeds have become a major problem for many farmers reliant on GM crops, and they are now driving up the volume of herbicide needed each year by 25%."

That's one of the conclusions of a study published by Dr. Charles Benbrook, a professor at Washington State University *(USA)* reported by Brian Clark on October 2, 2012 in the on-line journal *Science Daily* .

Reviewing the research report, the article states,

"… the use of herbicides in the production of three genetically modified herbicide-tolerant crops – cotton, soybeans, and corn – has actually increased."

The natural survival instinct of plants eventually enables them to develop a resistance to virtually any form of toxin. Thus, the conclusion was environmentally inevitable:

"Herbicide-tolerant crops worked extremely well in the first few years of use, Benbrook's analysis shows, but over-reliance may have led to shifts in weed communities and the spread of resistant weeds…" [1]

Monsanto's *glyphosate,* used on GMO crops to kill the other plants, is now helping these plants to become immune to more toxins.

"IS THERE A RISK OF THE GMO GENE MOVING TO WEEDS?"

That's the question in an on-line *UW Extension* discussion by then-Associate Professor and Extension Weed Scientist, Dr. Chris Boerboom, with the University of Wisconsin College of Agriculture and Life Sciences *(USA)*. *(Dr. Boerboom moved to North Dakota State University in 2012.)*

"The answer is yes and no, depending on the crop," he answers. "The risk depends if the crop can make fertile crosses with weedy relatives." Then he adds, "For crops that can cross with weeds, the scientific probability that a GMO gene will escape to a weed is 100%. It's just a question of time. The rate that a gene might move to a weed depends primarily on the type of pollination."

Putting some numbers to the issues, he says, "For 60 crops grown in the U.S., crop-weed hybrids occur for 15 crops and 34 crops have weedy relatives, although it is not well known if they can form hybrids."

The implications are obvious:

> If the GMO genes are passed onto weeds, then Monsanto's GMO seeds could be spawning entirely new varieties of weeds which would be difficult to control, or kill.

As Dr. Boerboom observes, "Obviously, if the gene is for herbicide resistance, the weed would become resistant, a problem." [2]

———

Farmers across the United States and agriculture departments of three (3) separate universities have now revealed that GMO crops and *glyphosate* are adding to the farmers' problems, not to their solutions.

Monsanto's GMO crops and related assurances regarding *glyphosate's* effectiveness did not contemplate the power of nature.

> IN SUMMARY, while the planet is being increasingly poisoned by toxin-filled GMO crops and *glyphosate*, the Super-Weeds are increasing – in quantity, size, and strength!

[1] http://www.sciencedaily.com/releases/2012/10/121002092839.htm
[2] http://www.uwex.edu/ces/grains/gene_to_weed.html

SUMMARY OF CONTAMINATION

Various formal research studies reveal that the environment is being poisoned. There are a myriad of unquantifiable repercussions connected with the toxin-filled GMO crops and their companion *glyphosate* in the world's soil, air, and water resources.

In addition to the formal studies by scientists, there is an abundance of anecdotal evidence – all pointing to the poisoning of the planet.

The toxin-filled GMO crops and their accompanying pesticides and herbicides contaminate the entire environment: air, soil, and water. This, in turn, creates a poisoning and disruption of the entire ecosystem.

The GMO toxins affect all those who inhabit the earth: essential bacteria and other micro-organisms, worms, insects, bees, butterflies, Lepidoptera, birds, fowl, amphibians, fish, animals… and people.

The GMO toxins are systematically poisoning the planet!

PART 2
ANECDOTAL EVIDENCE
of
GMO DANGERS

REVEALED in
SCIENTIFIC ARTICLES
and
INDIVIDUAL STUDIES

BIOLOGICAL ORGANS
and
ABNORMALITIES

ALLERGY

An 'allergy' (from Greek 'allos' meaning 'other,' plus 'ergon' meaning 'action' or 'energy') is a hypersensitivity disorder of the immune system which occurs when someone's immune system reacts to something to which it is exposed, either through the air or through eating/drinking.

Since the Creation of GMO Crops, Food Allergies Have Dramatically Increased.

Scientists have long suspected that GMO crops cause food allergies. However, because of the nature of allergies, at present there is no conclusive evidence *specifically* connecting a particular allergy to a particular GMO 'food product.'

Part of the difficulty in establishing a relationship is that proteins which have the potential to cause allergies do not always result in an allergic reaction. Many proteins can only cause a reaction if they come into contact with a person who has a corresponding sensitivity.

Allergic reactions are interrelationships between individual immune systems and specific substances. To diagnose a specific allergy is difficult unless a specific allergic reaction occurs. The potential for any particular protein to be a food allergen for any particular person is impossible to predict with any accuracy.

The entire matter is also made more complicated because many people believe they suffer from food allergies when it is actually not the case. While up to 20% of Americans sometimes believe they have a food allergy, true food allergies are an immunological reaction and occur in less than 2% of the adult population and 5% – 8% of the child population. [1] [2]

"We believe this raises serious new questions about the safety of GM foods."

That was the alarm expressed by John Graham, the spokesman for York Laboratory, Europe's leading facility for testing antibody reactions to food and drinks *(United Kingdom).* York Laboratory conducts annual evaluations of food allergies, and reports on them. This latest evaluation regarding GM foods produced special concerns.

This was one of the many studies on which Organic Consumers Association *(USA)* has frequently reported. OCA has consistently informed the public of the abundance of circumstantial evidence that a wide variety of allergies are related to GMOs, and that childhood food allergies accelerated since the introduction of GMO crops in the 1990s. [3]

———

There are an abundance of unusual instances when allergies and medical maladies from GMOs are strongly suspected, but cannot be scientifically proven. There are numerous examples of people reporting headaches, nausea, rashes, and fatigue, and visiting doctor after doctor searching for a cure. For many people, these problems cease when they stop eating GMO 'food products,' particularly GMO corn.

There is an abundance of anecdotal evidence and studies that link allergies to GMO crops, even if one cannot point to a specific biological tissue. Because of the complex chemical nature of allergies, there has yet to be scientific certitude regarding any direct relationship between any particular GMOs and specific allergies.

However, in addition to warnings spawned by various research studies, the circumstantial and anecdotal evidence has become overwhelming across the globe. Part of this circumstantial evidence is that when GMO diets are discontinued, the medical maladies decline or disappear... both in humans and in animals (which we eat, or whose milk we drink).

———

"… it appears that in the genetic engineering of soy, a soy allergen was created that is 41% identical to a known peanut allergen, ara h 3. This new allergen, now found in soy, is recognized by 44% of peanut allergic individuals."

That's one of the observations by the Allergy Kids Foundation and its founder and author, Robyn O'Brien, who also point out that

"recent studies out of the University of London *(England)* conducted by Gideon Lack support this undisclosed research and highlight the role that conventional soy (and soy formula) play in the development of the peanut allergy."

The conclusion is,

"As a result of these studies, the British Dietetic Association advises parents to avoid exposing infants under the age of one to soy." [4]

[1]   http://www.plantphysiol.org/content/126/1/5.full
[2]   http://jxb.oxfordjournals.org/content/54/386/1317.full
[3]   http://www.organicconsumers.org/articles/article_5296.cfm
[4]   http://www.allergykids.com/defining-food-allergies/soys-role-in-peanut-allergy/

IMMUNE SYSTEM

In reviewing a study by the prestigious American Academy of Environmental Medicine (AAEM), Kristen Harding, M.D. published an article in *healthyALTEREGO.com* on August 28, 2011 entitled *'Is Your Immune System Confused? A Look at GMO Foods'*

Dr. Harding begins by pointing to potentially one of the most dangerous aspects of GMO crops:

Inserting the *Bt* Gene into the Crop Causes a Plant to Produce its Own Pesticide!

It has been known for some time that the 'good bacteria' in our digestive system are affected by these toxin-generating gene mutations – which proliferate once they are inside of our intestines.

Among other things, "This could have huge implications in antibiotic resistance down the road." The GMO genes may be making the human bodies resistant to certain antibiotics!

Dr. Harding reiterates that there are an abundance of unknown and unpredictable side effects, including some which confuse the entire immune system. For example, some GM plants create proteins that look like known allergens[1], including:

- GMO soybeans which have a protein sequence that appears to be a shrimp allergen;
- GM canola contains one that appears to be a dust mite allergen;
- *Bt* corn has one that matches egg yolk allergen.

Dr. Harding observed that soy allergy in Britain increased 50% after genetically modified soy was introduced; and, cooked GM soy "was found to contain seven times the amount of a known soy allergen."

Skin rashes and respiratory reactions occurred when the cotton crop was sprayed with a *Bt* pesticide. Similar reactions occurred in India in response to the *Bt* cotton crops which were genetically engineered to contain the *Bt* toxin.

"GMO foods can wreak havoc in several ways" (and she points out several):

- GMO crops can form new antigens, namely molecules in the body which stimulate a reaction
- GMO crops can transfer these 'antibiotic-resistant genes' directly into our intestines, and 'gut'
- GMO crops can create protein changes in the plant structure
- GMO crops can actually 'turn on' or ' turn off' genes in the organism
- GMO crops retain the residues of the herbicides which are sprayed on them, and which people then eat

Finally, she warns, because these new proteins are designed to look like other proteins that could harm our bodies, "our immune system may mistake them and attack. This can lead to food allergies and autoimmune diseases." [1]

[1] An 'allergen' is a substance that can cause an allergy.

[1] http://www.healthyalterego.com/index.php/2011/08/is-your-immune-system-confused-a-look-at-gmo-foods/

ALZHEIMER'S DISEASE

GMOs and Alzheimer's Disease … yet another reason why we should avoid GMOs!

That's the title of an October 18, 2013 on-line article in *Grown To Heal – Nutrition.com.* The article discusses another of the problems created by the toxin *glyphosate,* as it steadily accumulates in our bodies over the years when we eat GMO 'food products.' This pertains to the brain and how *glyphosate* can lead to the severe form of dementia known as Alzheimer's Disease.

Glyphosate was originally patented as a chelator in 1964 by Stauffer Chemical Company. In 1974 it was patented by Monsanto and introduced as a herbicide. The purpose was to kill the weeds which affected crops. Of course, it also killed the crops themselves. So Monsanto invented Roundup Ready crops – which could absorb these toxins and still grow. Most GMO crops contain *glyphosate.* However, 'growing' does not mean the crops become internally nutritious… and healthy to eat!

The article explains how, as a chelator, *glyphosate* binds to minerals and prevents the host organism from using these nutrients. This process helps the toxin kill weeds (and pests). But once it is inside of the GMO crops, understandably, it prevents the nutrition process there too. Thus, it creates nutrient deficient food.

"'Micronutrients such as iron, manganese, and zinc can be reduced by as much as 80-90 percent in GE plants. – Mercola'

The result:

"Research shows that without adequate amounts of zinc, the proteins in our brains clump together – this is a hallmark of Alzheimer's." [1]

Dr. Don Huber, professor of plant pathology at Purdue University and recognized as one of the world's experts in GMOs, explains that, "*Glyphosate* contamination is a major part of the overall hazards of

GE foods, as the chemical *cannot* be washed off – it is incorporated into every cell of the plant."

Glyphosate, the same chelator which affects weeds, plants, and pests, remains in our body! It immobilizes nutrients, preventing them from being available for our body's basic health and development. In an October 6, 2013 interview Dr. Huber said,

> *"You may have the mineral [in the plant], but if it's chelated with glyphosate, it's not going to be physiologically for you to use, so you're just eating a piece of gravel."* [2]

"Glyphosate May Be Worse Than DDT, Which Has Now Been Linked to Alzheimer's Disease, Decades After Exposure"

That's the title of a February 13, 2014 article in *Mercola.com* which discusses how absorbing *glyphosate*, the principal active chemical in Roundup, may have a more severe impact on the human brain than DDT, and lead to Alzheimer's Disease.

The sixth leading cause of death in the U.S., and with an estimated 5.4 million people currently affected, Alzheimer's Disease is predicted to afflict more than 25% of American adults in the next 20 years.

A number of studies have now linked DDT to Alzheimer's Disease. "According to Dr. Don Huber, an expert in an area of science that relates to the toxicity of genetically engineered (GE) foods, glyphosate – the active ingredient in Monsanto's Roundup herbicide – is actually *FAR worse* that DDT." [Emphasis in original]

Of course, if someone has been eating these *glyphosate*-filled GMO crops for many years, then, like DDT, the residual effect will exhibit itself in later years of life.

Dr. Huber summarized his overall view:

> "What we have in glyphosate is the most abused chemical we have ever had in the history of man... When future historians write about our time...when it comes to glyphosate, they're going to write about our willingness to sacrifice our children and jeopardize our existence,

while threatening and jeopardizing the very basis of our existence, the sustainability of our agriculture…" [3]

[1] http://www.growntohealnutrition.com/#!GMOs-and-Alzheimers-Diseaseyet-another-reason-why-we-should-avoid-GMOs/c1snt/1E3D7B2E-B5D1-4903-989E-D79E2656AF99
[2] http://articles.mercola.com/sites/articles/archive/2013/10/06/dr-huber-gmo-foods.aspx
[3] http://articles.mercola.com/sites/articles/archive/2014/02/13/glyphosate-ddt-alzheimers.aspx

ANENCEPHALY

"Glyphosate, Brain Damaged Babies and Yakima Valley – A River Runs Through It"

That's the title of a July 28, 2013 article in *Farm Wars* by Barbara H. Peterson, discussing "A high rate of birth defects has confounded Washington [state] health officials, who have been unable to identify a cause."

The disturbing statistics reveal that while the U.S. has one or two case of anencephaly[1] for every 10,000 annual births, in three Washington counties (Yakima, Benton, and Franklin) from January 2010 to January 2013 the number was 8 times as high!

Anencephaly is a condition that prevents the normal development of the brain and the bones of the skull of a newborn baby. The condition occurs when the neural tube, a layer of cells which gradually develop into the brain and spinal cord, fails to close during the first few weeks of embryonic development. Nearly all babies with anencephaly are either stillborn, or die within hours or days of the birth.

The 1,000 square miles of agricultural land in the Yakima River valley includes orchards for many of the famous Washington apples and cherries, as well as pastures, grapes, hops, and the standard field crops. The state has a Noxious Weed Control Board, but the state directed that these weeds on land and in the water be eradicated with *glyphosate*. As Peterson says, "… one would think that the level of Glyphosate in the Yakima waterways would be monitored since this has been several years in the making. Think again."

Despite the continuous use of *glyphosate*, the only study which Peterson could find pertained to the year 2000 when 146 pesticides were applied. Although most (51%) of the pesticides were analyzed for the study, "Only glyphosate (Roundup Rodeo) was applied in large amounts, but not analyzed in this study."

"Glyphosate has been linked to the same birth defect that the Washington State Department of Health reported to have found a high incidence of –   anencephaly[1]."

192

(Rull et al. provided evidence of an association between maternal exposure to glyphosate herbicides and anencephaly, a neural tube defect, as well as with neural tube defects NTDs in general [71.72] – consistent with retinoic acid-linked teratogenicity[2].) " [1]

[1] *'Anencephaly' (from Greek 'anenkephalos': 'an' meaning 'no'; 'enkephalos' meaning 'brain') is the absence of a major part of the brain, skull, and scalp that occurs during embryonic development.*
[2] *'Teratogenicity' is the capability of producing fetal malformation, from the Greek word 'teratos' meaning 'monster.'*

Largely because of the delaying tactics caused by the chemical industry, and the complexity of brain research, there is a lack of published studies which connect *glyphosate* directly to specific brain issues. Yet, similar to allergies, the research is now beginning. Apart from scientific studies, an abundance of anecdotal evidence is being systematically gathered all around the world.

[1]   http://farmwars.info/?p=11137&utm_source=feedburner&utm_medium=
email&utm_campaign=Feed%3A+FarmWars+%28Farm+Wars%29

AUTISM

'Autism' stems from the ancient Greek word 'autos' which means 'self', since the autistic person has an abnormal introversion and egocentricity, characterized by the acceptance of fantasy rather than reality.

Autism is a group of brain development disorders which are collectively referred to as 'autism spectrum disorder' (ASD). It is called a 'spectrum' since it includes a variety of symptoms and disabilities or impairments, generally classified as 'pervasive developmental disorders' (PDDs) or the ASD. They include: autistic disorder, the standard form of autism; Asperger's disorder, generally referred to as 'Asperger Syndrome'; pervasive development disorder not otherwise specified (PDD-NOS); Rett's disorder, generally called 'Rett syndrome'; and, childhood disintegrative disorder (CDD). [National Institute of Mental Health, of the U.S. National Institutes of Health, citing the 'Diagnostic and Statistical Manual of Mental Disorders, Fourth Edition – Text Revision (DSM-IV-TR)'] http://www.nimh.nih.gov/health/topics/autism-spectrum-disorders-pervasive-developmental-disorders/index.shtml

In the above citation, the National Institute of Mental Health states, "Scientists don't know the exact causes of autism spectrum disorder (ASD), but research suggests that both genes and environment play a role."

Non-GMO Diet Recommended to Avoid Autism

"The Lyme Induced Autism Foundation Prescribes 100% Non-GMO Diet [and] Joins Moratorium on Genetically Modified Foods".

That is the official announcement made in July 2009 by the Lyme Induced Autism Foundation (LIA Foundation), *(USA)* because of the considerable amount of anecdotal and circumstantial evidence pointing to a connection.

The LIA Foundation pointed out that children with autism often have allergies to corn, soy, and dairy products by the time they are tested and diagnosed. Now, the vast majority of corn and soy products are genetically modified. So is much of the milk – from cows injected with GMO bovine growth hormones, i.e. rBGH.

It is now well-known that GMO 'food products' have affected various organs of the body, including the digestive system, and may have contributed to certain allergies.

The LIA Foundation formally stated,

"There is an urgent need for independent research to evaluate the role that GM foods play in contributing to the prevalence or severity of autism, Lyme disease, and related conditions." [1]

"Do GMO Foods Cause Autism? Read About the GMO Crops Autism Connection"

That's the title of a September 25, 2012 article by Caryn Talty in the on-line journal *'healthy-family.org'* which reported what some scientists observe:

lab animals fed a GMO diet experience some of the same symptoms as autistic children, such as anti-social behavior, listlessness, and lack of focus.

The scientists also notice that, like animals fed a GMO diet, most children diagnosed with autism have digestive disorders, such as inflammation, intestinal permeability, and imbalances in the intestinal flora (bacteria).

In discussing GMO crops, Dr. Michelle Perro, a California *(USA)* pediatrician with 30 years of experience, said,

"You can extrapolate that the same thing may be occurring in babies clinically. They are not digesting their food. They are malabsorbing… and I'm seeing that commonly now."

Dr. Perro reported that:

"Digestive issues are skyrocketing among her patients… More parents are finding that they have a baby allergic to all formulas on the market and they are starting to question GMO corn and soy as culprits."

The article notes (and graphs) what many observers have noticed:

Autism has dramatically increased in the United States – but has not dramatically risen in Europe where GMO crops are largely banned, or in other parts of the world.

These observers, from the science community as well as sociologists, point to the fact that autism began its skyrocketing rise in the United States in the 1990s, *when GMOs came into existence.* [2]

"As of March 2013, the CDC estimates that one in every 50 school children are diagnosed with autism spectrum disorder (ASD)…"

That's one of the statistics from the Center for Disease Control *(USA)* cited in the *Harvard College Global Health Review*). This number must be compared with lower ASD for the rest of the world, for example in China where the rate is 1.1 in every 1,000 children. [3]

(In an apparent attempt at academic sophistication rather than empirical reality, the Harvard article tried to discount the abundance of global empirical statistics. They wonder if this has a lot to do with the lack of psychological diagnosing throughout the globe, compared to the abundance of psychiatrists in the US. Of course, the issue is that the autism rates began climbing when GMOs came into existence. Perhaps the authors of this article at Harvard did not notice that psychologists had already been around for decades.)

"It appears there is a direct correlation between GMOs and autism."

That is according Dr. Arden Andersen, a medical doctor and agronomist in the *USA*, one of the many scientists who are seeking to find evidence directly linking GMOs and autism. This comment was quoted in an article by Jeffrey Smith in the on-line blog *Institute for Responsible Technology* of which he is the Executive Director.

This was one of the many points raised by Jeffrey Smith, a long-time critic of GMO food products, who has warned about possible connections as well. He has written extensively on the subject of GMOs, including specifically on the subject of GMOs and autism.

The article also cites a comment by an autism specialist discussing GMOs and animal studies,

"The symptoms you describe are exactly what we are finding in our autistic children."

The relevant point is that:

"The animals in those studies were fed the same GM soy and corn eaten by children and adults in the US." [4]

The insect-killing *Bacillus thuringiensis* (*Bt*) gene has been inserted/blasted into these crops; and, these crops contain a gene which helps the crop resist herbicides, enabling them to sustain a heavy dose of toxic sprays. Then, the crops *absorb* the toxic pesticides and herbicides. Thus, by the time the 'food products' from these crops are eaten, they *contain* a variety of poisons from several different sources!

There is an abundance of evidence suggesting a connection between GMOs and autism, particularly since diet is now known to have such a major biological impact on the brain, the psyche, and the emotions.

"Products of the human gut microflora in relation to autism and its symptoms appear to have been largely ignored in the past."

That was the conclusion of an article entitled, *'Autism and the Human Gut Flora'* by Dr. Max Bingham of the Food Microbial Sciences Unit of the University of Reading in Berkshire, ***United Kingdom,*** explaining the relationship between the mental process and the digestive system.

He concludes his study by saying,

"Products of the human gut microflora in relation to autism and its symptoms appear to have been largely ignored in the past... While it is clear that abnormal metabolites from the human gut flora may contribute to autistic symptoms, it is certain that many other systems and pathways are involved. It is possible that many are functioning simultaneously but at varying levels between individuals... This may explain the similarity of autism and other chronic behavioural disorders such as Asperger Syndrome, PDD, ADHD, ADD, and Rett syndrome." [5]

By introducing the variety of toxins contained in GMO crops into the human gut microflora, we are disturbing the entire process of metabolism.

"The little brain in our innards, in connection with the big one in our skulls, partly determines our mental state and plays key roles in certain diseases throughout the body."

That's the message in a February 12, 2010 article in *Scientific American* by Adam Hadhazy entitled *'Think Twice: How the Gut's "Second Brain" Influences Mood and Well Being.'* The article discusses a book written by Dr. Michael Gershon, chairman of the Department of Anatomy and Cell Biology at Columbia University Medical Center *(USA)*, called *The Second Brain.*

It is now known that over 90% of the body's serotonin[1] is produced in the digestive process, over 30m nuero-transmitters (brain chemicals) are involved with digestion and the gut bacteria, and that a key neuro-transmitter, acetylcholine, is intimately involved with human digestion. "The [intestinal] system is way too complicated to have evolved only to make things move out out of your colon," says Dr. Emeran Mayer, professor of physiology, psychiatry and biobehavioral sciences at the David Geffen School of Medicine at the University of California, Los Angeles, (UCLA), **(USA).**

Therefore, poor digestion leads to physical, emotional, and psychological disorders. What we eat has a major affect on our emotional and mental health.

Dr. Gershon explains that

"… the same genes involved in synapse formation between neurons in the brain are involved in the alimentary synapse formation…. If these genes are affected in autism, it could explain why so many kids with autism have GI[2] motor abnormalities." [6]

NOTE: Consuming a diet which has been shown to be partially indigestible will create problems affecting the brain as well as the body. Thus, when the federally-sponsored US school lunch program is comprised largely of GMO 'food products,' the rash of mental and emotional maladies can become epidemic.

[1] *'Serotonin' is a hormone found in the digestive tract, the central nervous system, blood platelets, and the pineal gland—deep in the center of the brain. ('Hormones' are chemicals which the body produces that control and regulate certain activities in the cells and organs. Hormones are essential for every activity in life, including reproduction, growth, metabolism, digestion, and mood control.)*
[2] *'GI' is the abbreviation for the 'gastrointestinal tract,' sometimes called 'the digestive tract' or 'the alimentary canal,' a 30 foot tube which extends throughout the body from the mouth to the anus.*

"Nearly every substance that helps run and control the brain has turned up in the gut. Major neuro-transmitters like serotonin, dopamine, glutamate, norepinephrine and nitric oxide are there."

That was the thesis of a detailed article by Dr. Michael Gershon entitled, *'AUSTISM SPECTRUM DISORDERS (ASDs) and GUT FLORA,'* and published by the Wellness Center of Shillington (Pennsylvania, **USA**).

He went on to explain that small brain proteins are in the gut, and so are major cells of the immune system. He then disclosed a shocking discovery:

"… the gut is a rich source of benzodiazepines – the family of psychoactive chemicals that includes such ever popular drugs as Valium and Xanax." [7]

———————

It is now being confirmed, what the ancients knew centuries ago: What we eat affects every part of our body, including our minds and emotions. If we eat properly, we can avoid many diseases and medications. It has now been scientifically established that the proper functioning of our digestive system is essential for our mental and emotional stability.

When GMO foods interfere with our digestive system, they not only affect our physical health, but our mental and emotional health.

NB   Although many scientists point to a connection between GMOs and autism, others wonder if there is some relationship between autism and the aspartame which has been put in food and liquids for several decades. (NB Aspartame was originally created by G. D. Searle, part of Monsanto; the brand name was originally NutraSweet.) As Dr. Gershon suggests, there are a number of possible items in the diet that can contribute together to these maladies.

[1]   http://www.lymeinducedautism.com/gmopositionpaper.html
[2]   http://healthy-family.org/do-gmo-foods-cause-autism/
[3]   http://www.hcs.harvard.edu/hghr/online/autism-on-the-rise-a-global-perspective/
[4]   http://www.responsibletechnology.org/autism
[5]   http://www.ei-resource.org/articles/autism-articles/autism-and-the-human-gut-flora/
[6]   http://www.scientificamerican.com/article.cfm?id=gut-second-brain
[7]   http://wellnesscenterofshillington.com/?p=78

BIRTH DEFECTS/FEMALE INFERTILITY

"Most Offspring Died When Mother Rats Ate Genetically Engineered Soy."

That's the title of an article by Jeffrey Smith pertaining to a much-publicized study in **Russia** by Irina Ermakova, a scientist at the Institute of Higher Nervous Activity and Neurophysiology of the Russian Academy of Sciences who presented her research findings in October 2005.

Ermakova's study consisted in providing Monsanto's Roundup-Ready GMO soy flour to the diet of 45 female rats, while 44 other rats were fed non-GMO soy or no soy of any kind. The diet period of the research began two weeks before the rats conceived, continuing through pregnancy and nursing.

Several startling developments occurred. When the rat pups were born, those from mothers fed with GMO diets were smaller than the others; after two weeks 36% of them weighed less than 20 grams, while fewer than 6% of the other groups had such a low weight.

Then, within three weeks, 25 of the GMO-soy group died (55.6%), while only 3 of the non-soy 44 rats died (9%). [1]

"Warning: This Common Food Causes Devastating Offspring Effects in New Research Study."

That's the heading of a May 2010 article on *Mercola.com*, in which Dr. Joseph Mercola, *(USA)* the internationally recognized health physician, provided additional analysis to this same Russian study in conversations with Jeffrey Smith five years later.

Smith, who had had conversations with Dr. Ermakova, told Dr. Mercola that the Russian research had another strange development: when the soy was fed to male rats, the color of their testicles changed from pink to blue. In addition, the structure of the cells in the testicles was different, even having "a completely different blood flow."

Dr. Mercola confirmed that similar studies had similar results, "mice fed GM corn had increasingly fewer and smaller babies the longer they stayed on the GM diet... There are also other reports about pigs, cows and other livestock having reproductive problems when fed genetically modified feed."

Dr.Mercola summarized another study: a two-year study of a GM diet fed to hamsters. The hamsters on the GM soy diet had "a fivefold higher infant mortality rate", and

"nearly all of the third generation hamsters lost the ability to have babies altogether... nearly the entire third generation of GM soy eaters were sterile!" [2]

N.B. Dr. Ermakova was not allowed to complete her research. Under some form of pressure her boss cancelled further research on GM food and animals, her documents were burned, and her samples disappeared. Then there were attempts to denigrate the quality of her research and to destroy her reputation. (A similar situation occurred with the renowned chemist and nutritionist, Dr. Arpad Pusztai, in Scotland when he disproved Monsanto's claims about its GMO potatoes.[See POTATOES.])

[1] http://responsibletechnology.org/gmo-dangers/health-risks/articles-about-risks-by-jeffrey-smith/Most-Offspring-Died-When-Mother-Rats-Ate-Genetically-Engineered-Soy-October-2005

[2] http://articles.mercola.com/sites/articles/archive/2010/05/22/jeffrey-smith-interview-april-24.aspx

---

EMBRYO/FETUS

Because of the critical importance of the Canadian Sherbrooke Hospital Center study referred to in EMBRYO/FETUS above, it was reviewed in the **United Kingdom** by Sean Poulter in the UK publication *Mail Online* in May 2011 which reported on the implications of this research for mothers and their offspring. The need for further study of GMO crops and their implications on human health was becoming increasingly obvious.

Also obvious were the attempts by the GMO industry to attack the credibility of the scientists. The review noted that the international public relations efforts of the chemical companies were already in full swing in an attempt to discredit the results of this research. The **Agriculture Biotechnology Council, which speaks for the GM** industry, questioned the reliability and value of this research that reveals the serious health issues of the GMO products.

However, the *Mail Online* points out that,

"Most of the global research which has been used to demonstrate the safety of GM crops has been funded by the industry itself."* [1]

*Many of the so-called 'studies' by the GMO industry have been discredited, while other 'internal studies' of the chemical companies are hidden from the public. On the other hand, since independent research on the GMOs began, Monsanto and the chemical industry have spent millions of dollars attempting to suppress and to discredit independent research. The GMO industry also spends millions of dollars each year, in legal actions and lobbying campaigns, to prevent labeling the contents of their 'food products' so that the public will not learn what chemicals are inside of them.

"The toxins designed into genetically modified crops are finding their way into the bloodstreams of <u>all</u> pregnant women and their fetuses. This shocking result belies the genetic modification industry's claims that such toxins are destroyed by the digestive tracts of people who eat the animals fed these GMO crops."

This is how Heidi Stevenson reported on this same study in an article published in *GAIA Health.* The September 17, 2012 article is entitled, *'GMO Toxins Are in Nearly All Pregnant Women and Fetuses.'*

Stevenson pointed to the unexpected conclusion that, "Interestingly, both *glyphosate* and *glyphosinate* were found in large percentages of non-pregnant women, but neither was found in pregnant women or their fetuses." She alluded to the possibility that some form of metabolic change in pregnant women could account for this, but laments, "One might have hoped that would be adequate to prevent the toxic effects of GMO feed crops. Unfortunately, it appears that the opposite occurs…"

For some reason, the toxins in GMO 'food products' themselves remain in the pregnant women, and in their fetal cords. The laboratory results show how strongly the *Bt* toxins in the GMOs show up in the mothers and the fetal cords:

- 100% of the mothers and fetal cords retain the 3-MPPA toxin;
- 93% of the mothers retain the Cry1Ab toxin;
- 80% of the fetal cords retain the Cry1Ab toxin. [2]

[1] http://www.dailymail.co.uk/health/article-1388888/GM-food-toxins-blood-93-unborn-babies.html
[2] http://gaia-health.com/gaia-blog/2012-09-17/gmo-toxins-are-in-nearly-all-pregnant-women-fetuses/

UTERUS

"In simpler terms, according to senior UK pathologist Stanley Ewen, something in the GM soy diet was 'wrecking the ovary and endometrium of the rats'."

That's how Jeffrey Smith quoted Dr. Ewen in an article he authored in September 2010 for the *Huff Post Green* which was entitled, *'Genetically Modified Soy Diets Lead to Ovary and Uterus Changes in Rats.'*

Dr. Ewen is the eminent pathologist in the ***United Kingdom*** who was involved in the exposure of the GMO potato problem in Scotland with Dr. Arpad Pusztai. Jeffrey Smith explained that the female rats which were "fed GMO soy appeared to have their ovulation cycle in full gear… In addition, the lining of the uterus (endometriim) had more cells than normal and the glands were dilated."

Dr. Ewen explained that the proliferative growth of the endometrium cells indicates alterations in essential reproductive hormones. He speculated on the implications for women who eat GM soy, including changes in important   reproductive hormones.

He speculated if this could generate excessive production of estrogen and interfere with the *estrus* (fertility) cycle, or perhaps even cause damage to the pituitary gland, which releases many hormones that affect growth, sexual development, metabolism, and the system of reproduction. [1]

––––––––––––

".... another hormonal shift caused by GMO soy increases the risk of retrograde menstruation – where instead of leaving the body through the normal route, menstrual blood travels backward through the fallopian tubes, leading to endometriosis.[1]"

That's according to Michael Danielson in an article entitled, '*Hazards of GM Food: Female Sex Organs Affected by GMO Soybeans,*' which was published in *Eugenics, Food* in September 2010 *(USA)*.

The article also mentions how Dr. Ewen refers to *glyphosate* as "an endocrine buster" and says that it "interferes with aromatase, which in turn produces estrogen." [2]

The article points out that there is an ever-growing abundance of evidence that *glyphosate* destroys endocrine and reproductive cycles in creatures that consume it. Of the many potential consequences is endometriosis, which can lead to infertility.

––––––––––––

It has now been demonstrated for years that *glyphosate* is toxic to the placenta, and that placenta cells can die even when exposed to Roundup. These GMO crops are *designed* to absorb these toxins. Then they pass these toxins, and others, on to those who eat them – both animals and human consumers.

1 'Endometriosis' is a gynecological disorder which occurs when cells lining the uterus (endometrium) begin to grow in other areas of the body outside of the uterine cavity. This can lead to various other disorders, such as pain, irregular bleeding, or infertility.

[1]   http://www.huffingtonpost.com/jeffrey-smith/genetically-modified-soy_b_735528.html
[2]   http://www.noonehastodietomorrow.com/eugenics/food/2539-2539

CANCER

"GMO CORN LINKED TO CANCER TUMORS"

That's the title of an article by Mike Adams of *Natural News* in *'FOOD MATTERS – You are What you Eat'* discussing the study referred to above.

This article addresses the long-term consequences of eating GMO foods which pertain directly to the issue of cancer. It was also reported that the rats which drank only trace amounts of Roundup – *even amounts legally allowed in the water supply* – developed a 200% to 300% increase in large tumors. [1]

In a related article on September 19, 2012 in *Natural News.com,* Mike Adams referred to the study as "the most thorough research ever published into the health effects of GM food crops and the herbicide Roundup on rats," and added his own evaluation,

> "News of the horrifying findings is spreading like wildfire across the internet, with even the mainstream media seemingly in shock over the photos of rats with multiple grotesque tumors … tumors so large the rats even had difficulty breathing in some cases. **GMOs may be the new thalidomide."** [2]
> *[Emphasis in original.]*

Strangely, this was the first study of its kind to analyze the long-term effects of eating GMOs, since the US government officially allowed Monsanto to promote its 'food products' – without any studies of the effects of these GMO seeds and toxic herbicides on the population!

———————

"GM food can cause cancer"

That's the heading in a summary of GMO food toxins in *Golden Harvest Organics (USA)* which provides a variety of information on GMO studies in Europe and the United Kingdom.

One is an article in the *Sunday Herald* newspaper by the Environment Editor, Rob Edwards, with the headline *'EATING genetically modified (GM) food could give you cancer.'* The article summarizes,

"Dr. Stanley Ewen, a consultant histopathologist at Aberdeen Royal Infirmary, says that a cauliflower (mosaic) virus used in GM foods could increase the risk of stomach and colon cancers." [3]

Research in Europe, the United Kingdom, and many other countries outside of the United States continues to disclose the health risks of GMO crops, and of *glyphosate*. In the United States, much of the research is done by those on the payroll of Monsanto and the other chemical companies … with the expected "results" occasionally reported.

[1] http://foodmatters.tv/articles-1/gm-corn-linked-to-cancer-tumors
[2] http://www.naturalnews.com/037249_gmo_study_cancer_tumors_organ_damage.html
[3] http://www.ghorganics.com/GM%20food%20can%20cause%20cancer.htm

---

COLON

The colon (from Greek 'kolon' meaning 'large intestine') is also called the large intestine. It is the last part of the digestive system. It extracts salt, water, and some fat soluble vitamins from solid wastes before they are eliminated from the body. Billions of bacteria coat the colon and its contents, in order to achieve a healthy balance inside of the body.

"Eating GM Food Could Give You Cancer Says Scientist"

That's how it was explained by Rob Edwards, Environmental Editor of *The Sunday Herald* in September 2012 when he reported on the testimony of Dr. Stanley Ewen, a consultant histopathologist at the Aberdeen Royal Infirmary in Aberdeen, *Scotland*.

Dr. Ewen told the Scottish Parliament's Health and Community Care Committee that he has "great concern" about a cauliflower mosaic virus which is used as a "promoter" in genetically modified foods. He explained that this virus acts like a tiny engine to drive implanted GMO genes to express themselves. This would mean that the 'foreign' pesticide *GMO bacteria would proliferate inside of the human gut* along side of the healthy human bacteria.

When he presented his analysis to the Parliament's Health Committee, Dr. Ewen informed the Committee that this mosaic virus

> "is infectious, and could act as a 'growth factor' in the stomach or colon, encouraging the growth of polyps. The faster and bigger polyps grow, the more likely they are to be malignant."

With 29 years of experience as a histopathologist, Dr. Ewen even warned the people living near the GMO crop trials in Aberdeenshire, Ross-Shire, and Fife in Scotland that their food and water will be contaminated by these GMO experiments. [1][2]

"Literally, some GMO foods might be altering our healthy bacteria so they'll now produce concentrated pesticides in our guts for the rest of our lives."

That's how Kim Evans expressed it in a June 22, 2010 article in *Natural News.com* when reviewing an analysis by pro-biotic expert Dr. S.K. Dash, president and Director of Research at UAS Laboratories, in Eden Prairie, MN *(USA)*.

Confirming similar conclusions of Dr. Ewen in **Scotland**, this additional warning about the malignant GMO affects on the colon was enunciated by Dr. Dash when he explained how the healthy bacteria in our intestines are the first line of our immune defense.

The colon is the last part of the digestive system, and extracts salt and water from the digested solid wastes before they are eliminated from the body. The colon is the site where the gut flora, large bacteria ferment the unabsorbed materials that have been passed along from the previous digestive process. It is where the gut flora breaks down the remaining solid materials, and contributes to the immune system, and regulates the growth of harmful, pathogenic bacteria.

Every disease imaginable, including cancer, is connected to these healthy micro bacteria, whose job is to protect us from a wide variety of maladies. The human body contains trillions of these tiny bacteria, which can double in number every 20 minutes.

According to Dr. Dash, even one serving of GMO foods has been found to actually alter the genetic structure of our healthy bacteria. This causes them to continually *create* abnormal proteins inside of us, instead of healthy ones needed to deal with the waste products and other materials in the colon.

> So, instead of being our healthy *protectors*, by eating GMO 'food products' our colons are actually being turned into *producers* of toxins! [3]

[1]   http://www.rense.com/general32/Eating.htm
[2]   http://www.ghorganics.com/GM%20food%20can%20cause%20cancer.htm
[3]   http://www.naturalnews.com/029041_GMOs_toxicity.html

———————

DIGESTIVE SYSTEM

"GE [genetically engineered] organisms become part of the bacteria in our digestive tracts and reproduce continuously inside us... "

That is one of the conclusions in an article published in the May 31, 2011 issue of the *Alliance for Natural Health* entitled, *'Genetically Engineered Food Alters Our Digestive Systems!'*

The article continues,

> "The idea of having genetically engineered genes permanently living inside our guts has staggering implications." [1]

One of the "staggering implications" to which the article refers is that if/when the antibiotic GMO genes were to transfer into our bodies (and immune system), they could create antibiotic-resistant diseases. And if these GMO genes continue to reproduce by themselves, we may not be able to control the consequences... including developing medications to fight newly-created diseases.

[1] http://www.anh-usa.org/genetically-engineered-food-alters-our-digestive-systems/

INTESTINES

In October 2011 the Commonwealth Scientific & Industrial Research Organization of *Australia* (CSIRO)

"...tacitly admits that Agribusiness causes most bowel cancer."

That's one of the admissions by Australian authorities referred to in an October 20, 2011 on-line article in *GAIA HEALTH*.

"Dr. David Topping of CSIRO says that 80% of colon cancers are preventable, and that the cause is removal of most soluble fibers from grains during mass processing to produce the food stuffs that so often pass as foods today."

The producers of the GMO "food stuffs" who removed the soluble fibers have learned that these fibers feed the 'good bacteria' in our digestive system. These 'good bacteria' metabolize the fibers, thereby producing "compounds which promote the health of the bowel, the liver, and indirectly the whole body." *By removing various components in the food seeds, unknown and unpredictable consequences occur.* [1]

When GMO genes are inserted/blasted into food seeds, other ingredients in those seeds are displaced or removed; the same with soluble fibers. The result is that the digestive system cannot process these chemical 'foods.'

The intestinal lining of pigs deteriorated and the critical microbial balance was drastically changed when the pigs were provided a GMO diet.

That was the conclusion of the plant pathologist Professor Don Huber of Purdue University, Indiana *(USA)*, who conducted research on the effects of GMOs on various parts of the anatomy.

Among those who reviewed this matter was Angela Hoover in the April 1, 2013 issue of *Health & Wellness.*

Dr. Huber reported that evidence of GMOs affecting intestines and other internal organs has been accumulating since 1999, when the world's leading general medical journal, the *Lancet,* published the first evidence of GMOs causing GI tract distress.

He revealed that the cells of the stomach lining and intestines of rats were significantly altered after eating a GM diet for only 10 days.

Anecdotal evidence was also rampant, since butchers disclosed that GMO-fed livestock have thin small intestines which can rupture easily. These organs are stronger in animals fed a non-GMO diet. (Because US livestock intestines are of such poor quality, US meat processors import intestinal sausage casings from New Zealand.)

Dr. Don Skow, a livestock veterinarian for over 40 years *(USA)*, reported an increase of inflammation and infection of the lower part of small intestine of farm animals after the introduction of GMO animal feed in the US in the 1990s.

Dr. Huber's studies illustrate the accumulating evidence that GMO-fed livestock have a disturbed intestinal flora balance[1], which is essential for proper digestion.

Hoover puts the matter in perspective by pointing out that this same thing is happening to people:

"Autistic patients not only demonstrate structural deformities in their digestive tracts, but also have intestinal flora that has gone wild."

The 'good bacteria' inside of our digestive system is essential for digestion, immunity, allergy prevention, detoxification, and the production of nutrients. The GMO diet is affecting the gastrointestinal system of people, and particularly children. Dr. Michelle Perro, a California pediatrician with decades of experience, observed that for some reason children are not properly digesting their food.

British research scientists pointed out nearly a decade ago that part of the DNA which is inserted/blasted into GMO crops can transfer into the DNA of our intestines, our so-called 'gut bacteria.' And, these 'foreign' GMO transferred genes continue to reproduce and multiply inside of our bodies – **even after we stop eating GMOs.** [2]

¹ *The 'flora' in the gut (intestines) is a complex set of microorganisms (trillions of them) which reside in the digestive tract. Their function is to ferment energy from undigested food, help the immune system, and help restrict the growth of harmful bacteria.*

[1] http://gaia-health.com/gaia-blog/2011-10-20/agribusiness-to-use-gmos-to-fix-a-plague-it-caused-bowel-cancer-and-test-it-on-the-public/
[2] http://healthandwellnessmagazine.net/content/features/poor-gut-health-and-autism-linked-through-gmos-genetically-modified-organisms/

LIVER

GMO Wheat Can Lead to Liver Failure.

In September 2012 Dr. Jack Heinemann, molecular biologist at Canterbury University in *New Zealand* and the director of the Center for Integrated Research in Biosafety, warned that genetically-engineered wheat contains an enzyme suppressor which, when consumed by humans, could cause permanent liver failure and death.

Dr. Heinemann reported that the enzyme suppressor in the wheat could also attack a natural human enzyme which produces *glycogen*, a hormone molecule which helps the body's regular blood-sugar metabolism. The bodies of people who consume genetically-engineered wheat would be contaminated, affecting this hormone, which could lead to liver failure.

Dr. Heinemann said in a press conference,

> "What we found is that the molecules created in this wheat, intended to silence wheat genes, can match human genes, and through ingestion, these molecules can enter human beings and potentially silence our genes."

"The findings are absolutely assured. There's no doubt that these matches exist … and therefore we are calling for a particular battery of experiments to be done before humans eat this wheat."

His comments were confirmed by Professor Judy Carman, a biochemist and Director of the Institute of Health and Environmental Research (IHER), Flinders University, Adelaide, *Australia*, who added,

> "… children who are born with this enzyme not working tend to die **by the age of about five**." *(Emphasis in the original)*

She continued, "You need to do proper long-term toxicology studies[on animals] … you need to check for cancer, you need to see if there are any reproductive problems, and you need to check for allergies." [1]

Referring to GMO crops, Dr. Heinemann said *using* GMO crops is also different and even more complicated than trying to *contain* them, and added,

> **"There's no evidence that they can be contained, and there is considerable evidence that we cannot contain them."** [2]

[1]   http://www.naturalnews.com/037170_gm_wheat_liver_failure_gmo.html
[2]   http://www.sott.net/article/262585-Its-not-just-Monsantos-genetically-engineered-wheat-You-may-already-be-eating-rogue-GE-crops

PROSTATE

"Many studies have noted some links associated between IGF-1 levels and increased risk of cancer, especially breast and prostate cancer."

This is a quote from The Organic Trade Association *(USA/Canada)* on their website, on which they report a number of studies concerning IGF-1 levels in milk due to the GMO bovine growth hormone (rBGH) developed for cows (to increase milk production).

Insulin-growth factor 1 (IGF-1) is an essential hormone that is produced by the liver and body tissues. Human and bovine IGF-1 are essentially identical. The body's production of IGF-1 is regulated by a growth hormone.

That natural growth hormone (in animals and humans) that stimulates growth, cell reproduction, and regeneration is called 'somatotropin.' 'Bovine somatotropin' (BST) refers to this hormone in cows. BST is a protein naturally produced in the pituitary glands of cows.

The IGF-1 levels in cows are now being artificially increased through the GMO process of the chemical companies.

In order to stimulate milk production, Monsanto developed a different version of BST called 'recombinant bovine somatotropin' (rBST) by genetically modifying an E. coli bacteria. The result is called 'recombinant growth hormone' (rBGH). This rBGH increases the levels of insulin-growth factor 1 (IGF-1) in cows.

By accelerating the internal process of their organs, this increases their production of milk. This can lead to increased amounts of IGF-1 in the milk itself – and end up in those who drink it.

One of the studies reported by the Organic Trade Commission is from The European Commission – Food Safety, *(Italy)* in March 1999, in a *"Report on Public Health Aspects of the Use of Bovine Somatotropin."* This study also confirms:

"rBST [rBGH] is known to increase the levels of insulin-like growth factor 1 (IGF-1) in cows, which can lead to increased IFG-1 in milk." [1]

This IGF-1 increase can lead to the growth of cancer cells.
(See MILK.)

"The role of IGFs in cancer is supported by epidemiological studies…"

That's according to another article, published in *oxford.journals.org,* entitled, *'Role of the Insulin-like Growth Factor Family in Cancer Development and Progression,'* in the *Journal of the National Cancer Institute*, 92:1472-89, 2000.

"The role of IGFs in cancer is supported by epidemiological studies, which have found that high levels of circulating IGF-1 and low levels of IGFBP-3 are associated with increased risk of several common cancers, including those of the prostrate, breast, colorectum, and the lung."

The research was conducted by two (2) research scientists, Professor Herbert Yu, Director of the Cancer Epidemiology Program at the University of Hawaii, *USA,* and Professor Thomas E. Rohan, Chairman of the Department of Epidemiology & Population Health at the Albert Einstein College of Medicine *(USA).*

In the Conclusion of the study, the authors of the research state:

"Laboratory experiments demonstrate that IGFs are able to stimulate the growth of a wide variety of cancer cells and to suppress apoptosis[1]. In addition to their direct affect on cancer cells, IGFs also interact synergistically with other mitogenic[2] molecules and counteract antiproliferative molecules that are involved in cancer development and progression." [2]

IN SUMMARY, substantial research now documents that increases in IGF-1 levels by the GMO bovine growth hormone in milk can lead to cancer.

[1] *'Apoptosis' is the process of programmed cell death that occurs in multicellular organisms.*
[2] *A 'mitogen' is a chemical substance which encourages a cell to commence cell division.*

[1]   http://www.ota.com/m/advocacy/hottopics/rBST.html?printable=1
[2]   http://jnci.oxfordjournals.org/content/92/18/1472.full.pdf

---

STOMACH

"Before the FDA decided to allow GMOs into food without labeling, *FDA scientists* had repeatedly warned that GM foods can create unpredictable, hard-to-detect side effects, including allergies, toxins, new diseases, and nutritional problems."
[Emphasis in the original.]

That is how the Institute for Responsible Technology summarized the present state of affairs in an article entitled, *GMO Dangers.* The article discussed many of the known dangers involved with GMO 'food products.' Referring to one study concerning the stomach, the article points out:

"The stomach linings of rats fed GM potatoes showed **excessive cell growth**, a condition that could lead to cancer." [1]
[Emphasis in the original.]

[1]   http://www.responsibletechnology.org/gmo-dangers

MALE INFERTILITY

SPERM

Scientists have created 'contraceptive corn' – "researchers have discovered a rare class of human antibodies that attack sperm … corn plants that make anti-sperm antibodies."

This was an article that appeared over 10 years ago, on September 9, 2001, in *The Observer*, in the **United Kingdom**.

The article explained that,

"By isolating the genes that regulate the manufacture of these antibodies, and by putting them in corn plants, the company has created tiny horticulture factories that make contraceptives. Contraceptive corn is based on research on the rare condition, immune fertility, in which a woman makes antibodies that attack sperm. "

The article wonders out loud if, "Waiving fields of maize may one day save the world from overpopulation." [1]

A May 2013 article in www.antigmofoods.com points out that since Mitch Hein, the president of Epicyte, the company which made this discovery, gave his 2001 press release, "all discussion of the breakthrough vanished. The company itself was taken over in 2004 by Biolex and nothing more was heard in any media about the development of spermicidal.com... Did it go underground? ... Is this killer cereal already turning up on our breakfast tables?" [2]

In 2012 Biolex Therapeutics filed for Chapter VII in the bankruptcy court, and sold many of its chemicals assets and technology to a Netherlands-based pharmaceutical company, Synthon.

There is no public word on what happened to this 'contraceptive corn'!

[1]   http://www.theguardian.com/science/2001/sep/09/gm.food
[2]   http://www.antigmofoods.com/2013/05/gm-corn-set-to-stop-man-spreading-his.html

TESTICLES/TESTOSTERONE

"Men! Save Your Testicles (and Humanity): Avoid Roundup and GMO/GE Roundup Ready foods"

That's the heading of a July 29, 2013 article by Dr. Elizabeth Vaughan, a specialist in integrative medicine, which refers to a June 2013 study in Brazil – and to several other studies concerning 'GMO foods' and *glyphosate* (one of the toxins in Roundup). Commenting on the study, she points out the significance of what the researchers in **Brazil** discovered:

- That even exposure to low doses of Roundup (36 ppm, 0.036g/L for as little as 30 minutes induced cell death in Sertoli cells in young (prepubertal) rat testis.

- Healthy Sertoli cells within the testicles are vital, since they are responsible for maintaining the health of sperm cells, and for normal male sexual development.

- No more sperm can be generated if all of the Sertoli cells[1] die.

The scientists conducted 30 minute incubation tests with *glyphosate* alone (36 ppm), and reported an increased $Ca2+$. *Glyphosate* reduces the effective supply of *glutathione* (an antioxidant) and results in damage to cellular communication, cellular factories, and to the integrity of the cell wall.

Dr. Vaughan also referred to several other well-known studies. [1]

[1] *'Sertoli cells' are the somatic cells of the testes which are essential for the formation of the testes and for spermatogenesis. These cells facilitate the progression of germ cells to spermatozoa.*

[1] http://www.drvaughan.com/2013/07/men-save-your-testicles-and-humanity.html

ABNORMALITIES
of
OTHER
BIOLOGICAL ORGANS

GENES

"New GMO Wheat May 'Silence' Vital Human Genes"

That's the title of an April 23, 2013 article in *Mercola.com* by Dr. Joseph Mercola summarizing the results of Professor Heinemann's research in ***Australia***. (See *GENES*)

"Heinemann reported that his research revealed over 770 pages of potential matches between two GM genes in the wheat and the human genome. Over a dozen matches were 'extensive and identical and sufficient to cause silencing in experimental systems,' he said."

Dr. Mercola pointed out that eating this GMO wheat could lead to major changes in the way glucose and carbohydrates are stored in the body. This could be serious for adults, but even deadly for children.

Dr. Mercola explained that, like DNA, RNA is one of the major macromolecules, and "Double-stranded RNA (dsRNA) is responsible for regulating over one-third of human genes."

He pointed out that the chemical companies are now creating GMO crops "designed to change their RNA content in order to regulate gene expression." [1]

The children of the world are the laboratory!

Current GMO crops involve DNA modification, and are designed to create a new protein to achieve the various objectives of these chemical 'foods,' whether to deal with weather conditions, e.g. drought, freezing temperatures, etc., or to combat and kill pests.

This new GMO wheat, involving RNA, would alter the genes and the carbohydrate content.

RNA, ribonucleic acid, is an important molecule with long chains of nucleotides and performs multiple vital roles in coding and regulating gene expression; it also forms the genetic material of some viruses. RNA has a much shorter chain of organic molecules (called 'nucleotides') than DNA, and is more prone to hydrolysis (breaking its chemical bonds by adding water). Because of their short internal structures they can achieve chemical catalysis (a rapid rate of chemical reactions).

This RNA approach to creating GMO crops 'turns off' certain genes, and thereby modifies the growth patterns and internal dynamics of the crops. According to the ***Australian*** study, this could ultimately affect the genes in human bodies, with serious unpredictable… negative… consequences.

Because it can take years, or decades, to see the cumulative results of these GMO 'chemical crops,' once again 'the children of the world are the laboratory.'

[1]   http://articles.mercola.com/sites/articles/archive/2013/04/23/gm-wheat.aspx

---

HAIR
"GMO and Morgellons Disease"

That's the title of a March 2008 (updated November 2013) article by Barbara H. Peterson in *Global Research.*

There have been many anecdotal incidents of hair growing, which some people suspect are the result of GMO food; however, there is no evidence. Morgellons Disease is a strange skin disease with strong fiber-like materials coming out of sores or wounds that erupt in the skin, accompanied either by pain or intense itching. Few people are affected; hence, there is little research on it. Its origins are unknown. The first known case was in 2001.

Recent research has shown that these 'fiber-like materials' contain a substance called 'Agro-bacterium,'

"… which, according to New Scientist, is 'used commercially to produce genetically-modified plants.' Could GM plants be 'causing a new disease?'"   [1]

There is an increasing amount of anecdotal evidence concerning GMO 'food products' and various medical maladies and biological problems. That's why it is so essential to have studies done on the GMO crops, in order to ascertain what is, and what is not, attributable to the GMO chemically-created 'food products.'

Needless to say, the studies concerning the consequences of eating GMO 'food products' should be done BEFORE they are eaten by animals, people, and children.

[1]   http://www.globalresearch.ca/gmo-and-morgellons-disease/8464

LUNGS (GMO Tobacco)

The lungs are the essential respiratory organ for many animals and many other creatures which breathe air.

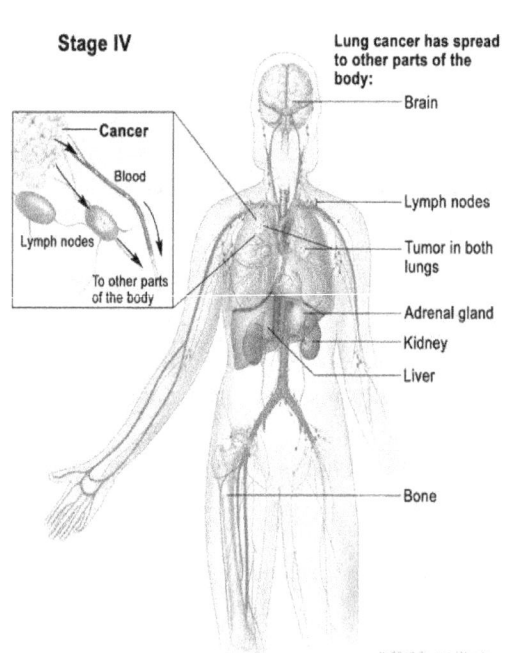

The function of the lungs is to transport oxygen from the atmosphere into the blood stream (from where it is then distributed to all of the body's cells as life-sustaining fuel), and to expel carbon dioxide (which has accumulated in the bloodstream) back into the atmosphere. Just as the lungs spread oxygen to all parts of the body, they can also spread toxins to all of the body's cells.

Image from: http://www.cancer.gov/cancertopics/pdq/treatment/non-small-cell-lung/healthprofessional/page3

"Ninety percent of U.S. tobacco is GMO; hey, smokers, you're smoking pesticide!"

That's the title of a June 10, 2013 article by S. D. Wells in *Natural News*, pointing out that "… farmers who use GM pesticides are spraying up to TEN TIMES MORE *Roundup* and other poisons on the crop, adding exponentially to the toxicity of the smoker's nightmare…"

Tobacco farmers use a variety of herbicides, pesticides, and fungicides to kill so-called 'pests' such as the tobacco budworm (*Heliothis virescens*), the tobacco hornworm (*Manduca sexta*), the tobacco wireworm (*Conoderus vespertinus*), and the aphid (*Myzus persicae*).

These poisons are then absorbed by the tobacco plants, and end up in the cigarettes. Then the *glyphosate* in Roundup and the other toxins mix with the **thousands** of other chemical additives in the cigarettes, including the ammonia-treated nicotine, "… and creates a chemical cocktail for the nervous system to engage."

When smokers inhale, these additives also mix with the bacteria already in the lungs, in the heart, and in the brain. These human organs then absorb the GMO bacteria and chemicals – which are designed to explode the stomachs and digestive tracts of beetles, worms, and other insects, as well as to destroy their reproductive abilities. By ingesting these poisons, "… humans are destroying their same genes." [1]

As far back as 2006 in an article entitled, '*Pesticides Found In Cigarette Smoke*,' *livescience* reported on a Colorado School of Mines study which revealed some of the pesticides that even survive into the smoke after the cigarettes are burned at 1,700 degrees of heat at the tip of the cigarette. These toxins included: Trifluralin (a known endocrine disrupter which affects the reproductive system and metabolic system), Pendimethalin (a known endocrine disrupter that affects the thyroid), and flumetralin (a suspected endocrine disrupter, already banned in Europe in tobacco). Kent Voorhees, a member of the School's study team, commented that, "... no data exists to establish the possible synergistic effect of these pesticides with each other, or with the other 4,700-plus compounds that have been identified in tobacco smoke."

Of course, one of the disturbing questions is: what happens to this combination of toxic chemicals which are *not* burned up, but reside in the lungs of the smoker – and in his/her digestive tract and heart? [2]

"Farmers Sue Big Tobacco, Monsanto for knowingly poisoning them with deadly pesticides that cause birth defects"

That's the title of an April 17, 2012 article by Ethan A. Huff in *Natural News*, reporting on **Argentina** farmers who are suing Phillip Morris and Monsanto. Dozens of farm workers claim that their children suffered "devastating birth defects" when these corporate giants persuaded the farmers to abandon their regular tobacco crop and plant "a new tobacco crop which is specific to Phillip Morris cigarettes."

To effectively grow this "new crop" apparently requires increased amounts of herbicides and pesticides, including Monsanto's Roundup – "... which suggests that the new crop may actually be a genetically-modified (GM) tobacco variety produced by Monsanto."

In a variety of medical maladies from which these children are now suffering "...the corporate biotechnology [of Monsanto and Phillip Morris] appears to have played a direct role ...,"and the farmers were not forewarned of the dangers. According to the report, these include "... cerebral palsy, psychomotor retardation, epilepsy, spina bifida, intellectual disabilities, metabolic disorders, congenital heart defects, Down syndrome, missing fingers, and blindness." [3]

According to *GMO Compass*, GM tobacco is being "field tested" in more than 60 areas in over a dozen countries, but it seems to be unknown how many people or populations are involved in this "field testing." Meanwhile, GM tobacco is already in some cigarettes, including in the U.S. [4]

According to a review of records of the U.S. Department of Agriculture at the time, the multi-billion dollar tobacco giant Phillip Morris was experimenting with producing GM cigarettes as far back as 2007, ostensibly to reduce the carcinogens. The company "… has run dozens of field trials for genetically modified tobacco varieties," more than twice the number of field trials compared to other tobacco companies at the time. Phillip Morris' intention was to create a mutation to introduce into their various tobacco products, "… presumably avoiding a genetically modified organism label." [5]

The chemical industry is spreading more poisons… to more people … than the tobacco industry ever did. Not to miss an opportunity, the GMO industry is now partnering with their fellow poison producers, the tobacco industry, to expand the crop production of the 'nicotine delivery devise' known as cigarettes.

Together, they can create more addicted customers and help each other profit – by poisoning the planet's entire population.

[1] http://www.naturalnews.com/040703_GMO_tobacco_chemicals_in_ciga rettes.html#

[2] http://www.livescience.com/4083-pesticides-cigarette-smoke.html

[3] http://www.naturalnews.com/035592_Big_Tobacco_Monsanto_birth_de fects.html

[4] http://www.gmo-compass.org/eng/database/plants/304.tobacco.html

[5] http://www.wired.com/wiredscience/2008/03/philip-morris-t/

SKIN

The skin is by far the largest organ of the body, covering an area of approximately 20 square feet. Its purpose is to protect the inner organs of the body from microbes and other elements, to help regulate body temperature, and to permit the sensations of touch, heat and cold to guide the body in its survival impulses.

More Anecdotal Evidence From Around the World: GMOs Cause Skin Diseases

There is a strange skin disease, called Morgellons Disease, which is characterized by the growth of strange fiber-like tissues. Those who have this disease have a growth of these 'hairs' under their skin, protruding from their skin, and often growing out of sores on their bodies. Sometimes the victims of this disease feel that something is crawling under their skin. The first known case was discovered by Mary Leitao in her son in 2001 – after GMO crops were invented. She named the disease after a 17th century study in *France* which identified similar symptoms. [1]

Those who suffer from this malady have mysterious strands that appear to be cellulose (which is not manufactured by the human body). The biochemist Vitaly Citovsky, professor in the Department of Biochemistry and Cell Biology at Stony Brook University in New York *(USA)* discovered that the fibers contain a substance called '*Agrobacterium tumefaciens.*' Citovsky says,

> "Agrobacterium[1] is capable of genetically transforming not only plants, but also eukaryotic species, including human cells, and is used in the production of some genetically modified organisms."

IN SUMMARY, there is now a demonstrated chemical connection between Morgellons Disease and GMO crops.

[1] *'Agrobacterium' is a bacteria found in the soil which genetically engineers live cells into a wounded part of a plant. It is part of the GMO genetic engineering process.*

"Unless skincare products are certified non-GMO... there is a good chance they contain GMOs."

That's the warning of Josephine Beck in an August 22, 2013 article in *Natural News.com* entitled '*Possible negative impacts of GMOs on health and skin: How to avoid GMOs in skincare products.*'

While pointing out the currently unknown risks of using skincare products containing GMO toxins, she refers to some anecdotal evidence of skin conditions such as acne and eczema, and scientists who already forecast some of the known dangers.

Another research scientist, Dr. Joe Cummins, Professor Emeritus at the University of Western Ontario, *Canada*, observed that sufferers of Megellons Disease tested for *Agrobacterium tumefaicens*. He concludes that there may be a link between Morgellons Disease and GMO crops. [2]

"Nightmare on Elm Street's Dinner Table; Thank you, Monsanto!"

That's the caption of an April 2008 article Dr. Rima E. Laibow, MD, Director of the Natural Solutions Foundation *(USA)*.

Dr. Laibow acknowledges that as of yet there is no direct, definitive evidence. Yet, like many scientists, because of the anecdotal evidence she suspects this horrible disease is associated in some way with GMO crops. Referring to Morgellons Disease, she says,

"A study of the fibers show that they contain DNA from **both** a fungus and a bacterium which are used in the commercial preparation of genetically modified foods and non-food crops (such as cotton). The fibers themselves are primarily cellulose, which the human body cannot break down or manufacture." [3]
[Emphasis in original.]

Russian scientists discovered that, by the third generation, rat pups fed GMO soy had hair growing in recessed pouches in their mouths.

In April 2010 the biologist Alexey V. Surov with the Russian Academy of Sciences reported on a joint study by the National Association for Gene Security and the Institute of Ecological and Evolutionary Problem, both in *Russia*. In the study three generations of hamsters were fed varying diets, including GMO soy.

The third generation of GMO-fed hamsters experienced growth of hair in their mouths. [4]

Since it has now been discovered that GMO crops produce ectopia[1] hair, the anecdotal evidence is steadily increasing that the 'hair' produced by Morgellons Disease is GMO-related.

[1] *'Ectopia' is the abnormal location or position of a body part or organ, which can occur congenitally or as part of an injury or experiment. (From the Greek 'ektopos' which means 'out of place')*

"Skin Disease Linked to GMOs – Don't Let This Happen to You!"

That's the title of a September 2011 article by Barbara H. Peterson in *Farm Wars* in which she describes how she developed "skin rashes" and "bumps" which "oozed clear liquid." Antibiotics and other medicines did not work; so she began to stop eating GMO 'food products' and ate natural foods instead.

"When I stopped eating the contaminated food, the itching subsided and the rash got better. I tried this with several foods, one at a time, and sure enough, each one that was most certainly GM, I had a reaction."

In her research she also learned about similar, and worse, skin diseases in India where GMO cotton (*Bt* cotton) is grown. The *Bt* cotton in India has created its own plague of problems with the health of farmers and farm workers, and with the physical survival of farmers, thousands of whom commit suicide because of various issues with the *Bt* cotton.

After several years of avoiding GMO 'food products' she is now back to health. [5]

IN SUMMARY, like other bodily organs, anecdotal evidence is accumulating around the globe that GMO 'food products' are involved in the development of skin diseases – which were not previously experienced before the chemical companies invented the GMO 'food products.'

[1]   http://www.globalresearch.ca/gmo-and-morgellons-disease/8464

[2] http://www.naturalnews.com/041727_gmos_skincare_products_morgell
     ons.html
[3] http://drrimatruthreports.com/gm-files-horrifying-new-disease-contains-
     identical-material-to-gm-food/
[4] http://voiceofrussia.com/2010/04/16/6524765.html/
[5] http://farmwars.info/?p=6920

URINE (HUMAN)

"Herbicides Found in Human Urine"

That's the title of a January 2012 article by Dirk Braendli and Sandra Reinacher in the German *ithakajournal – viticulture ecology climate-farming* regarding the Delinat Institute for Ecology and Climate-Farming referring to a study by the University of Leipzig in **Germany**.

"To determine if only individuals who are in direct contact with contaminated feed or glyphosate laced compounds are at risk for glyphosate poisoning a study was conducted in December 2011 of an urban population in Berlin. The urine of city workers, journalists and lawyers, who had no direct contact with glyphosate, was examined for glyphosate contamination. The study found glyphosate in all urine samples at values ranging from 0.5 to 2 ng glyphosate per ml urine (drinking water limit: 0.1ng/ml). None of the examinees had direct contact with agriculture."

These are concentrations of between 5 and 20 times the safe standards for drinking water, and "None of the examinees had direct contact with agriculture"!

The assumption is that "Glyphosate probably entered human populations over the past 10 years through its increasing presence in daily foods such as meat and dairy products, vegetable and fruit produce and grains products."

Despite this toxicity, "… authorities in the EU raised the legal limit of glyphosate in bread and wheat to 100 times the legal limit for vegetables. For feed grains the legal limit was raised 200 fold, this without that these limits are being enforced by any form of relevant random sampling." [1]

The conclusion is that, because of the GMO crops and the increased use of *glyphosate* (particularly in Roundup) *glyphosate* poisoning is now spread throughout the entire population.

[1]   http://www.ithaka-journal.net/druckversionen/e052012-herbicides-urine.pdf

GMO CROPS
and the
RESULTING
'FOOD PRODUCTS'

CANOLA

'Canola Oil,' ("Canada Oil Low Acid") is a genetically-engineered oil from the rapeseed plant. Historically, it was used as industrial oil for lubricants, bio-fuels, inks, candles, soaps, and even lipsticks. Its original name was LEAR, for 'Low Euric Acid Rapeseed.' Rapeseed is so toxic that bugs and animals won't eat it. This genetically-modified oil is now used in a variety of foods and GMO 'food products.'

Turning Lubricating Oil into Cooking Oil

In the mid-1990s Canola Oil was genetically engineered, creating a new form of GMO hydrogenated oil. 'Hydrogenated' means that, using high pressure, hydrogen is forced into the empty areas of a fat molecule, and turns vegetable oil into a saturated fat. This is how margarine is produced *[margarine also elevates cholesterol, and has a number of other ingredients – in any case, bugs refuse to eat it¹]*.

Once it was decided that this genetically engineered creation could be sold as a 'food product' it was named 'Canola,' an abbreviation of 'Canada Oil Low Acid'. This enabled it to be marketed as new healthy cooking oil from Canada, and a substitute for vegetable oil.

By 2005 over 87% of Canola Oil in the United States was genetically modified, and by 2009 over 90% of the Canadian crop was GMO.

As the nutritionist Dr. Josh Axe *(USA)* says, there have been no long term research studies of CanolaOil. *(At least none have been published! Presumably Monsanto scientists have conducted long-term studies internally, but the results have not been publicized.)* However, Dr. Axe observes that there have been numerous anecdotal reports of kidney, liver and neurological health problems. He says,

"This would make sense, since there are other reports that GMO products like corn and soy also can cause negative health effects." [1]

232

Although there have not yet been any independent studies, since Canola Oil involves a chemical process of turning a traditional lubricating oil and bio-fuel into a chemical 'food product', it is included here as a matter of caution.

[1] http://www.draxe.com/canola-oil-gm/

¹ NB: Cows, pigs, geese, squirrels, rats, and other creatures will also not eat GMO seeds or crops unless they have nothing else to eat.

CORN (MAIZE)

"Biotech Lies Exposed: Genetically-Modified Corn contains practically no nutrients but is loaded with chemical poisons"

That's the title of an April 10, 2013 article by Jonathan Benson of *NaturalNews.com* which revealed more details of corn studies, emphasizing that the

> "… non-GMO corn is **20 times richer in nutrition, energy and protein** compared to GMO corn…"

and that in non-GMO corn the "… potassium levels were **more than 13 times higher**," testing at 9.2 ppm." [1]
[Emphasis in the original]

In his book *Seeds of Deception*, Jeffrey Smith discusses how animals refuse to eat GMO corn and other GMO crops, some of which he describes in sections entitled, *'Wisdom of Squirrels, Elk, Deer, Raccoons, and Mice,' 'Wisdom of the Cows and Hogs,' 'Wisdom of the Geese,'* and even *'Wisdom of the Rats.'*

The obvious point is that since animals refuse to eat GMO 'food products,' humans should realize how toxic these 'food products' are. [2]

Animals which eat a GMO diet often die, including chickens, caterpillars, butterflies, and various other creatures who accidentally encounter wind-blown GMO toxins.

For a general review of the toxicity of GMO corn, you can also go to the general articles by Dr. Joseph Mercola, an internationally recognized natural health physician. One published on September 15, 2012 is entitled, *'How Can the Wealthiest Industrialized Nation be the Sickest?'* In it he discusses many health issues and makes reference to another book by Jeffrey Smith, *'Genetic Roulette: The Documented Health Risks of Genetically Engineered Foods.'*

Some of the medical issues discussed are: autism (which now affects one in 88 children, compared to one in 25,000 in the 1970s); Type 2 diabetes (whose rates have increased by 176% between the years 1980 and 2010); Alzheimer's Disease (which have doubled since 1980); and the reality that: life expectancy has decreased while infant mortality has increased. [3]

"If you want to avoid obesity, then avoid eating genetically engineered (GE) corn, corn based products, and animals that are fed a diet of GE grain."

That's the opening line from of a July 24, 2012 article entitled, *'Obesity, Corn, GMOs'* by The Cornucopia Institute in Wisconsin *(USA). [This article is also referred to above, in OBESITY.]*

The article reports,

"The results show a positive link between GE corn and obesity. Animals fed a GE corn diet got fatter quicker and retained the weight compared to animals fed a non-GE grain diet."

The animals were fed a diet of GE corn and soy. What is even more conclusive regarding the consequences of eating a GMO diet is that,

"The studies were performed on rats, mice, pigs and salmon achieving the same result."

The scientists even discovered that rats even "got fatter faster" if they ate *fish which had consumed GE grain.* The article warns that,

"[humans] could get the same life altering effects."

The study also showed that these animals were "less able to digest proteins," which would not only relate to a rise in obesity but to other diseases,

"which include diabetes, digestive disorders, inflammatory bowel disease, colitis, autism spectrum disorders (ASD) (ADD), autoimmune diseases, sexual dysfunction, sterility, asthma, COPD, and many more." [4]

IN SUMMARY, studies by scientists around the world have now shown that GMO corn is toxic to a variety of biological organs.

———————

There is another toxic danger from GMO corn: GMO corn is also used as a bio-fuel, ethanol, which infects the lungs.

[NOTE: During 2012 and 2013 Monsanto and other chemical companies have been working with the Obama administration to obtain approval of a new variety of GMO corn, a 2,4-D – dicamba-tolerant corn, an ingredient used in one of Monsanto's other products – Agent Orange. The Save Our Crops Coalition has called dicamba "one of America's most dangerous herbicides for non-target plant damage."] [5]

A Political Note Regarding GMO corn: By flooding Mexico with its GMO corn, Monsanto has destroyed the centuries-old maize culture of Mexico – where thousands of varieties of maize originated. Consequently, tens of thousands of these farmers ('compesinos') and their young offspring have been displaced, and are now flooding to the United States… many illegally. [6]

[1] http://www.naturalnews.com/039864_gmo_corn_nutrients_minerals.html

[2] http://www.amazon.com/s/ref=nb_sb_noss_1?url=search-alias%3Daps&field-keywords=seeds%20of%20deception&sprefix=seeds+of+d%2Caps&rh=i%3Aaps%2C

[3] http://articles.mercola.com/sites/articles/archive/2012/09/15/genetic-roulette-gmo-documentary.aspx

[4] http://www.cornucopia.org/2012/07/obesity-corn-gmos/

[5] http://www.bloomberg.com/news/2013-05-10/monsanto-dow-herbicide-tolerant-crops-to-get-reviews.html

[6] See page 85 of The Poison Planters on amazon.com.

PRODUCTS made from GMO CORN

According to the United States Department of Agriculture, by 2013 over 85% of all corn planted in the US was GMO corn.
[1]

There are hundreds of 'food products' and non-food products (e.g. motor fuel, lubricating oil, animal feed, etc.) made from GMO corn.

Some of the 'food products' are: baby food, baked goods, bread, cakes and cookies, canned fruits, cereals, cheese and cheese products, corn chips, doughnuts, English muffins, food coloring, ice cream, instant foods, pancake mixes, peanut butter, potato chips, powdered sugar, precooked frozen foods, salad dressings, soups, spray cooking oil, tomato sauces. [2]

"5 Reasons High Fructose Corn Syrup Will Kill You"

That's the title of an article by Dr. Mark Hyman , Chairman of the Institute for Functional Medicine and six times New York Times best-selling author *(USA)*.

High Fructose Corn Syrup (HFCS) is an inexpensive sweetener made from genetically modified corn.

HFCS is a group of corn syrups that have undergone various forms of chemical 'processing', largely altering the enzymes, to convert much of the cornstarch (a polymer of interlinked chains of glucose molecules) into fructose in order to enhance the sweetness. In Canada HFCS is called 'glucose/fructose.'

Summarizing the reasons presented by Dr. Hyman to avoid HFCS:

i. Too much sugar in any form causes obesity and disease; but the existence of HFCS in so many products causes an over-consumption of sugars.

ii. Since HFCS is a chemical 'food product' and is not biologically identical to cane sugar, it is not processed the same way by the body. 'Food products' made with fructose do not require digestion, and are rapidly absorbed into the blood stream.

"High doses of free fructose have been proven to literally punch holes in the intestinal lining allowing nasty products of toxic gut bacteria and partially digested food proteins to enter your blood stream…"

[The resultant] "inflammation …. is at the root of obesity, diabetes, cancer, heart disease, dementia, and accelerated aging."

iii. HFCS contains contaminants – including mercury – that are not regulated or measured by the FDA. Various studies have confirmed this disturbing realization.

iv. Independent medical and nutrition professionals do not support the use of HFCS – even though the corn industry claims that they do.

v. HFCS is almost always a marker of poor-quality, nutrient-poor, disease-creating industrial 'food products' or 'food like substances.'

As Dr. Hyman points out, HFCS is often not digested, but travels directly into the blood stream. Fructose then travels directly to the liver and triggers the production of fats such as triglycerides and cholesterol which lead to liver damage. The rapidly absorbed glucose also triggers an elevation of insulin levels.

"Both these features of HFCS lead to increased metabolic disturbances that drive increases in appetite, weight gain, diabetes, heart disease, cancer, dementia, and more." [3]

―――――――

HFCS has been shown to contribute to obesity, cardiovascular (heart) disease, diabetes, and hyperlipidemia[1].

High fructose corn syrup (HFCS) is not a natural sugar from canes or beets. HFCS is a 'chemically-processed package' of genetically-engineered sweeteners.

The process to convert some of the glucose in corn syrup into fructose was developed in 1957. It resulted in a product which was 42% fructose and 58% glucose, thereby dramatically increasing the sweetness and making it an inexpensive competitor to sucrose (table sugar derived from cane sugar or sugar beets).

HFCS generally consists of 24% water and the rest is a combination of the various sugars. HFCS is regarded as a 'cheap sugar' since sugar is too expensive to add as a sweetener in most products on the market.

Due to its low cost, there are thousands of 'food products' which contain HFCS. Hundreds of these 'food products' are deceitfully mislabeled as "natural".

These 'food products' include all of the items listed above and their derivatives, some of which are:

(1) breakfast cereals (even those from major companies that are advertised as healthy, such as Kellogg's, Post, General Mills);

(2) fruit juices (which are not 100% juice), including juices from Ocean Spray, Capri-Sun, Tropicana, and other big names;

(3) sodas and various soft drinks;

(4) Yogurt, including such names as Dannon and Yoplait;

(5) nuts;

(6) breads (including such major names as Pepperidge Farm and Sara Lee who advertise 'whole grain marketing' but don't mention the HFCS inside);

(7) baked goods and pastries;

(8) macaroni and cheese;

(9) Candy;

(10) salad dressings;

(11) popcorn;

(12) health foods;

(13) nutrition bars;

(14) processed snacks;

(15) many fruits and vegetables, particularly those packaged in liquids;

(16) baking and cooking ingredients. This is just to name a few of the general categories of the 'food products'! [4]

(One of the most widely used chemically-created 'GMO corn products' is ethanol!)

Anything you eat which tastes sweet, and does not contain only sugar, is probably "flavored" with HFCS. Since 85% of all corn grown in the US is GMO corn, GMO toxins are contained in these HFCS products.

For a general discussion of the dangers of HFCS, please review the article below on Organic Consumers Association by Will Allen of Cedar Circle Farm, Vermont *(USA)*. Cedar Circle Farm and Education Center is a flower and certified organic vegetable and berry farm whose purpose is to provide education in agriculture and to produce organic foods. [5]

[1] 'Hyperlipidemia' is a term meaning high lipid (fat) levels in the blood. It usually means high cholesterol and high triglyceride levels, and can accelerate the process of atherosclerosis (hardening of the arteries).

[1]   http://www.ers.usda.gov/data-products/adoption-of-genetically-engineered-crops-in-the-us/recent-trends-in-ge-adoption.aspx#.UmWeYXC2Zv4

[2]   http://www.kycorn.org/documents/cornuses.pdf

[3]   http://drhyman.com/blog/2011/05/13/5-reasons-high-fructose-corn-syrup-will-kill-you/#close

[4]   http://www.celestialhealing.net/Food_contain_HFCS.htm

[5]   http://www.organicconsumers.org/articles/article_26209.cfm

COTTON

Cotton, from the Arabic word 'qutn' is any of a variety of shrubby plants of the genus Gossypium with soft downy flowers which surround oil-rich seeds. The flowers are often used for clothing and other materials; the seeds are often used for food products; both are often used for animal feed.

GMO cotton (*Bt* cotton) is a genetically engineered crop designed to combat the bollworm. It was created by genetically altering the cotton genome to include a protein from the *Bacillus thuringiensis*. This transgene 'inserted' into the plant's genome produces toxin crystals which the plant itself does not create.

When ingested by insects or other organisms, it dissolves the lining in their intestines, thereby enabling a more continuous flow of potassium. The unregulated flow of potassium results in the death of the epithelial cells[1], creating gaps in the membrane, and allowing bacteria and the *Bt* toxins to enter the body cavity, and thereby causing the death of the organism. Essentially,

Like Other GMO Crops, When the Insects Eat the Crops, Their Stomachs Explode.

Although first discovered in Japan in 1905, the *Bacillus thuringiensis* and its potential applications were rediscovered in 1905. It was used to kill the Mediterranean flour moth. Since the German scientist Ernst Berliner discovered this bacterium in the German town of Thuringia, he named it *Bacillus thuringiensis (Bt)*.

In 1995, as molecular biology advanced, Monsanto 'inserted' this bacterium into the cotton seed and *Bt* cotton was born.

Bt cotton was 'introduced' into India even before it received an official government approval. Now approximately 25% of agricultural land in India is planted with cotton, making India 3rd in cotton production, behind the U.S. and China.

Among the man-made difficulties   created by the *Bt* cotton are:

- the increasingly high cost of the *Bt* cotton seeds themselves

- the increasing costs of the herbicide, Roundup

- the unexpected costs of additional herbicides that are required for pests which are *not* killed by the *Bt* cotton

- the cost of borrowing money in the hope of having expanded cotton yields which don't always occur

- the litigation costs involved when the *Bt* cotton seeds unintentionally end up in a neighboring farm and legal issues arise*

- the selling of fraudulent GMO seeds with the result that they are not protected from *glyphosate* (Roundup)

- the poisoning of non-GMO farms by the spread of the increased use of *glyphosate* (Roundup) on the GMO crops.

- the usual health issues associated with the GMO toxins

This combination of catastrophes has caused tens of thousands of Indian farmers to go bankrupt, and to commit suicide.

[1] *'Epithelial cells' are the cells that cover the epithelium, the membranes covering the internal organs and other internal surfaces in the body*

* *Monsanto has what are referred to as the 'seed police' who, on a global basis, monitor the spread of GMO crops and prosecute farmers who use Monsanto's seeds without paying for them, even if the farmers are neighbors who do so unintentionally because the seeds were accidentally blown onto their farms by the wind. The 'seed police' are very active in India.*

"Monsanto's seeds are seeds of suicide."

In an article of March 30, 2013 for *AL JAZEERA,* the renowned author and founder of the Research Foundation for Science, Technology, and Ecology, in **India**, Dr. Vandana Shiva, quoted the statistics just in the Maharashtra region which has the highest concentration of *Bt* cotton, and the highest number of farmer suicides:

nearly 54,000 farmer suicides since 1995, of which 33,752 occurred since 2003. She adds,

> "The price of seed jumped 8,000 percent; Monsanto's royalty extraction and the high cost of purchased seed and chemicals have created a debt trap." [1]

She discussed the situation again in a June 24, 2013 article in the on-line publication *Global Research* entitled, *'The Seeds of Suicide: How Monsanto Destroys Farming.'* Referring to the Maharashtra region again, she explained a Government of India (GOI) report that almost 75% of the rural debt is due to purchases of Monsanto's seed monopoly. She summarized by saying,

> "As Monsanto's profits grow, farmers' debt grows. It is in this systemic sense that Monsanto's seeds are seeds of suicide." [2]

"Human beings lack the enzymes necessary to cleave the linkages between the sugars in cellulose [derived from cotton]."

In addition to being used for clothing, cotton is heavily involved in our food supply.

One of the principal products of cotton is cellulose. Cellulose is a molecule comprised of carbon, hydrogen, and oxygen, and is found in the cellular structure of virtually all plant matter. Cotton is the purest natural form of cellulose.

Due to the increasing awareness of the need for high fiber content, cellulose has become one of the most popular food additives. Without disturbing the flavor, it contributes to the bulk and fiber content of food, drink, and sauces. And, it has no calories. However,

> "Unfortunately, human beings lack the enzymes necessary to cleave the linkages between the sugars in cellulose." Thus, the digestive process is disturbed. [3]

Due to the spread of this "food additive," every day of the week humans consume 'food products' which contain cellulose.

Melody Meyer, of *United Natural Foods and Organic Matters* blog, provides a list of foods and 'food products' which involve cotton or cellulose. These cheese, cream, milk powder, processed fruits, cooked vegetables, canned beans, pre-cooked pastas, pre-cooked rice products, soups, yeasts, seasonings, sweeteners, soybean products, breakfast cereals, bakery items, and even dietetic foods as a non-caloric filler. Cotton seed oil is also used to produce Vitamin E, and Cotton Seed Oil is the primary ingredient in Crisco.

She also points out that animals we eat, or whose milk we drink, are often fed cotton seed meal or cotton gin by-products known as "Gin Trash." This includes cotton seed, stalk, leaves, burrs, and twigs. Gin Trash is also sold to food companies for further processing and use in cotton seed oil, "additives" and "fillers" for livestock feed, and for soil compost mix. [4]

Thus, in the final analysis, we don't even know how much toxin-filled GMO cotton we are actually ingesting into our bodies – either directly or indirectly by eating beef and pork.

[1] http://www.aljazeera.com/indepth/opinion/2013/03/20133281355372925
0.html
[2] http://www.globalresearch.ca/the-seeds-of-suicide-how-monsanto-
destroys-farming
[3] http://antoine.frostburg.edu/chem/senese/101/consumer/faq/what-is-
cellulose.shtml
[4] http://foodreference.about.com/od/Food-Additives/a/What-Is-
Cellulose.htm

FRUIT

From the Latin word 'fructus' meaning 'stem,' in botany fruit is part of a flowering plant. A fruit is the matured ovary of a flower containing the seed, and the surrounding ovule ("small egg") becomes the fruit. Fruits usually are in trees or on vines. (A vegetable is usually considered to either grow in the ground, e.g. edible roots, tubers, stems, or to be leaves, seeds, or softer parts of plants.) In culinary terms, a 'fruit' is generally any sweet-tasting plant, usually containing some kind of seeds.

APPLES

The origin of the word 'apple' is unknown, but many believe it is derived from the Old English word 'appel' which, in turn, derived from the Old Teutonic word 'apful.' The fruit itself is believed to have originated in the Asian country of Kazakhstan, and was discovered there by Alexander the Great.

Botox Apples?

According to a May 10, 2013 article by David Knowles in the on-line publication *Daily News (USA)*,

"Dubbed 'botox apples' because they are designed to prevent bruising and browning, Arctic Granny Smith and Arctic Golden Delicious apples made by Canada's Okanagan Specialty Fruits have been under review by U.S. regulatory agencies since 2010 and could become the second genetically modified fruit to be allowed in the country."

(NB Currently, the other fruit is Rainbow papaya.)

Like Monsanto, the Okanagan company opposes labeling any of the genetically modified apples which will result from this chemical-engineering process. In a striking example of 'double-speak,' the president of Okanagan, Neal Carter, cynically presented the company's position by saying, "We as a company don't support mandatory labeling because we feel it basically undermines the regulatory process." [1]

Washington State apple growers are opposed to this attempt to bring genetically modified apples into the U.S. market, since they fear it will contaminate U.S. apples and cause foreign countries, particularly the European Community, to ban U.S. apples.

The issue is now moving forward.

[1]   http://www.nydailynews.com/news/national/gmo-apples-don-bruise-brown-stores-article-1.1340831

ORANGES

The orange is believed to have originated 2500 B.C. somewhere between southern China and northeastern India where it was called 'naranga.' When it appeared in southern Europe, Sicily, from the Arab traders, the 'n' was dropped (probably for linguistic ease) and its name was pronounced 'arangia,' and was eventually reduced to 'orange.'

Biotech scientists are now helping Florida orange growers to create genetically modified oranges to fight a bacteria.

In the U.S. Florida orange growers are seeking a way to combat the ever-increasing spread of the bacteria-carrying psyllid, which is responsible for a bacterial infection of 'citrus greening' called *huanglongbing*.

In June 2012 they were exploring how large quantities of a spinach protein could be engineered into orange trees, and what the repercussions would be. The matter remains under development. [1]

[1]   http://grist.org/food/orange-you-ready-for-a-tall-glass-of-gmos/

MILK

"Milk and the Cancer Connection"

"Should you be concerned?" asks Dr. Hans R. Larsen in an article entitled *'Milk and the Cancer Connection.'* His answer: "Yes, you certainly should, particularly if you drink milk produced in the United States."

Dr. Larsen reviews several of the studies on the subject of bovine growth hormone (rBGH) and the   "Cancer Connection":

- As far back as 1990 researchers at Stanford University *(USA)* discovered that IGF-1 promotes the growth of prostate cells and the accelerated growth of breast cancer cells.

- In 1995 scientists at the National Institutes of Health *(USA)* disclosed "that IGF-1 plays a role in the central progression of many childhood cancers and in the tumours in breast cancer, small cell lung cancer, melanoma, and cancers of the pancreas and prostate."

- In September 1997 a link was discovered between high concentrations of IGF-1 and prostate cancer by international research scientists.

- In 1998 Harvard Medical School *(USA)* research scientists confirmed previous findings that high IGF-1 levels in the blood are linked to the risk of prostate cancer.

Dr. Hansen concludes by saying,

"The evidence of a strong link between cancer risk and a high level of IGF-1 is now indisputable." [1]

Therefore, the health risk of drinking rBGH milk is overwhelming, because

Bovine growth hormones (rBGH) are *scientifically designed* to increase IGF-1!

The Health Protection Branch of the Canadian government *challenged* the entire FDA study, and even alleged that the *FDA misreported* the results.

When Monsanto presented a study, using rats (not cows!), to show how innocuous their bovine growth hormone (rBGH) is, the Canadian government challenged the entire study. The Canadian report (referred to as the Gaps Analysis Report) stated that 20% to 30% of the rats fed rBGH in high doses developed antibody responses to rBGH:

indicating that rBGH was absorbed into their blood – and would likely be absorbed into the blood of   humans who drink rBGH milk.

Since rBGH increases the levels of IGF-1, the signals increasingly point to the possibilities of cancer.

According to the Health Protection Branch of the government of **Canada**, an increased risk of mastitis (inflammation of the udder) may be associated with rBST. This has resulted in an increase in different bacteria, as well as pus and blood secretions – all of which could be passed along in the milk. This could have health implications for humans, and create an antibiotic resistance in farm-borne human pathogens.

The Gaps Analysis Report says, "The BST-induced mastitis is harder to treat than naturally occurring mastitis and duration of treatment is longer due to high incidence of infection with S.aureus...[1]

"There is a one-third higher incidence of antibiotic-resistant bacteria. BST use increases the amounts of drugs in general to treat the various adverse effects it causes in cattle." [2]

[1] *'S.aureus' (Staphylococcus aureus) is a bacterium frequently found in the human respiratory tract and on the skin, and is a common cause of respiratory disease, skin infections, and food poisoning.*

Because of Monsanto's policy of refusing to disclose the results of many of its internal studies, there have been insufficient 'known' studies on the health effects of the bovine growth hormone (rBGH). Also, Monsanto and the chemical industry have (so far) successfully prevented the labeling of their 'food products.' So, no one knows for sure what chemicals are contained in them – or what the various consequences are to human health for ingesting them.

However, numerous independent research studies over the past two decades have been conducted in over 30 countries and revealed what *some* of the consequences are. This research indicates possible medical dangers to people, including various forms of cancer.

Also, the existing research has revealed disturbing biological/medical issues for the cows... which could create even more medical issues for those who eat meat, or those who drink milk – particularly for babies and children.

[1] http://www.notmilk.com/drlarsen.html
[2] http://ucbiotech.org/biotech_info/PDFs/Chopra_rBST_Nutrilac_Gaps_A
     nalysis_Report.pdf

PAPAYA

'Papaya' (probably through Spanish from the Arawakan West Indian word 'pawpaw' or 'papaw') is a tree-like plant native to the tropics of the Americas, namely the Caribbean, Mexico, and Central America. It produces a fruit which is used as a food, a cooking aid, and even in some medicines.

A GMO papaya was created to combat papaya ringspot virus (PRSV), which devastated the papaya crop on the Hawaiian Islands in the 1950s and 1960s. In the process the plants developed a pathogenesis[1].

The virus has been known to affect crops in various parts of the world, from Asia to the Middle East. A similar virus called, PRSV-W, attacks watermelon, squash, and other cucurbits.[2]

To combat this virus, two transgenic (GMO) varieties of papayas were created. They were created in a manner analogous to vaccinating humans, namely to insert a mild strain of the virus itself directly into the plant. As probably expected, one of the side effects was to create pathogenesis in the plants; so the plants began to generate their own pathogens.

One of the many broader side effects of this development was to create GMO contamination throughout the islands. On Hawaii Island itself the contamination has been estimated to be nearly 50% of the crop. This development has led to a decline of lucrative exports of papaya, since many countries ban GMO crops.

The contamination occurs through the air, by the GMO pollen being carried by the wind, or by animals, insects, birds, or even humans. Seed contamination also spreads by GMO seeds contaminating the traditional seed supply.

There have been insufficient studies to determine the magnitude of the contamination of the crops, or of the health consequences to humans and animals that eat GMO papaya. [1]

However, it is now increasingly documented that the *genetically engineering process* itself causes internal disruptions in seeds, with unknown and unpredictable health consequences.

[1] 'Pathogenesis' is the development of a disease.
[2] 'Curcurbits' are mostly climbing or trailing plants of the Curcurbitaceae family, which includes squash, pumpkin, cucumber, watermelon, and cantaloupe.

[1] http://hawaiiseed.org/local-issues/papaya/

PEAS

GMO Peas Created Immune Reactions in Mice

The 'pea' (singularized from the Old English 'pease' –OED) is botanically a pod fruit 'Pisum sativum,' since it contains seeds developed from the ovary of a flower; but in culinary terms it is a vegetable. Its multiple varieties and variations are part of cuisine all over the world.

"Genetically Modified Mush"

That's the title of a 2006 Editorial in the on-line journal *nature biotechnology* which reports on a research project conducted in *Australia* involving genetically modified peas fed to mice.

This study involved six field trials over a five year period, between 1996 and 2001, by two (2) research scientists, T. J. Higgins of

Australia's Commonwealth Scientific and Industrial Research Organization (CSIRO) and Maarten Chrispeels of the University of California (**USA**).

CSIRO published a paper with the results of their experiments, which revealed that genetically modified peas created immune reactions in mice. This could lead to the possibility of creating serious allergic issues in humans.

The objective was to genetically create a transgenic pea (*Pisum sativum*) which then produces an 'a-amylase 1 inhibitor' (a protein with insecticidal properties originally isolated from the common bean, *Phaseolus vulgaris*) and insert this protein into the pea.

This would be similar to other GMO seeds, with alternative DNA genes inserted into the seeds. This protein inhibitor suppresses the insect's ability to digest starch, and causes the insect to starve to death. This would kill any insects which ingest these seeds – by destroying the insects' digestive systems or exploding their stomachs or intestines.

However, the results were not as safe as originally hoped. "Unlike mice fed on a diet of wild-type peas (lacking the a-amylase inhibitor) or bean (containing the native inhibitor), animals that had previously ingested transgenic peas exhibited elevated levels of antigen-specific IgG1 in serum[1], enhanced delayed-type hypersensitivity responses in skin and increased reactivity to other food antigens."

It appears (once again) that it was not necessarily the toxin itself, but the *genetic engineering process* which may have created health issues. The reason is the same:

> There is no way to evaluate what *internal* damage is done to seeds when the GMO process inserts/blasts alternative DNA into a seed.

Peas are a major business in Australia, worth over AU$100 ($88) million per year at the time of this study, and there was a need to find a GM crop which would deal with infestations of the pea weevil (*Bruchus pisorum*). However, the possible negative side effects were judged too great to continue the   project. [1]

Since the project was discontinued, there were no further (reported) studies to test the reactions which could lead to human health problems. Whether similar immune problems, allergy issues, or other maladies would affect people remains an open question.

Nevertheless, the first GMO pea experiments produced toxic results.

[1] An 'antigen' is any substance that causes your immune system to produce antibodies against it. An antigen could be a bacterium formed inside of the body, or a foreign substance such as chemicals, pollen, viruses or bacteria. Anything which elevates the antigens can have negative effects on the immune system and trigger an immune reaction.

[1]   http://www.nature.com/nbt/journal/v24/n1/full/nbt0106-2.html

---

POTATOES

Chemically-Created GMO Potatoes May Become Part of the 'Fast Food' Industry.

As of 2013 another company is attempting to reintroduce GMO potatoes into the food chain. The company is J.R. Simplot Company, which has generated billions of dollars of revenue over the decades by selling frozen French fries to McDonald's and the other fast-food companies. Like other *chemical* companies that produce GMO 'food products,' Simplot is in the *chemical* business: It produces fertilizer for agriculture.

The US Department of Agriculture has been reviewing a petition from Simplot to sell another variation of genetically modified potatoes. Slipping GMO potatoes into the fast-food market appears to be a back-door strategy to begin marketing this new GMO 'food product' into the food chain.

McDonald's sells 9 Million pounds of French fries to the world every day! Perhaps GMO 'potatoes' will be coming to a McDonald's near you. If so, MacDonald's may face another legal action from Professor John Banzhaf of the George Washington University Law School who initiated the law suits against the tobacco industry, and had a previous legal victory over MacDonald's for its claim that its French fries were cooked in "100% Pure Vegetable Oil." [1]

As Dr. Pusztai pointed out over a decade ago, the toxicity appears to come from the *GMO process* itself. Since there is unknown internal damage to food seeds by forcefully inserting GMO components into them – and unknown synergistic reactions among the various toxic chemicals involved, and how they interact – the repercussions on human health cannot even be effectively evaluated and quantified.

This conclusion was reiterated by Bill Freese, a policy analyst for the Center for Food Safety:

"The biotech approach is to change the food on a genetic level in quite frankly risky ways with inadequate regulation to adapt a crop to an industrial food system that's really unhealthy in so many ways." [2]

The future may involve adding even more chemically-created 'food products' to the fast-food industry's diet… so poison can be ingested more rapidly!

[1] http://www.prlog.org/11638180-law-suit-over-natural-foods-follows-multi-million-dollar-victory-over-mcdonalds.html
[2] http://truthstreammedia.com/gmo-potatoes-coming-soon-to-a-mcdonalds-near-you-2/

RICE

'Rice' (from Sanskrit 'vrihi-s', 'rice') is believed to have originated in China over 10,000 years ago, and is the second most widespread food crop in the world (after maize).

GMO Rice Could Dominate and Destroy Regular Rice Crops.

There are no long-term studies on the health consequences of consuming GMO rice.

The first two varieties of GMO herbicide-resistant rice were created in 2000, and approved in the United States. During the next several years a number of varieties were approved in several other countries. These various types of herbicide-resistant rice have different names: Monsanto's GMO rice is called "Roundup Ready rice"; Bayer's is called "LibertyLink"; and Bayer is working on another variety. However, so far there has been no major commercialization of any of them.

A form of GMO rice has been created which its inventor, Ingo Potrykus, calls 'golden rice.' He claims that it will help prevent blindness and death in children by providing up to 60% of the Vitamin A they require on a daily basis. (Rice is known for having only small amounts of iron and Vitamin A). In 2005 the chemical company Syngenta took the next step and replaced one of the genes which creates an enzyme called *phytoene synthase* with a gene from maize. The claim is that it produces 20 times more beta carotene, which combines with another molecule to create Vitamin A. [1]

Asian countries, led by China, are attempting to breed different varieties of GMO rice. Again, there is not a widespread commercialization of GMO rice compared to the spread of other GMO crops. There are also no long-term studies as to the health consequences of the varieties of GMO rice.

―――――――――

"If the EPSP-synthase gene [GMO gene] gets into the wild rice species, their genetic diversity, which is really important to conserve, could be threatened because the genotype with the transgene would outcompete the normal species."

This issue was reviewed in the August 16, 2013 issue of *nature - International weekly journal of science* by Jane Qiu in an article entitled, *'Genetically modified crops pass benefits to weeds.'*

Dr. Brian Ford-Lloyd, a plant geneticist at the University of Birmingham, in the ***United Kingdom***, explained the findings of a recent study:

"This is one of the most clear examples of extremely plausible damaging effects [of GM crops] on the environment."

"If the EPSP-synthase gene [GMO gene] gets into the wild rice species, their genetic diversity, which is really important to conserve, could be threatened because the genotype with the transgene would outcompete the normal species."

Dr. Ford-Lloyd's concern was triggered by the conclusion of research done by Dr. Lu Baorong, an ecologist at Fudan University in Shanhai, **China**, which showed that if the GMO genes are spread into the wild (by the wind or through various methods of pollination), the ability of these now-genetically modified wild crops to resist certain pests would be enhanced. The invading pests would then focus their attack on the normal (weaker) rice crops of farmers, and destroy them. This would upset traditional rice farming throughout China. It would have serious repercussions for farmers around the globe.

In his own review of this Chinese study, Dr. Norman Ellstrand, a plant geneticist at the University of California, Riverside *(USA)* commented that the "traditional expectation" that this development would not occur is now challenged. He concludes, "… the study shows that novel products still need more careful evaluation." [2]

The chemical industry has consistently assured farmers and governments around the world that this kind of spread of GMO seeds into the atmosphere and onto neighboring farmlands would never occur. But it continues to happen.

[1] http://www.slate.com/articles/health_and_science/new_scientist/2013/10/golden_rice_inventor_ingo_potrykus_greenpeace_and_others_wicked_for_opposition.html
[2] http://www.nature.com/news/genetically-modified-crops-pass-benefits-to-weeds-1.13517

SOY

GMO Soy and the Health of Babies

"Genetically engineered foods contain new proteins that children have not been previously exposed to. I believe this may be responsible in part for the profound increase in allergies and immune dysfunction that I am witnessing."

That's the warning of Dr. Michelle Perro, pediatrician at the Institute for Health and Healing, in California, (*USA*), one of 'America's Top Physicians' for 5 consecutive years.

Dr. Vyvyan Howard, professor of Bio Imaging and Toxic Pathology, University of Ulster, Londonderry, *Ireland*, explains,

> "Swapping genes between organisms can produce unknown toxic effects and allergies that are most likely to affect children."

The Institute for Responsible Technology also warns,

> "Numerous doctors and medical organizations say, 'Stop eating GMOs, and especially stop feeding them to children, who are most at risk." [1]

According to the US Department of Agriculture, in 2013 over 93% of all soy bean grown in the United States were GMO. [2]

> YET: *GMO soy is a major ingredient in baby food*!

"… it appears that in the genetic engineering of soy, a soy allergen was created that is 41% identical to a known peanut allergen, ara h 3. This new allergen, now found in soy, is recognized by 44% of peanut allergic individuals."

That's one of the observations by the Allergy Kids Foundation, which also points out that "recent studies out of the University of London *(England)* conducted by Gideon Lack support this undisclosed research and highlight the role that conventional soy (and soy

255

formula) play in the development of the peanut allergy." That point out that,

"As a result of these studies, the British Dietetic Association advises parents to avoid exposing infants under the age of one to soy." [3]

[1]   http://responsibletechnology.org/docs/BabyFoodCampaignBroch.pdf
[2]   http://www.ers.usda.gov/data-products/adoption-of-genetically-engineered-crops-in-the-us/recent-trends-in-ge-adoption.aspx#.UmWeYXC2Zv4
[3]   http://www.allergykids.com/defining-food-allergies/soys-role-in-peanut-allergy/

SUGAR BEETS

'Sugar' (from Arabic 'sukkar' or Persian 'shakar' or Sanskrit 'sharkara') is a plant which apparently originated in India. Botanically called 'Beta vulgaris,' it is cultivated largely because it has a high concentration of sucrose in its roots.

"They only offer risk."

That's how Andrew Kimbrell, executive director of the Center for Food Safety, referred to GMO sugar beets in an article in the on-line publication *Rodale News (USA)*.

Referring to a 2011 decision by the US Department of Agriculture (USDA) to approve the planting and sale of genetically modified sugar beets without the completion of an environmental impact study (EIS), he warned,

> "They're going by the seat of their pants. They've never, ever done this before."

One of the environmental issues is that sugar beets are wind-pollinated crops – so they contaminate other crops. Also, sugar beets are related to weeds; so they can become herbicide resistant – like the 'super-weeds' which are being created and becoming immune to herbicides by the exposure to *glyphosate* (Roundup).

The sugar beet, called *Beta vulgaris*, is responsible for approximately 20% of the world's sugar production; sugar cane produces the balance. Sugar is created through the *photosynthesis* process in the leaves, and then stored in the root. The root of the plant contains a high concentration of sucrose, which is used globally as a sweetener.

Although the US is one of the principal producers of sugar, it still imports approximately 15% of the sugar consumed by its population. (There are strict import tariffs on imported sugar.) According to the chief scientist at Consumer Union, Michael Hanson, PhD, of the domestically produced sugar in the US, approximately 54% is produced by the sugar beet and the other 46% from sugar cane.

The US sugar industry is heavily subsidized. "Currently, the government has plans to pump $1.4 Billion into the sugar industry between 2008 and 2017." [1]

In addition to the specific concerns regarding GMO sugar beets, there are the general concerns over GMO 'food products':

- How much *glyphosate* are the GMO seeds absorbing, and passing into the food supply? And into animal feed?

- How do the toxins which are inserted/blasted into the GMO seeds affect humans who eat them?

- Inserting/blasting 'foreign' DNA into the seeds causes a disruption of the internal dynamics of the seeds, with unknown consequences.

- The *genetically engineering process* and *the synergy of the combination of toxins* are known to create unpredictable and uncontrollable effects on those who ingest the GMO 'food products,' whether humans or animals.

As of 2011, over 90% of the sugar beet acres planted in the U.S. are GMO!

[1]   http://www.rodalenews.com/genetically-engineered-sugar-beets-0

TOMATOES

*'Tomato' (from the Spanish, in Mexico, 'tomate' from the Nahuatal
Uto-Aztecan 'tomana' meaning 'to swell') was called "the swelling
fruit" and was cultivated in Mexico prior to 500 BC. It was 'brought
out' of Mexico in the 16th century.*

———————

**"The type of stomach lesions linked to tomatoes could lead to
life-endangering hemorrhage, particularly in the elderly who
use aspirin to prevent blood clots."**

That's one of the observations in a review in ***India*** of a number of
studies on GMO 'food products.'

This discussion was on the first genetically engineered 'food product.'
It was the tomato, created by Calgene and called the 'Flavor Savor
Tomato.' In 1987 the scientists in the Calgene laboratories identified
and cloned a tomato fruit enzyme *polygalacturonase* (PG gene) with
antisense DNA instructions for the purpose of slowing the process of
ripening, and by 1992 it was considered ready.

In 1994, with its usual corporate acquiescence, the FDA approved it
by saying that it's "… as safe as tomatoes bred by conventional
means."

Despite the FDA's official assurances of the safety of the first GMO
crop, later analysis revealed that,

"Out of 20 female rats fed the GM tomato, 7 developed stomach
lesions." [1]

———————

"There was very little flavor to save."

Part of the objective of this genetically engineered tomato was to
prevent softening and rotting.

Although approved for sale in 1994 by the FDA, the product was
taken off the market because it was too delicate to transport.
Apparently the taste was also an issue. A professor of horticulture at

Cornell University, *(USA)*, Christ Watkins, said, "There was very little flavor to save." [2]

As a product, the genetically engineered tomato did not initially survive the long shelf life which was intended – but the research led to other GMO 'food products.'

In 1996 Calgene was acquired by Monsanto and began greater research into GMO vegetable oils, including canola and cottonseed.

Perhaps the GMO tomato will return. An article by J.D. Heyes in the July 31, 2013 issue of the on-line journal *Natural News.com* discusses an attempt to reintroduce GMO tomatoes, an effort being led by University of California, Los Angeles (UCLA) professor Alan Fogleman. The current focus is to grow GMO tomatoes which produce a peptide [amino acid compound] that could mimic the HD cholesterol (the good cholesterol) in order to reduce heart disease.

Fogleman and his UCLA team fed mice a diet of tomatoes which had been genetically engineered to produce 6F, a small peptide which mimics the main protein (ApoA-1) of HDL, the 'good cholesterol.' The objective is to reduce the plaque build-up in arteries (atherosclerosis) and reduce heart disease.

The short-term effects seem to be positive; but, as usual, there have been no long-term studies to determine the ultimate repercussions of chemically altering the body's natural process. So, even if such an effort appears to be successful, no one can begin to predict what the negative side effects might be. As the article points out:

Short-term studies don't disclose the long-term consequences of eating GMO 'food products.' Short-term gratification often has bad long-term consequences. [3]

[1] http://www.academia.edu/542384/A_Review_on_Impacts_of_Geneticall y_Modified_Food_on_Human_Health
[2] http://www.mnn.com/green-tech/research-innovations/photos/12-bizarre-examples-of-genetic-engineering/flavr-savr-tomato#
[3] http://www.naturalnews.com/041418_tomatoes_gmos_groceries.html

ZUCCHINI

'Zucchini' (from the Italian 'zucchino,' a diminutive of 'zucca' meaning 'gourd, squash') is botanically a fruit, but in the culinary community it is usually regarded as a vegetable. It is regarded as a summer squash from the Cucurbita pepo species, like the pumpkin and other squashes.

Monsanto's problem in trying to sell GMO squash seeds is that when squashes are infected by a viral disease, they are often affected by several different ones at the same time.

In 1995 one of Monsanto's seed brands, Asgrow Seed Co., genetically engineered a yellow squash which was resistant to zucchini yellow mosaic virus and watermelon mottle virus 2; in 1996 they transferred the GE virus-resistance from the yellow squash to zucchini by conventional breeding (yellow squash and zucchini are the same species). In 1997 Asgrow genetically engineered its GMO squash to resist another virus, cucumber mosaic virus.

Monsanto has had a problem in selling these seeds, because when squashes are infected by a viral disease, they are often infected by several viral diseases at once. So the farmer must continue to spend money to control various diseases which may develop. Monsanto could not keep up with the number of disease-resistant genes which have to be inserted into the squash and zucchini seeds to combat these diseases.

So this particular GMO seed has not yet become sufficiently profitable to sell to farmers. [1]

[1] https://scholarworks.iupui.edu/bitstream/handle/1805/813/GE%20plant%20virus%20resistance.pdf

ANIMALS, INSECTS, and FISH

COWS

Toxic GMO Crops are Fed to Farm Animals

"How Pervasive are GMOs in Animal Feed?"

That's the heading of a July 16, 2013 article by Ryan Beville in the blog of GMOiNSiDE.org entitled *'WE HAVE A RIGHT TO KNOW WHAT'S IN OUR FOOD!' (USA)*

In addition to the 'bovine growth hormones' in cows – the GMO industry provides the feed for the nation's livestock. This includes dairy cows, beef cattle, pigs, sheep, goats, poultry, fish, and rabbits – all of which are fed GMO corn.

"In the U.S., livestock has been fed genetically engineered crops since these crops were first introduced in 1996 and each of the top 6 GMO crops (soy, cotton, corn, canola, sugar beet, and alfalfa) are heavily utilized by the U.S. and global animal feed market."

The article points out that commercial animal feed comes directly from harvested crops... and it comes from the leftovers of 'processed' crops. Currently 88% of all corn and 94% of all soybeans are genetically modified. And,

"98% of this [GMO] soy and 79.5% of this [GMO] corn goes directly into feeding animals and fueling cars in the U.S."

GMO cotton, and the various parts of the GMO cotton crop, are also ingredients for animal feed – as well as for some human foods.

One of the most widely used sources of protein in animal feed for livestock, poultry, and fish, is Canola meal. In the U.S. 90% of the canola crop is genetically modified, and in Canada 97.5% is genetically modified.

The U.S. is the world's largest purchaser of canola oil and meal for animal feed.

GM alfalfa was approved in 2011, and now dairy cows are the primary consumers of alfalfa hay … including the cows that are also being injected with another GMO chemical, the 'bovine growth hormone' (rBGH). [1]

Toxin-filled GMO crops are now widespread in animal feed.

So, are cows now being poisoned in two (2) different ways: by the rBGH injections they receive, and by the GMO feed they eat?

What does that do to the meat we eat and to the milk we drink?

"Bovine Growth Hormone: Milk does nobody good…"

That's the title of an article by Mike Ewall, the founder of the Energy Justice Network *(USA)*.

In the paragraph called "Pus" he refers to Monsanto's own label on POSILAC, the brand name for rBGH, which was originally developed and marketed by Monsanto in 1994. The warning label for the cows says,

"Cows injected with POSILAC are at an increased risk for clinical mastitis (visibly abnormal milk). The number of cows affected with clinical mastitis and the number of cases per cow may increase … In some herds, use of POSILAC has been associated with increases in somatic cell counts [pus and bacteria]."

The warning label includes additional issues, such as

"use of POSILAC *[bovine growth hormone]* may result in digestive disorders such as indigestion, bloat, and diarrhea…" [2]

Yet, this was formally approved by the FDA and sold to the public.

[1] http://gmoinside.org/gmos-in-animal-feed/
[2] http://www.ejnet.org/bgh/nogood.html

FISH

"Frankenfish on the Menu? FDA Gives Initial Approval"

That's the title of an on-line article in *livescience (USA)* on December 26, 2012 by Marc Lallanilla discussing how the Food and Drug Administration (FDA) has now given preliminary approval to a genetically modified Atlantic salmon which the biotech developers call 'AquAdvantage.'

A Massachusetts company called AquaBounty is genetically modifying Atlantic salmon, "with DNA material from a Chinook salmon and an eel-like species called an ocean pout. These genes cause the fish to grow twice as fast as wild salmon, according to the British newspaper *The Telegraph*..." (The link below shows the difference between the GMO fish and a natural fish.) [1]

The gene taken from the Chinook salmon was a growth hormone; and the gene taken from the ocean pout was a 'genetic switch.' This genetic modification allows the resultant fish to grow during the entire year, not merely during the usual warm summer months.

The fish grow to full size in half the standard time of 3 years that it takes a wild Atlantic salmon to grow in nature.

Apart from the environmental dangers, there are potential perils for humans who ingest genetically modified fish. One of the immediate dangers is that no labeling is required on these GMO fish and whatever 'fish products' are derived from them. So consumers will not know if they are buying (and eating) natural fish or chemically-created GMO 'fish products.'

Among the various potential dangers to humans is one claimed by the Organic Consumers Union:

"... AquAdvantage contains elevated levels of the growth hormone IGF-1, which is linked to prostrate, breast, and colon cancers."

Another peril is pointed out by the research analyst Nina Mak with the American Anti-Vivisection Society *(USA)* who warns that,

"The AquAdvantage salmon studies, by their very design, underreport or fail to detect health problems and abnormalities in the fish… Yet we know that genetic engineering is fraught with failures and unintended consequences." [2]

———————

In a separate development, back in 2010, a transgenic (genetically modified) trout created by an aquaculture professor at the University of Rhodes Island, Terry Bradley, can develop a muscle mass 15-20% larger than the average trout. Professor Bradley led a team which injected 20,000 rainbow trout eggs with a variety of DNA types which were designed to inhibit *myostatin*. *Myostatin* is a protein which slows down the muscle growth; and the professor wanted to accelerate the muscle growth. Accelerating the muscle growth is one of the genetic engineering techniques which make the fish bigger and stronger, and leads to the issues described above.

Two pieces of DNA are involved: "One, taken from the relative of the cod called the ocean pout, promotes the activity of the gene that encodes growth hormone. The other, taken from a Chinook salmon, is a version of the growth-hormone gene itself." When these two are put together, "The result is a fish that reaches marketable size in 18-24 months, as opposed to 30 months for the normal variety." [3]

Applying basic logic, many scientists assume that these GMO fish will not have time to properly develop and mature as they have done for millions of years of evolution. So, among the questions are 'how much nutrition do they lack, which will also be lacking in the 'food products' that they become?' and 'what alterations occur in their behavior?'

Because of their increased size (and modified behavior?) the accelerated-growth fish have been shown to dominate. Thus, natural fish will not be able to compete with chemically-created man-made fish.

And, we do not know what characteristics will evolve in those 'Franken-fish.'

"Freshwater mussels have been found to be acutely sensitive to pure glyphosate, surfactant ingredients and to the glyphosate – containing herbicide Roundup. Freshwater carp showed changes to liver cells and mitochondria (parts of all cells) after exposure to Roundup herbicide at levels 20 and 40 times lower than would be expected from normal agricultural practice."

That was part of a June 2013 publication by Friends of the Earth Europe in which they summarize various studies performed by different scientific groups in the ***European Union***. The publication was entitled *'The environmental impacts of glyphosate.'*

In addition to the genetic engineering of fish, the use of Roundup and the amount and spread of *glyphosate* in the water supply has increased, including in streams, rivers, and groundwater (drinking water). It is now affecting fish, frogs, toads, tadpoles, and other amphibians. [4]

So, fish and 'fish products' are being affected by attempts to genetically engineer their growth, and by being exposed to the continuous increase of *glyphosate* which is poisoning the water supplies of the world.

[1] http://www.livescience.com/25799-frankenfish-salmon-gmo.html
[2] http://news.msn.com/science-technology/gmo-salmon-debate-frankenfish-or-wunderfish
[3] http://www.economist.com/node/16295564
[4] http://www.foeeurope.org/sites/default/files/press_releases/foee_5_environmental_impacts_glyphosate.pdf

---

INSECTS

"GMO multi-toxin crops continue to backfire as more insects become resistant to crop chemicals"

That's the title of an article by Ethan A. Huff in the April 29, 2013 issue of *Natural News.com.*

Summarizing research performed by the University of Arizona College of Agriculture and Life Sciences *(USA)*, an article published in the *Proceedings of the National Academy of Sciences* reports that:

"Promises made by the biotechnology industry about the alleged robustness of its genetically modified (GM) crops are proving to be false …"

The research reveals that pests are developing a growing resistance to multi-toxin GMO crops. The study evaluated a variety of toxins which are inserted into the seeds, including *Bacillus thuringiensis* (*Bt*), focusing on GMO corn and GMO cotton.

It turns out that the pests are outsmarting the Monsanto scientists, as the pests are developing immunity to these multi-toxins.

"In fact, the pest response to multi-toxin GMOs is so complex and unpredictable that it [the multi-toxin combination] is already shaping up to be a complete failure."

Even worse, *Monsanto's latest GMO technique of inserting a variety of toxins into a single crop has strengthened the resistance of pests to toxins.* This could make the spread of pests even worse for farmers, since the pests are now immune to some of these poisons.

In addition, previous research by the Arizona College already revealed that western corn rootworm beetles are also developing a resistance to multi-toxin GMO crops. [1]

———————

"Monsanto Corn May Be Failing to Kill Bugs in 4 States, EPA Says"

That's the headline in a December 6, 2011 article in *Bloomberg Businessweek.com* by Jack Kaskey.

The EPA report discussed was partially based on a July 2011 Iowa State University *(USA)* study which showed that rootworms had developed an evolved resistance to the insect-killing *Bacillus thuringiensis* (*Bt*) in GMO crops.

The study pertained to the severe damage done to crops by pests, pests which had developed a tolerance of the plants' insecticide. The *Bt* insecticide in the GMO crops was unable to stop the damage from the pests – in several states.

Business Week quotes an internal document of the EPA:

"Resistance is suspected in at least some portions of four states in which 'unexpected damage' reports originated." [2]

While containing toxins that have been proven to be harmful to animals and humans, the GMO crops are now losing their ability to protect the crops from pests.

[1] http://www.naturalnews.com/040120_gm_crops_monsanto_chemical_re
sistance.html
[2] http://www.businessweek.com/news/2011-12-06/monsanto-corn-may-
be-failing-to-kill-bugs-in-4-states-epa-says.html

PETS

GMO Foods Are Toxic to Pets

"Pet Food Perils -- Lurking GMOs May Hurt Our Pets"

This was the headline of a July 2013 article on the on-line journal *Natural Awakenings* by Dr. Michael W. Fox, a veterinarian with doctoral degrees in medicine and animal behavior *(USA)*. The summary of the article was:

"In the mid-1990s, as genetically engineered or modified (GE, GM, or GMO) corn and soy were becoming increasingly prominent ingredients in both pet food products and feed for farm animals, the number of dogs reported suffering from a specific cluster of health problems increased."

Dr. Fox revealed that veterinarians and dog owners reported such problems occurred more often among dogs that ate pet food containing GM crops.

The medical issues most often cited were allergies, asthma, atopic (severe) dermatitis and other skin problems, irritable bowel syndrome, leaky gut syndrome, inflammatory bowel disease, colitis, recurrent diarrhea, vomiting and indigestion, as well as abnormalities in the liver, pancreas, and immune system functions.

Dr. Fox referenced a 2011 study in the journal *Cell Research* which claimed that novel proteins are created in the genetically engineering process that attack the immune system and cause allergies "especially in the mothers of offspring fed GMO foods."

He also mentioned the common complaint that there is "diminished nutrient content" in GMO foods – a theme which constantly arises when discussing GMO crops. Thus the animals may suffer from malnutrition, with a variety of consequences. [1]

––––––––––––

'The Dangers of Genetically Modified Ingredients in Pet Food'

That was the title of another article, authored by the integrative veterinarian, Dr. Karen Becker, and published November 12, 2012 in the on-line journal *Healthy Pets* by *Mercola.com*.

In this article Dr. Karen Becker *(USA)* discusses a variety of animal studies conducted around the world – all of which revealed serious medical and biological issues for those animals that were fed a diet of GMO foods.

One of the animal studies which Dr. Becker cites was conducted in 2009 by two research scientists from the Department of Forensic Medicine and Toxicology at the University of Athens Medical School *(Greece)*, Artemis Dona and Ioannis S. Arvanitoyannis.

The Greek research scientists conclude:

"The results of most of the rather few studies conducted with GM foods indicate that they may cause hepatic, pancreatic, renal and reproductive effects and may alter hematological, biochemical and immunologic parameters the significance of which remains unknown."

"The above results indicate that many GM foods have some common toxic effects." [2]

SUMMARY: Research continually demonstrates that pet food products containing GMO ingredients are harmful to pets.

[1] http://www.naturalawakeningsmag.com/Natural-Awakenings/July-2013/Pet-Food-Perils/

[2] http://healthypets.mercola.com/sites/healthypets/archive/2012/11/14/genetically-modified-corn.aspx

DRAMATIC INCREASE
in USAGE of
HERBICIDES/PESTICIDES

GMO Crops Expand – Not Reduce – the Use of Herbicides/Pesticides

---

"Monsanto defeated by Roundup Resistant Weeds"

That's the title of an article by the Institute of Science in Society from a report on November 28, 2011 by Dr. Eva Sirinathsinghji.

The article summarizes the situation:

> "Monsanto is surrendering to glyphosate weeds...They are spreading at exponential rates in US farms and are increasingly documented in Australia, Argentina, Brazil, Chile, Europe, and South Africa. "

Resistance to *glyphosate* has been shown to develop as a result of the increasing large-scale use of Monsanto pesticides, particularly Roundup. When the article was written in 2011, resistant weeds already covered over "4.5 million hectares [11,115,000 acres] in the US alone, while world-wide coverage is thought to have reached 120 million hectares [296,520,000 acres] by 2010...The US has the worst problem, with 13 different species in 73 different locations."

Explaining how Monsanto described the situation as recently as 2007 as "manageable," by 2009...

> "Sixteen glyphosate-resistant species had already developed by this point, many of which could not be killed or even uprooted by combine harvesters due to their size and strength."

Among Monsanto's "solutions" are:

- to have 'pesticide cocktails' of various pesticides combined, and in increasing amounts

- to add more chemicals to the GMO seeds to enable these seeds to *absorb* more pesticides which are sprayed on the neighboring weeds. [1]

Of course, these new GMO seeds with additional chemicals are the ones which produce the 'food products' we eat.

"Contrary to claims made by the chemical industries, glyphosate use increased 6,504% from 1991 to 2010 according to data from the USDA: National Agricultural Statistics Service (NASS)."

This was part of a report by N.L. Swanson in an article entitled, *'GMO Crops Increase Pesticide Use'* which was published in the September 2013 issue of the on-line journal *Farm Wars. (USA)*

The article, including charts and graphs, pointed out:

"In a 2011 study by the U.S. Geological Survey, glyphosate was frequently detected in water, rain, and air in the Mississippi basin… Because glyphosate is in our air, water and food, we are likely accumulating low doses over time."

It adds, "Glyphosate residues of up to 4.4 mg/kg have been detected in stems, leaves, and beans of glyphosate-resistant soy, indicating metabolism of the herbicide."

"This means that the Roundup Ready plants are absorbing the herbicide and you cannot simply wash it off."   [2]

"Superweeds: How Biotech Crops Bolster the Pesticide Industry"

That's the title of an article on July 1, 2013 in the on-line journal *food and water watch* which discusses how Food & Water Watch examined studies by the U.S. Department of Agriculture (USDA) and the U.S. Environmental Protection Agency (EPA) when documenting the increased use of herbicides. *(USA)*

"Food & Water Watch evaluated data from the International Survey of Herbicide Resistant Weeds that reveal burgeoning herbicide-resistant weeds caused by the over-reliance on glyphosate for broad control of weeds."

Among many of the continuing promises of the chemical industry is that GMO crops will increase crop yields, lower the operating costs of farmers around the world, and reduce the environmental impact of farmers who use insecticides and pesticides on their fields.

"Yet nearly 20 years after their introduction, genetically engineered crops have not provided the benefits promised by the companies that patented them."

Food & Water Watch has a video to discuss this issue, and the ramifications. [3]

"The end result will be to starve people in Africa and feed corporations in the US and Europe."

That's the conclusion of a September 2013 article by 'Food Sovereignty Ghana' *(Ghana)* in the on-line publication *MG Modern Ghana.* The article is entitled, *'Why Is Kofi Annan Fronting For Monsanto? The GMO Assault On Africa By Crossed Crocodiles.'* *('Crossed Crocodiles' is a blog in Africa.)*

The article announces:

"Kofi Annan has joined with President Obama, Monsanto, AGRA, and the Gates foundation to promote and execute food aid that replaces bags of wheat, rice and corn (agricultural dumping) with bags of pesticides, herbicides, chemical fertilizers and genetically engineered seeds. The end result will be to starve people in Africa and feed corporations in the US and Europe."

AGRA ('Alliance for a Green Revolution in Africa') is the latest public relations flagship for spreading Monsanto's GMO seeds into Africa. The Chairman of the Board and one of AGRA's leading spokesmen is Kofi Annan, the former Secretary General of the United Nations.

The article points out that, "Under the guise of 'sustainability' the [Gates] Foundation is spearheading a multi-billion dollar effort to transform Africa into a GMO-friendly continent."

Since many of Monsanto's GMO 'food products' are banned by countries in Europe, Monsanto is focusing on less sophisticated markets… with "foreign aid" money from the United States government paying for this "food aid."

Some of the known participants are Barack Obama, Bill & Melinda Gates Foundation, Howard G. Buffett Foundation, and leading African and government officials and diplomats. Although the financial involvement of most participants is unknown, among the known investors is the Gates Foundation which purchased 500,000 shares of Monsanto for approximately $23.1 million.

According to the article,
  "Family farmers, who produce 75% of the world's food, will gradually be displaced, driven off their land, and the land will be poisoned and ruined. There will be less food, less healthy food. More people will starve, while more corporations will get fat." [4]

Part of the current Monsanto project in Africa is the Water Efficient Maize for Africa (WEMA) project. This project is part of Monsanto's response to the failure of its MON810 maize in South Africa. After that South African failure was recently revealed (October 2013), Monsanto and its government and financial supporters decided to export their seeds to the less sophisticated sub-Saharan African countries.

––––––––––

"…it will destroy the diversity, the local knowledge and the sustainable agricultural systems that our farmers have developed for millennia and that it will thus undermine our capacity to feed ourselves."

That's how an earlier Monsanto project in Africa was described.

The current WEMA project follows an earlier attempt (1998) by Monsanto called 'Let the Harvest Begin' – which Monsanto and its allies also promoted as "helping Africa." As this previous project proceeded, except for South Africa at the time ALL of the African delegates to the United Nations' Food & Agriculture Organization negotiations on the 'International Undertaking for Plant Genetic Resources' opposed this project as commercial exploitation of Africa, saying,

"…this campaign gives a totally distorted and misleading picture of the potential of genetic engineering to feed developing countries." [5]

Now, even South Africa has joined the other nations of Africa in condemning Monsanto's GMO crops.

Now, Monsanto provides a new set of promises to "help Africa." So, "with a sleight of hand," Monsanto is dumping its "defective MON810 maize" onto the countries of sub-Saharan Africa.

[1] http://www.i-sis.org.uk/Monsanto_defeated_by_herbicide_resistant_superweeds.php
[2] http://farmwars.info/?p=11515
[3] http://www.foodandwaterwatch.org/reports/superweeds/
[4] http://www.modernghana.com/news/488639/1/why-is-kofi-annan-fronting-for-monsa.html
[5] http://www.orpheusweb.co.uk/john.rose/africa.html

ENVIRONMENTAL CONTAMINATION

GMOs Contaminate Soil, Air and Water for Bacteria, Insects, Animals – and Humans

AIR and WIND CONTAMINATION

"Argentina's Genetically Engineered Hell"

That's the headline of an October 22, 2013 article in the online publication of *gmeducation.org.*

The article, like many similar articles during the past decade, discusses the massive increases in the use of pesticides because of the creation of anti-toxic resistant GMO crops. A major part of the problem is that the winds spread these poisons, through the air into schools and homes, and into the water supplies.

One case cited was Sofia Gatica who lost her new-born son to kidney failure, and eventually won a court fight which resulted in Argentina's first criminal conviction for illegal spraying. By this legal victory in **Argentina**, and the professional medical testimony required, the court confirmed that these poisons were responsible for her son's death.

Doctors warn of the health consequences to over 12 million people who live in Argentina's farm belt who are exposed to excessive spraying of pesticides, largely spraying GMO soy crops. The report says,

> "A government study there found alarming levels of agrochemical contamination in the soil and drinking water, and 80 percent of the children surveyed carried traces of pesticide in their blood."

GMO technology and the associated herbicide and pesticides poisons have made Argentina into the world's third largest producer of soybeans. But those herbicides and pesticides are being carried by the winds around the country.

"The Associated Press documented dozens of cases around the country where poisons are applied ... [and] the spray drifts into schools and homes and settles over water sources..."

An Associated Press analysis of official data revealed that pesticide use expanded from 9 million gallons in 1990 to over 84 million gallons today "as pests become resistant to the poisons." This continual increase in the expansion of these toxins has unpredictable human consequences.

Dr. Andres Carrasco, molecular biologist from the University of Buenos Aires *(Argentina)* discovered that injecting

a low dose of *glyphosate* into embryos can alter the levels of retinoic acid[1].

This resulted in spinal defects in frogs and chickens similar to those observed in the farming areas where large amounts of pesticides are in use. [1]

[Note: Sofia Gatica has since become an anti-Monsanto protestor. In that context she has received many threats, including death threats, as reported in a November 20, 2013 article in *GMWatch.* [2] She was also recently assaulted.]

[1] *Retinoic acid is a nutrient created in the body from Vitamin A, and it aids the growth and development of cells, especially in the embryo.*

"GM Soy: The invisible ingredient 'poisoning' children"

That's the title of a May 2, 2011 article by Louise Gray in the *United Kingdom* on-line publication of *The Telegraph* describing the wind-blown spread of poison in Paraguay due to the expanded use of pesticides for anti-toxic GMO crops.

Part of the discussion pertains to Petrona Villasbona, a mother of eight children, whose 11 year old son Silvino was subjected to the pesticides sprayed on the crops. Silvino complained to his mother, who took him to the hospital. Within hours, after bouts of pain and paralysis, he died. After years of campaigning, Petrona Villasbona was able to get the matter into court, where the farmers involved were convicted of murder. It remains unclear if the farmers were ever sent to jail. However, by virtue of the conviction, and the required medical evidence by those testifying, the court in *Paraguay* validated that the poisonous death of Silvino was caused by the GMO crops and the related pesticides.

The article discusses how Paraguay, "… ruled by despotic dictators for centuries, the country is famous for being a hot bed of drug smugglers, Nazi war criminals, and even al-Qaeda…" and "… is on the front line of the new craze for growing 'green gold'." [3]

Monsanto has been linked to the Paraguayan government, as discussed in a July 24, 2012 article by Ethan A. Huff in *Natural News*, entitled *"Monsanto Linked to Coup That Ousted Paraguayan President."* This article summarizes part of the issue of the domination by political dictators and large corporations:

> "Among these corporate influences was Monsanto, which over the years has converted much of Paraguay's arable land into plantations that grow GM crops." [4]

There have been many discussions of Monsanto's role in 'influencing' government officials around the world, including, of course, the United States, in order to foster the sale of their GMO seeds. As the above article references, these 'influencing techniques' are alleged to even include orchestrating elections in foreign countries.

The issue of poisoning the air by GMO crops and the *glyphosate* (Roundup) sprays that accompany them is widespread around the globe. Examples abound on all continents. In a multitude of cases it involves the direct poisoning of the air by the herbicide and pesticide sprays, particularly *glyphosate*. In other cases it involves poisoning the soil and the water, or the flora and fauna, the bacteria and insects, the birds and the bees.

> The fundamental question is 'How can we even quantify how much poison, and what kinds of poisons, the toxin-filled GMO crops are spreading into the atmosphere, the soil, and the water?'

"Farmers Continue to Fight Monsanto's 'Seed Police'"

That's the title of an article in the July 26, 2012 issue of *EcoNews* on *ecowatch.com (USA)*.

In addition to the poisons carried by the wind from the excessive use of pesticides for GMO crops, there is a related issue. The wind spreads the GMO seeds themselves onto neighboring farms.

Those neighboring farmers must then clean up the GMO seeds at their own expense, to prevent their crops from being contaminated by the toxin-filled GMO seeds. Even worse, if they don't clean up those GMO seeds, they will also have to make royalty payments to Monsanto if any of their next year's crops have become contaminated by the GMO seeds (since Monsanto has a patent on these seeds).

The number of legal cases brought by Monsanto against small farmers is multitude, in the U.S., Europe, India, Latin America, and elsewhere. Monsanto enforces payments by maintaining their own police force, 'seed police' who travel around the world looking for such incidents, then taking the often-unsuspecting farmers to court. Dan Ravicher of the Public Patent Foundation (PUBPAT) which represents the 'Organic Seed Growers and Trade Association' against Monsanto stated,

> "Monsanto is known for bullying farmers by making baseless accusations of patent infringement."

"Every year Monsanto investigates more than 500 farmers for patent infringement with their notorious 'seed police'."

As of July 2012, Monsanto has brought lawsuits against 144 farmers, and, in addition, forced over 700 other farmers to settle out of court for undisclosed sums of money. Since small farmers do not have the financial resources to face a giant like Monsanto in court, the farmers are usually forced to settle – and pay Monsanto money, and end up using Monsanto's seeds if they can't clean all of them up off their farms. This expands Monsanto's list of 'customers.'

Seed and pollen can drift, or be blown by the wind, up to 15 miles. Therefore, farmers who plant GMO seeds can inadvertently contaminate neighboring natural farms miles away. There have also been accusations, in the U.S., India, Paraguay, and elsewhere, that Monsanto and its allies have secretly spread the GMO seeds in order to create a basis for making legal   claims against farmers.

Many farmers have given up planting natural corn and soy, because their neighbors have GMO crops which could contaminate them. As a result, in addition to the spread of GMO crops, the national food supply of organic corn and soy is reduced further every year by natural farmers no longer willing to take the risk of planting healthy crops. [5]

IN SUMMARY, just as politicians, bureaucrats, and academicians are being intimidated and corrupted by the GMO chemical companies, now small farmers and organic farmers themselves are increasingly becoming the targets.

Thus, in addition to the environmental pollution from the toxin-filled GMO crops and their related pesticides, the entire global farm system is being contaminated by the GMO seeds.

[1] http://www.gmeducation.org/food-and-health/p216779-argentina-s-genetically-engineered-hell.html
[2] http://www.gmwatch.org/index.php/news/archive/2013/15174-protester-receives-death-threat-over-anti-monsanto-protest-in-argentina
[3] http://www.telegraph.co.uk/earth/earthnews/8391748/GM-soy-The-invisible-ingredient-poisoning-children.html
[4] http://readersupportednews.org/news-section2/318-66/12596-monsanto-linked-to-coup-that-ousted-paraguayan-president
[5] http://ecowatch.com/2012/07/06/monsantos-seed-police/

WEEDS (SUPER WEEDS)

"GMO CROPS CREATE SUPERWEEDS"

That's the title of an October 16, 2013 article by Gina-Marie Cheeseman in the on-line journal *naturally savvy (USA).* The article discusses the spread of super-weeds, unintentionally created by the GMO chemical industry, and reviews the report by Food & Water Watch.

Ms. Cheeseman points to some of the issues in the study, that there are currently 14 species of weed in the United States which are resistant to *glyphosate,* 24 weed species globally, and that,

"The estimates by the agriculture industry are that 61.2 million acres of cropland are infested with glyphosate resistant weeds. Over a quarter (27%) of U.S. farmers reported more than one *glyphosate* resistant weed species in their fields in 2012, almost twice as many as the year before."

Weed resistance is expanding, including *glyphosate*-resistant waterhemp which went from five states in 2008 to 12 states in 2012; *glyphosate*-resistant Palmer amaranth[1] was only reported in eight states in 2008, but in 17 states in 2012; and *glyphosate*-resistant horseweed jumped from 12 states in 2004 to 21 states in 2012.

It is expensive for farmers to deal with these increasingly *glyphosate*-resistant weeds. This means they must purchase more *glyphosate*!

The chemical industry increased its sales of crop protective toxins from $26 Billion in 2001 to $64 Billion in 2012, and 50% of those sales are herbicides.

Meanwhile, the GMO seed sales have increased from $115 Million in 1996 to $15 Billion in 2012 – an increase of 130 times! [1]

[1] *'Amaranth' (from Greek 'amarantos' meaning 'unfading' and 'anthos' meaning 'flower') is the genus of cosmopolitan annual or short-lived perennial plants which have been cultivated for over 8,000 years as a flower or grain.*

"Farmers making plans to dodge glyphosate resistance"

That's the headline of a December 3, 2013 article in *[A] AGRICULTURE.COM* by Jeff Caldwell, Multimedia Editor for *Agriculture.com* and *Successful Farming* magazine.

The article describes how the *glyphosate* resistant weeds have become a growing problem in 2013. Pointing to weed management specialist, Dallas Peterson, of Kansas State University Extension *(USA)*,

"A key factor in the development of resistant weeds appears to be frequent and exclusive use of glyphosate for weed killer."

What is professor Peterson's recommended solution? : "…to avoid exclusive use of glyphosate."

"The number of glyphosate-resistant weed species around the country is increasingly regularly, with states like Illinois and Kansas seeing as many as half a dozen resistant weeds." [2]

People are already talking about 'Franken-weeds.'

[1]   http://naturallysavvy.com/live/gmo-crops-create-superweeds
[2]   http://www.agriculture.com/news/crops/farmers-making-pls-to-dodge-glyphosate_2-ar35883

CONCLUSION

Genetically-Modified Organisms, GMOs, Have Been Demonstrated to be Toxic to the Environment, to Insects and Animals, to People – and to the Unborn.

This has been the conclusion of research studies involving hundreds of doctors and research scientists in at least **thirty (30) countries,** for the past twenty (20) years. We do not know how many other studies were performed which did not go through the rigorous process of being reported in 'Peer Review' medical journals, or were conducted by individual biologists and medical doctors.

Obviously, Monsanto, Syngenta, Dow, DuPont, Bayer, and the other chemical companies have done their own internal research. However, they will not provide any data which contradicts their marketing plans or discredits their public posture. Worse, they even refuse to allow food companies to label the contents of their GMO 'food products.'

Scientists Around the World Say: To eat or drink GMO 'food products' is to ingest poison!

The studies referenced in this *Handbook* represent only a portion of the research done on the subject of GMOs and rBGH. These particular studies have been conducted over many years by doctors and research scientists in universities and laboratories in **30** countries, on every continent except Antarctica (where, by the way, some scientists are experimenting with growing a form of winter wheat...)

What we now know is

- GMO crops are *scientifically created* to be poisonous... to insects, in particular.

- GMO crops are *scientifically created* to *absorb* the poison *glyphosate.*

- By ingesting the 'food products' from these GMO crops, these poisons *enter* the bodies and *remain* in the bodies, blood, and intestines of animals... and of humans – and multiply.

- The toxin-filled GMO seeds and their constant companion, *glyphosate* (Roundup), are poisoning the soil, air, and water, and creatures which dwell in them.

We also see from the above research studies the multitude of dangers involved in GMO 'food products' or in rBGH milk … or eating animals which have a diet of GMO feed stocks.

In the past, farmers produced a variety of different plants and animal species. Now our diets are dominated by two: corn and soybeans – either directly or through the thousands of ways in which corn and soy are in our 'food products', in drinks, in vegetable oils, in sweeteners, and in our baby foods. Over 85% of corn and soy are now GMO.

What we don't know is

- how on a *long-term* basis these various chemicals damage, disrupt, or poison the various organs of our bodies

- how these various chemicals synergistically *interact with each other* inside of the 'host' human bodies

- how the genetically engineering *process* itself damages our bodies

- how these combinations of chemicals poison the foods we eat and the milk we drink

And, most importantly,

We don't even know how much we don't know!

So, dear reader, if you still have not lost your appetite, please eat *organic* foods.

Bon Appétite

APPENDIX

ORGANIC FARMS

One of the alternatives to GMO 'food products' is the healthy food produced by organic farms. For information on organic farms or to locate individual organic farms:

- Organic Consumers Association's list of Organic Farming Associations and Resources
  www.organicconsumers.org/organicgroups.cfm

- Alphabetical list of U.S. organic farms:
  http://www.localharvest.org/organic-farms/list.jsp

- Organic farms in U.S., by locality:
  http://www.localharvest.org/

- Eatwild's List of U.S., Canadian, and International Farms and Ranches
  http://www.eatwild.com/products/

- The Rodale Institute, one of the early leaders in organic farming, was founded in 1947. The Institute is "a curious blend of working farm, soil research station, tourist destination, international agency, and outdoor classroom."
  http://rodaleinstitute.org/2013/ask-the-famer-breaking-free-from-pro-gmo-myths/

- There is an international exchange called 'World Wide Opportunities on Organic Farms' (WWOOF) whereby individuals can work on organic farms in many countries. "In return for volunteer help, WWOOF hosts offer food, accommodation and opportunities to learn about organic life styles."
  http://www.wwoof.net/

SOME LEADING SUPPORTERS and JOURNALS of NATURAL and ORGANIC FARMS

- *Acres USA* (print and on-line publication)

- Gene Watch (UK)

- International Federation of Organic Agriculture Movements (IFOAM)

- Natural Health Revolution

- *NaturalNews.com*

- *New Zealand Organic*

- *Successful Farming (AGRICULTURE.COM)*

- The Cornucopia Institute

- *The Milkweed.com*

INFORMATIVE BOOKS ON FOOD AND GMOs

GMO FREE: Exposing the Hazards of Biotechnology to Ensure the Integrity of Our Food Supply, Mae-Won Ho and Lim Li Ching

The Unhealthy Truth, Robyn O'Brien

In Defense of Food; The Omnivore's Dilemma, Michael Pollan

Stolen Harvest: The Hijacking of the Global Food Supply, Vandana Shiva

Seeds of Deception, Jeffrey M. Smith

The Poison Planters (a reality novel), Charles Sutherland

ANTI-GMO ORGANIZATIONS in the U.S. (and some elsewhere):

- Organic Consumers Association
- *Alter Campagne* (France)

- Anti-GMO Foods and Fluoride Water

- Artists Against Monsanto

- Babes Against Biotech

- Canadian Biotechnology Action Network

- Center for Food Safety

- Center for Science in the Public Interest

- *Confédération Paysanne* (France)

- Dr. Joseph M. Mercola (Mercola.com)

- Dr. Vandana Shiva

- Earth Open Source

- Earth Save Canada

- Earth Watch

- Environmental Defense Fund

- Environmental Working Group

- Food and Water Watch

- Food Democracy Now

- Foundation for the Preservation of Honey Bees

- Friends of the Earth

- GE-Free New Zealand

- GM Watch

- GM Watch (UK)

- GM-Free Australia Alliance

- GM-Free Ireland

- gmeducation.org

- GMO Awareness (U.S. and Canada)

- GMO Free (U.S., Canada, Europe)

- GMO Inside

- GMO Justice

- GMO-Free Regions

- Greenpeace

- Greenpeace International

- Institute for Responsible Technology

- Institute of Science in Society

- Jeffrey Smith

- Justlabelit.org

- Kids Right To Know Club

- Label GMOs (U.S. and Canada)

- Label It (U.S. and other countries)

- March Against Monsanto

- Millions Against Monsanto

- Moms Across America

- Moms Against Monsanto

- Mothers Against Monsanto

- MoveOn.org

- Navdanya Research Foundation (India)

- No GMO

- Non-GMO Project

- Occupy Monsanto

- OGM Dangers

- OP: Anti-GMO Monsanto

- Organic Matters (Melody Meyer,
- Organic Seed Growers and Trade Association

- Pesticide Action Network

- Public Patent Foundation (PUBPAT)

- Right To Know

- Robyn O'Brien

- Save Our Crops Coalition

- Save Our Seeds (Europe)

- *Sociedad Peruana de Derecho Ambiental* (SPDA)

- Tami Canal

- The Refusers

- Transparency International United Natural Foods)

- VAS – *Verdi Ambienti e Societá Onlus-Italia*

- Weekly Women's GMO Free News

AUTHOR

Charles Sutherland was educated at schools and universities in the United States and Europe, including the University of Vienna and the London School of Economics and Political Science. As a student and international businessman for over 40 years, he has lived, studied,

worked in, or traveled to over 60 countries. He has sat on numerous Boards of Directors and has launched a wide variety of business ventures and philanthropic organizations in the United States, Latin America, Europe (including the former Soviet Union), Asia, and the Middle East. He has also been Director of Development of *The Washington Times*, and author of numerous articles and several books, including *Disciples of Destruction: The Religious Origins of War and Terrorism; Character for Champions; Red Tape: Adventure Capitalism in the New Russia* (co-author); *Clash of the Gods* (co-author); and *The Poison Planters*. He has two sons and lives in the Washington, DC area.

ACKNOWLEDGMENTS

First, it's essential to thank all of the medical doctors and research scientists around the globe who have spent countless hours over the years investigating the nature (and dangers) of genetically modified organisms. Many of these professionals have been vilified by the chemical companies and the chemical industry's supporters and surrogates. Beginning with Dr. Arpad Pusztai years ago, many scientists have had their reputations smeared, their credibility questioned, and their careers destroyed; some have even suffered physical threats, and sustained personal damages, for standing up to the chemical industry and its powerful (and financially supported) 'politicians' in various governments and the 'legal industry.'

Also, we all owe gratitude to the tireless opponents of the chemical industry's GMO poisoning of the world's agriculture. Many of these GMO opponents are organizations, scientific groups, and journals; many are writers; many are individual people. Some have been exposing these issues for a long time, such as Dr.Dan Huber, Dr. Charles Benbrook, Professor Michael Pollan, Dr. Vandana Shiva, Dr. Joseph Mercola, Jeffrey Smith, Robyn O'Brien, and others. Countless numbers of them have had their own reputations defiled and their names vilified, both openly and through sinister attacks. Some have been trying to shed light on these issues for many years, while others (like me) have only come recently to this table when we saw that it was set with toxic 'food products' created by chemical companies.

The disturbing health information in this *Handbook* has been researched and revealed for years by these various people. I merely assembled some of it for the convenience of the ordinary consumers – most of whom, I shockingly learned during my research, have never heard the term 'GMO'! If there are any errors, or if I have been inaccurate in summarizing any of these studies, the responsibility is obviously mine alone. Since there are links to each of these studies, the reader can check out the details for herself/himself.

Finally, having grown up in the farm country of Nebraska using a Smith-Corona typewriter and a mimeograph machine, the on-going act of learning was always more important (and easier) than chronicling the results. Now the opposite: like the expanding universe, modern recording technology continues to distance itself from me. Therefore, the graphic design and formatting were done by my son Daniel. Much assistance with my recalcitrant software and on-line research was done by my son Nathaniel. Both provided useful critical comments – solicited and unsolicited. *Because* of their efforts, this book has been completed; *despite* their efforts, any failings or poor decisions are mine alone. I wish that I had known as much as they do at their age, technically and intellectually. They will need it, since they live in a far more complicated and (to be euphemistic) 'morally diverse' world.

Appendix

ATTRIBUTIONS

The images for Birth Defects, Intestines, Prostate, and Sperm are from the National Institutes of Health.

- http://www.nlm.nih.gov/medlineplus/ency/imagepages/17144.htm
- http://www.nlm.nih.gov/medlineplus/magazine/issues/spring09/articles/spring09pg7-8.html
- http://www.nlm.nih.gov/medlineplus/magazine/issues/spring09/articles/spring09pg7-8.html
- http://www.nlm.nih.gov/medlineplus/ency/imagepages/19471.htm

The images for Breasts, Cancer, Lung, Obesity, Testicles, and Uterus are from the National Cancer Institute.

- http://www.cancer.gov/cancertopics/pdq/treatment/breast/Patient/page1
- http://www.cancer.gov/cancertopics/pdq/treatment/unusual-cancers-childhood/Patient/page6
- http://www.cancer.gov/cancertopics/pdq/treatment/testicular/Patient/page1
- http://www.cancer.gov/cancertopics/understandingcancer/cancer/AllPages
- http://www.cancer.gov/cancertopics/pdq/treatment/non-small-cell-lung/healthprofessional/page3
- http://www.cdc.gov/vitalsigns/adultobesity/infographic.html